# Mead's Other Manus

*Margaret Mead in Pere Village explaining the American Ballot.*

# Mead's Other Manus

*Phenomenology of the Encounter*

## Lola Romanucci-Ross

*Bergin and Garvey Publishers, Inc.*
*Massachusetts*

All photographs are courtesy of Lola Romanucci-Ross and Ted Schwartz.

Library of Congress Cataloging in Publication Data

Romanucci-Ross, Lola.
    Mead's Other Manus.

    Bibliography: p.
    Includes index.
    1.  Manus (Papua New Guinea people)   I. Title.
DU520.R66   1985      306'.0899912      84-21592
ISBN 0-89789-064-7


First published in 1985 by
Bergin & Garvey Publishers, Inc.
670 Amherst Road
South Hadley, Massachusetts 01075

56789   987654321

Printed in the United States of America

# Contents

# Foreword

*"The problem of the value of Truth presented itself to us, or was it we who presented ourselves before the problem? Which of us is Oedipus here? Which the Sphinx? It would seem to be a rendezvous of question and notes of Interrogation."*

Nietzche. *Beyond Good and Evil.*

This work emerged from my collection of field data spanning a period of over two years in the Admiralty Islands (New Guinea) in the culture area in the South Pacific known as Melanesia.[1] Highly detailed field notes, tape recordings, film and still photographs were used to record and analyze an "ethnographic present" of a culture that no longer exists in the form that I and my indigenous colleagues experienced it. My field notes of the New Guinea-Admiralty Islands Expedition are now housed in the Library of Congress along with those of Margaret Mead for this culture area. (Romanucci-Ross 1963-1967).

As I lived among the Manus groups to be presented here, I found it extremely difficult to reconcile what I had read in classical anthropological writings, as well as relevant monographs, with what I myself noted and experienced "among the primitives."[2] Such dissonance (apparently not idiosyncratic) was later noted by Kimball and Watson, who remarked that field workers are "rewarded for keeping their errors and their personalities hidden" (see Freilich 1970:36). Rabinow (1977) also wrote "the enterprise of inquiry is discontinuous with its results"; yet another anthropologist expressed the same feelings that reading much of anthropology was to him like reading fiction (Dumont 1977).

Lévi-Strauss, in giving us his personal, experiential and philosophical *Tristes Tropiques* (1955), found that "time, in an unexpected way, had extended its isthmus" between life and himself; "twenty years of forgetfulness" were needed before he could "establish communion with earlier experiences'' (pp. 13-18). Felicitous for an introspective work, but for the reconstruction of a culture in tropical discontents this might have its dangers, for a lapse of time could put one's mind to rest by creating comfortable lacunae where there once existed a series of puzzles.

Time has been my ally in quite another fashion, in the guise of seventeen years of observing a transformation in the thinking of anthropologists and readers of anthropology, as they have begun to question the very basis of how we know what we think we know (Romanucci-Ross 1980b), a problem which deprived me of equanimity even during my first experiences among American Indians as a graduate student. Only in the present intellectual climate do I feel encouraged to work on these materials in the only way that I ever wanted to present them. My intention here is not to describe or interpret an exotic culture for the reader, or to portray my own inner voyage of discovery in a "world on the wane," or to define who I was for these Manus peoples in the Admiralties, for I cannot know this. Nor is this an account of what they think of themselves, for that may not be possible to extrapolate except in "bits" of information that must, in any event, bear the stamp of the articulation of the writer. (Perhaps in this regard all we need to know is that they do not see themselves as we see them.)

The portrait of a culture should include: a historical dimension; the conscious models of behavior of the culture bearers; structural-functional aspects of the culture (i.e., how events are placed and how the system works); a nomothetic dimension (the search for general laws); and an idiographic dimension (determining how to treat a case that does not fit in with the general laws) (Romanucci-Ross 1982:220). In most cultural descriptions, these processes are "identified" and labeled by the researcher, with the "informants" supplying usable pieces of the puzzle. Our ability to generate knowledge of other cultures has been hampered by the superimposition of the investigator's myths, metaphors and similes onto the myths and experiences of others, although the mapping of minds on minds is in itself a cultural phenomenon and not without interest. Because we have not really applied our studies of other cultures to an understanding our own, we have persisted in the invention of new categorical grids as we "discover" other cultures. Some of these categories are structurally superfluous and at best reveal a lack of understanding of our categorizations. (Was it not "totemic" of a wine-bottling aristocrat in Southern France to explain to me, "Moi, je suis Barsac, mon beau-père il est Beaujolais"?).[3]

What I present here is about cognition and re-cognition, about the ways in which these Matankor (and other Manus) peoples reckon their own co-ordinates of space and time. It is about how they conceptualize their existential being-in-the-world through their senses, and about the manner in which they speak or otherwise communicate about "being" through their own "instancings." This is not a book of categories, then, but rather a book about linkages in the process of a series of encounters and the convergence of such a series to a construct. (Convergent series of interlocking constructs may then be described as "a culture"). We try to follow consciousness (theirs and mine) in ethnologizing to have a look at how explanatory principles (theirs and mine) might possibly emerge and evolve. In pursuit of the threads of my own co-ordinates in the field research situation, I hope to illuminate the process through which one anthropologist learned about a people and a culture, not in a mode known as "topical," but through the flow of events. How does this happen in time? What occurs before statements about "marriage exchanges" can be thrown into a universal meaning basket of all "marriage exchanges" in all cultures? How does the event of an anthropological investigation initiate and modify events later described in a metalogue about these events? Who defines an episode and its boundaries? Why does one kind of investigator elicit certain kinds of information but not others? We have rarely, if ever, been given this kind of information, and when we have caught glimpses of it, it has been *en passant*, bracketed off as an item of curious interest, unintended as "key" information.

The anthropologist is, in some important respects, like the shaman, the ecstatic healer whose ultimate purpose is to unite the person to the mystical body of society. Like the shaman, the anthropologist has his own impassioned *cogito*, a manner of knowing "objectively" but with underpinnings of emotion, or of apprehending in an emotive state, but with an overlay of consensually validated, hence "certifiable" knowledge (Romanucci-Ross 1983b). Both shaman and anthropologist enjoy the status of interpreter of symbols, cultural instruments for the perceiving and arranging of reality, and both produce configurations of knowing and being that compel mind, matter and experience. (For an outstanding example of the anthropologist compelling experience see Freeman (1983) on Margaret Mead, especially chapter 7; see also Romanucci-Ross 1983a).

Both shaman and anthropologist are alone but not lonely. Seeking solitude they are provided a context for their creativity by the culture. Both think analogically, overcome great difficulties and obstacles in their "travels" and have trials worthy of Perseus or other heroes of the early Greeks. Long sea voyages, devastating winds and storms, one-eyed monsters and evil adversaries to be overcome have always been voyages of self discovery as well, metaphors for finding oneself entrenched in the tradition of many cultures. In magical flight, far from creatures of their own kind, they both go to other worlds and return with their versions of them. In and out of vastly differing worlds with ease (the art is to be inside but also outside everything) they both have their own sub-cultural ontologies, epistemologies and ethics. Both unify real worlds and "dreamed of" designs, distorting data so that information flows in some channels but not others. We search in vain for a language of hermeneutics, i.e., an understanding of the informant's intent and of the discourse context. "How natives think" is presumed to emerge after one has observed the building of houses and canoes or the preparation for ceremonies and exchanges and rituals or puzzled out an acrostics of kinship. Formal recognition of the inadequacies of mapping our own categories onto the domains of others began the "emic" movement (an attempt to get "inside views") in anthropology; it served as notice to fieldworkers that the categories of others had to be elicited. (Pike 1967). Studies stressing "emics" have been useful, even if only about fragments and segments of other cultures and even if lacking a grammar to unite the fragments.

If there is a method to the following presentation it inheres in my total acceptance from a people of their own ethnographic facts, an ethno-ethnography, if you will. I accepted not only their own "facts" but the style of the discourse in which they were given to me, their own recognized levels of analysis, their own relational world. My attempts to avoid "receiving responses to queries" is what I have elsewhere called the *mode inferential* (Romanucci-Ross 1980a:308-309); this mode includes the respondent's notion: "I will give the response that must surely be wanted in this context as asked by this particular person — among the several replies I *could* give as correct." I was as interested in learning about rules for disorganiza-tion as for organization, the former often exemplified in anecdotes describing acceptable limits to system perturbation. This will be illustrated by native comments and by their accommodations to reli-gious missionary efforts, or to Australian efforts to Westernize them; or even in their own version of a native movement (known as a "cargo cult" to the white inhabitants), as the native leader of this constituency pushed hard for culture change. I tried to see their myths as they saw them, a centrifugal force for consensus about morality and for the retention of traditional epistemes (knowledge configurations), and *not* as "art forms" or explanatory principles.

The manner in which bits of culture are described, the contexts and sequentiality in which they are described, like so many boxes fitting into each other indicating the consideration of relevance by the teller, and the frame in which they were given to me, are here considered to be as important as the "facts" themselves. So too for the time-frame of an event and the events that triggered it. Social relations and structure are not self-evident; they must be distilled from many events that are selected from the time-space mass of the research paradigm. The selection of these events is always a product of the collusion or collision of the experience, the identity, the perceptions and biases of the investigator and the investigated. Event selection affects all expectations. Event selection implies a sense of chronology and event boundaries; it suggests the interplay between conscious models of behavior and underlying deep structures of what is considered appropriate behavior. An undisturbed population knows its own cultural stochastic processes, i.e., has the ability to predict the sequentiality of events and event probability in alternative states (Romanucci-Ross 1982:220-226).

A culture is always the product of a historical moment and the sex and temperament of the describer and the described. In the act of collecting data over time one evolves a consciousness of self and other. To the sense of self and other, sexual identity is not an "add on;" rather, it is fundamental, and attempts to ignore this generate consequences covering a wide range of behavior which subsequently surely leads to errors of interpretation. A culture then, is a created reality, but by this I do not mean it is a false reality. An exposition of the process by which it was created will validate the manner in which it is true.

Interpretation of cultural materials demands recognition that we are confronted with a series of personal inventions; the culture-bearer invents as he/she "acts out" and then further invents in reportage. Up to this point, as we begin to describe (read "interpret") we can at least count on the convergence of probabilities within a manageable range. This, however, is then followed by the inventiveness of the investigator in linguistic and cultural translation (with increased intensity if a problem of grand proportions is being addressed by the researcher). Little attention is paid to the fact that there is a person behind the cultural mask, one who is not usually unprepared for the intruder, benign or malignant. It is not usually the case that there is a conscious intent to deceive the investigator, but rather we should assume a resort to self-protection when we confront "informants" with direct inquiries on matters in which privacy is the main ingredient: sexual activities or preference, situations of conflict, claims to property rights and other behaviors regulated by moral codes.

It is time, then, that we begin to present materials in a "running analysis" that will illuminate the process of discovery of a culture, by all involved in the enterprise. We assert here that one can talk about a culture in its own terms, just as Carnap (1937) stated that the syntax of a language can be expressed in the language itself to an extent which is conditioned by the wealth of means of expression of the language in question. Too long has it been assumed that cultures we "study" do not have the wealth of expression for their own metalogues. As I worked on recording my field materials, it was with a determination not to fall heir to that fallacy. I was astounded by the gap between the array of analytic constructs and the discourse with which I had been prepared to grasp the living data, and by the ease with which these "primitives" transformed their own constructs (and mine) through what I can only describe as poetic devices. It was as though they wished to preserve their formal rules not only to maintain their own tradition, but to have those who came here and wanted to believe in them save face, so to speak, for the captured and codified rules are not incorrect. The following presentation should help resolve this seeming paradox and should indicate the many roads to *freedom* to be found in the unknown interior corridors of "a primitive culture."

Lola Romanucci-Ross

# Preface

The encounter between the investigator and the investigated in anthropological field research usually results in a description of the culture under study. The field encounter should, however, be viewed as a "co-mapping of experience and mind, and a simultaneous mapping of mind on mind" (Romanucci-Ross 1980a:304). What has been singularly lacking in reports of such encounters is an accounting that would take the investigator and the reader into the twentieth century, i.e., the recognition that phenomena consciously experienced and consciously examined will reveal unexpressed presuppositions. Margaret Mead welcomed this as well as other developments for the improvement of investigative techniques, but she was not one to "re-think" nor rewrite her interpretations based on past fieldwork.

The Manus of the Admiralty Islands of Melanesia were the people to whom she returned time and time again to study the phenomenon of social and cultural change. She often referred to these people as "my Manus" on those many occasions in which these cultures were summoned forth to furnish expository examples in professional dialogues or "exchanges." (This was not idiosyncratic with Mead, for most anthropologists appropriate "peoples" much as medical scientists appropriate diseases.)

For "Mead's Other Manus" I have a dual reference: the first is to those ecological groups in Manus that Mead did not study nor "see." She nevertheless described and characterized these groups in terms that her Manus Tru of Pere village used as they "saw" and talked about them. Secondly, "Mead's Other Manus" are the Manus Tru themselves, still committed to a belief in the wisdom of many facets of their traditional culture (with a proper dash of the Dionysian with which Mead hesitated to endow them) and much more like the rest of the world than those models of "cultural transformation" depicted in *New Lives for Old*. They pondered, as I did, the meaning of their presumed "rapid culture change" which Mead had pronounced painless and irreversible.

The Manus cultures herein (Matankor, Usiai and Manus Tru) emerge from a series of encounters in which the investigator, while interacting and while "recording," was committed to an exposition of the intimacy of those moments when each participant feels that he has grasped the reality of the other. Intentional relations of those involved become somewhat clear in the phenomenological attitude, in which investigation and description are directly experienced without "explanation;" for explanations generally cover for experiential gaps consisting of disregarded contexts. On another discourse level, the philosophical considerations in applying the phenomenological approach to the social sciences have been compellingly addressed by others, notably Merleau-Ponty 1967.

Phenomenology is the label given to a twentieth century philosophical movement (Spiegelberg 1960) whose objective is the investigation and description of phenomena consciously experienced, without theories about explanation and *as free as possible* from unexamined preconceptions and presuppositions. Some speak and write of a "phenomenological method" but that appears to be a case of contradictory concepts, since employment of "method" implies a concensus on the objectifiable nature of experience. I have chosen here to focus on the encounter as the "field" for exposition of how one can learn about self and other in pursuit of cultural description.

# List of Figures

# A Brief Introduction to the Field

The Sori and the Mokerang who live on small fringing islands off Manus proper are called "Matankor" by themselves and by others. (*Matankor* means "eyes of the place" in several Admiralty Islands languages.) Sori is on the North Coast and Mokerang on the Northeast of the main large island of Manus. The Sori are remote geographically and culturally, having been touched by "European" culture in only a most peripheral sense. The Mokerang have a history of culture contact from the "time of the Germans" to the present, persistent if not intense or continuous. The continuities of indigenous Mokerang culture in the face of these contacts are remarkable. The Lebei are an Usiai, or "bush people" group residing near Sori. On the South Coast of the Great Admiralty, or Manus proper, are the neighboring villages of Pere and Bunai, populated by speakers of a language called Manus Tru; these people are called "the Manus" by themselves and by others. (Bunai Village also contains Usiai speakers in its hamlets — a condominium of two ecological groups.)

The Admiralty Islands, more often called "Manus," are considered administratively part of New Guinea and are to be found in the culture area designated as Melanesia. Situated about 150 miles north of New Guinea (which is north of Australia), the Admiralties constitute a small archipelago, actually the northwestern extension of the Bismarck Archipelago, at 2 degrees South latitude and 147 degrees East longitude. The Admiralty group consists of the main high island of Manus and fifteen smaller outliers of the mixed volcanic and coral type. Manus is about fifty miles long and twenty miles wide; the interior is densely forested and largely mountainous, peaking at about 3000 feet. Mangroves along the coast are fringed with coral. At the time of my stay there, there were about 20,000 native inhabitants from approximately twenty-five linguistic groups.

There were several hundred Chinese and other non-whites and "Europeans," an Australian term denoting whites of any provenience.

Most of the "Europeans" and other non-natives lived in the administrative town of Lorengau, or at the nearby Australian Naval Base at Lombrum. Mokerang village was about a ninety-minute drive on a very bad jungle road, or a several-hours sail across the Bay from the Naval Base. Sori was isolated on the North Coast, requiring a long canoe trip of two days and the absence of the Northwest monsoons. During such a *Dyapay* (monsoon) time, one simply did not get out of Sori.

Admiralty Islanders classify themselves into three groups and they view the classification as ecologically-based. The seagoing Manus live by fishing and trade and were formerly domiciled in pile-houses over shallow lagoons between fringing reef and shore-line.[4] Since 1948 they have lived on the beach, however, urged by Paliau (the cult leader who later became political representative) to live "like men instead of fish." Another ecological type are the Matankor, such as the Sori and the Mokerang, who live on small islands around the large island of Manus and who combine fishing with gardening and tree crop cultivation. The third group, the Usiai, live in the interior of Manus and are referred to as "bush people." They are exclusively gardeners and occasional "small time" hunters. Despite inter-marriage, the tripartite classification persists.

The Admiralties were "discovered" by European navigators in the sixteenth century. They were then visited in 1767 and 1792, with unfelicitous results in encounters of brief duration by other European navigators, whalers, traders and possibly "blackbirding" slavers. In 1884 Germany estabished a protectorate over the Bismarck Archipelago, which included Manus. Germans then began the process of pacification. (It is interesting that many who lived there also saw it as "pacification" and told me that their parents welcomed the beginning of the end of the group massacres in Manus that had been in fashion before the arrival of the Germans). The Germans began most of the plantations still in operation during my field stay as well as commercial stations. In 1912 they established a local government and a police station and began to appoint natives to represent the administration in each village. Australia took Manus in 1914 and had it mandated to them in 1921 by the League of Nations. In 1946 the United Nations reaffirmed its status relative to Australia by making it a Trust Territory. After instituting internal self government in 1973, full independence was achieved by this area in 1975.

The Australians had begun by appointing three native officials for each village: a *luluai* as chief, an interpreter or *tultul* who was to be his assistant and a *doctor boy*, who would receive training in first aid and in the administration of simple medical care at the Administration Hospital. This Australian system was superimposed on the traditional, politically-atomistic system of village autonomy in such a way that the old pattern was preserved, i.e., each village was linked directly to the administration but intra-village relations were not affected by the new linkages and continued as they had in the past. The Australians also put a *paramount luluai* over the North and over the South Coasts; these were to be over all the *luluai* of single villages on their respective coasts. The prestige of the *paramount luluai* derived primarily from his having been a "big man" in the traditional status system and from his influence with the Administration in settling disputes. (Schwartz 1962:223). During World War II, a huge naval base was built by the Allies on Manus at Lombrum; it was a staging area and one of the arenas of actual combat.

From German times, men from some villages, but especially the South Coast villages, had the experience of working for "Europeans" on plantations or other occupations for which they were found adept. Missionization by various Christian factions began in the 1920s and is still continuing, with many missions considering their stay a permanent one.

## A Note on Use of Language

Melanesian Pidgin English is a language used as a *lingua franca* between members of groups, tribes and villages who have otherwise mutually unintelligible languages. It is also used between natives and "Europeans" when there is no other language held in common. It is not native, either in grammatical structure or vocabulary, to any who speak it. In the South Seas, English speaking sailors, traders and whalers brought this language to those who lived there. It was then known as Beach-la-Mar (from the name of the sea slug *beche-de-mer*, or trepang, of the genera *Actinopyga* and *Holothuria* and sold to the Chinese who used it in soup). This original "trader talk" left traces of vocabulary in the continuing "pidginization" process in the evolution of the language over time. Germans, Spanish and Polynesians, as well as Catholic Missionaries and others, made interesting and sometimes colorful contributions.

In what follows, I translate a word or phrase into English in parentheses. If the word or phrase is in Melanesian Pidgin English the translation will be preceded by "P.E." If what is being translated is in the language of the village in which I lived, or in the language currently under discussion, only the English equivalent will appear in parentheses. How to write Pidgin remains problematic. If one writes it phonetically it will have to be translated into English much of the time. I have chosen to follow Mead and to write it most often as English (insofar as that is possible) to facilitate understanding and pronunciation by the reader.[5]

## NOTES

1. The New Guinea-Admiralty Islands Expedition 1963-1967 was sponsored by the American Museum of Natural History (New York) and was financed by the National Institute of Mental Health (Bethesda). Researchers: Margaret Mead, Theodore Schwartz and Lola Romanucci-Ross. Mead had worked in Pere village on the South Coast with Reo Fortune in 1928, then again with Ted Schwartz in 1953. The 1963-1967 research project extended the study to the entire Admiralty Islands area, as we collected material to later describe an "areal culture" (Schwartz 1963).

2. It is perhaps noteworthy that I did not feel this alienation as I compared my field experiences and the anthropological literature, (for example, Pitt-Rivers (1957), Moss and Capannari (1982), Wylie (1974), Brandes (1980) or Hélias (1975) while doing research in peasant cultures in Europe. Is this because all of us are ourselves, along with our explanatory principles, derivatives of European models?

3. Another example among many: in European cultures the bodies of saints or miracle workers were sometimes dismembered into fragments and distributed within religious orders, with some bones placed in ornamental mountings. Some of these miraculous keepsakes can still be viewed at Notre Dame Monastery at Namur, the Prague Cathedral or the Swiss National Museum at Zurich, among other places. Skulls were particularly "powerful" and often had "stares" of inlaid jewels that can still be viewed in Tours, Provence or Naples (they are still revered by many). When, therefore, among some Manus groups one finds a recent history of the skull of the dead father in a large bowl protecting the extended family, is this a characteristic of paleolithic and thus "primitive" culture?

4. Pere village and the Manus Tru have generated books and articles by Mead 1930, 1934, 1956; Fortune 1933, 1935; Schwartz 1962, 1963. For publications relating to populations on the fringe Matankor Islands (Romanucci-Ross 1966, 1969, 1978, and T. Schwartz and L. Romanucci-Ross 1979.)

5. For an introduction to Pidgin English see Murphy (1966) and Hall 1954).

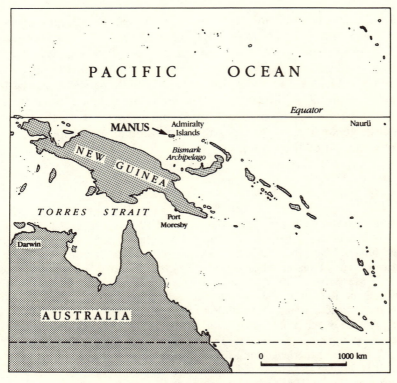

*The Location of the Admiralty Islands (Manus)*

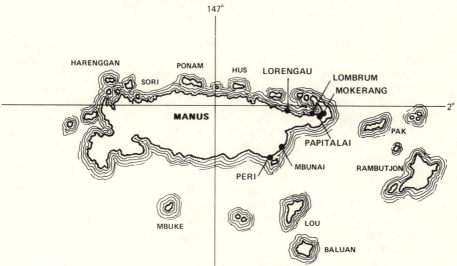

*Location of Some Villages and Islands of Manus*

# A Selected Cast of Characters

Kilepak — man of Pere village (Manus Tru speaker), our canoe captain.

Lokes — man of Pere village, (Manus Tru speaker), our companion and cook.

Lomot — young woman of Pere village (Manus Tru speaker), daughter of Kilepak.

Mesian — young woman of Bunai (Manus Tru speaker), member of anthropologists' household.

O'Malley, Jim — District Commissioner, Manus District of the Territory of Papua-New Guinea.

Paliau — leader of the "cargo cult" in Manus, later elected representative for Manus at the House of Assembly, Port Moresby.

Pwepwe — young woman of Sori, sister of the chief, Lohai, member of anthropologists' household.

Anthropologists — Margaret Mead, Ted Schwartz and Lola Romanucci-Ross comprising the New Guinea-Admiralty Islands Expedition for the American Museum of Natural History 1963-1967.

*Pere man making a fishtrap.*

# ONE

# Getting There

*October 6, 1963, Lorengau.* After the long flight from New York to Sydney and from Port Moresby to Lorengau, I find myself and our cargo in outrigger canoes headed for Pere village on the Southcoast of Manus. Ted, baby Adan and I settle in Bunai village near Pere so that we can prepare ourselves for our assignments: mine to study the Matankor people of Manus, his to go to the Sepik for a period of time and then return to Manus.[1]

Our cook is Lokes, who had worked for Margaret Mead in 1953, and who had been a young helper to her and Reo Fortune in 1928. He brings a woman with him; she is to help with housework and laundry. In the evening we are visited by a group from Pere (the sea-going Pere that Mead wrote about in *Growing Up in New Guinea*). Among these is John Kilepak, who is to be our canoe captain.

A buff moon, black silhouettes of palm trees, the soft slap of gentle surf on a silver and shimmering sea, and slit gongs wild with excitement — my first night on the South coast village of Bunai is remarkable for surpassing my expectations of what I had wanted to experience in the South Seas. As I step out of the shelter provided for us, shadows and outlines of "savages" dance to the rhythm of drumbeats and staccato yelps. They are trying very hard to give us a show of welcome. All I can think of is that Margaret would have been very surprised by this.

It is not what I expected after having read Mead's *New Lives for Old*, which is not to say that what she described did not contain *some*

1

aspects of "the verifiable" for the time she described it. But even Ted, who had been in Pere village in 1953−54, expressed astonishment at her resistance to his reports on "cult" behavior; Mead had by then already determined that the Manus were to be described as "rational" (Schwartz 1983:927). She did not want them to exhibit traits of Dionysian frenzies (Romanucci-Ross 1980a:306). Although my work is to be mainly on the North Coast and elsewhere, I later reflect on Mead's "most astonishing case of cultural transformation" when I return to Pere, where I look in vain for the "twentieth century" and the "model for rapid culture change" on which the literate world had, for a period, riveted its attention.

*October 9.* This is the day to try the *bung* (P.E. market). The Usiai, from the interior of the island are here to sell their products. Everything is of a quantity worth one shilling; they will not sell you anything for a sixpence, or half the quantity. One pineapple is 1s, ten bananas are 1s, one (crab) is 1s. The fishing people barter fish for vegetables amidst much bickering. Quite often many return home with much that they brought with them to sell or barter, in obvious enjoyment of having deprived an "unruly" customer.

But what I learn today, of great importance for my future research, is that there is no such thing as a casual remark. My first mistake was telling a vendor that the pineapples were too small. Subsequent knowledge of the culture informed me that this was a remark both insulting and meaningless to the vendor in this context. Too small for what? Compared to what? The pineapple had achieved its goal of becoming a pineapple. My second casual aside had wider repercussions: I noticed a young man and commented aloud to my companions that he wore a lovely necklace indeed. My companions told Lomot, wife of our cook Lokes, who told Lokes and a group of others nearby. Soon someone began a very long harangue to the crowd in the market place: "The Misis has been mistreated − this is reprehensible indeed − you may cheat among yourselves if you are that kind, and you obviously are − but Mastah and Misis are friends, dear and good friends. Now you should go home to your husbands and tell them what you have done."

Now all this occurred in native tongues to which I had had the privilege of listening for only three days, but it was all later translated for me into Pidgin. At this point I try to convey as best I can, for my Pidgin is hardly fluent, that I am mortified, ashamed, truly sorry, that whatever I had unleashed was not intended. They send back word that they know I had done no wrong, but indeed it was they who had. I live with ignorance and misery for a time, wondering if anyone will ever come to my house again. But that small mystery has to be laid aside as my interactions grow in complexity.

We have, in fact, many visitors who come to make exchanges, gifts that must be reciprocated. You must give just a little bit more than you have received. For example, today a man brought two fish and I gave him two sticks of tobacco (a very acceptable currency and exchange item). It seems as though people coming to call are trying to be very nice; but I keep working at getting the information I want: what happened at the *bung* this morning? Painfully, it evolved from several queries. The incident did revolve around the comment I had made about the necklace and particularly the breast ornament displayed around the neck and on the chest of a young man. It appears that as I expressed my delight, a friendly woman standing next to me asked him to give it to me. When he hesitated she became demanding, which frightened him. She appealed to an old man who had just wandered by the scene. This scene engendered the "market riot," an escalation of this aborted exchange.

Now I can explain my intent to our visitors, and all is well; I receive a necklace that a Pere woman made just for me, and that all agree is prettier than the one I had openly admired. I become the recipient of many *large* pineapple. All of this is a source of great embarrassment to me, and I shall be very careful about what emotions I express about anything in the future (an impossible goal!).

*October 10.*  Pidgin English, is not at all easy to learn. It is not simply impoverished English with truncated nouns and tenseless verbs, but rather a language that grew just like any other language, with bits and pieces of English, Polynesian, Melanesian, Chinese and Spanish, within the basic grammatical constructs of Oceanic languages. The greatest difficulty in learning Pidgin lies in overcoming a feeling that you already know it, which is why some "Europeans" who live here doing business never really learn it. They also probably don't want to learn it. At first one is struck with the comic effect of the language. Despite the linguists who tell us "all languages are equal," a language is also what people think it is. Pidgin does keep changing. "Worry," I learn, is one of the many words that are now incorporated into Pidgin and carry the English meaning.

Non-verbal languages do very well here, too. Pwaka, the village deaf-mute comes to tell us stories of planes, earphones, flags and bows and arrows, i.e., stories about World War II and the presence of Americans and Japanese in Manus. He draws on the sand and pantomimes. It is said that many in his hamlet understand his talk, and in any case, he does provide great entertainment for everyone. No one seems to feel that he is suffering a deprivation, not even, I think, Pwaka himself. Few others get so much attention.

We are planning my trip and my research on Sori Island. Lokes, the cook, will come with me and will be paid twelve pounds and ten shillings per month.

*October 21.* My first attendance at the religious services at the *house lotu.* The men are seated on one side of the church and the women on the other. The singing is much like a Catholic Mass. I meet Melien, a beauty by any cultural standard and schoolteacher from the North Coast who is substituting here. She promises to come for tea so that we can work on her language and on their kinship system. Melien studied first in Lorengau, then in Goroka on the Big Island of New Guinea. She likes teaching school but complains that the children are not as respectful to a female teacher as they are to a male. Mesian, one of the girls at our house taking care of my baby also went to school for eight years, but had to come home because of pregnancy. Her son is now one year old, and it seems she is engaged to be married to a boy from the island of Baluan who is not the father of her child. Mesian's Christian name, "Rosina" is tattooed on her arm — this seems to be a fashion for some of the girls. Mesian does receive one pound per month from the baby's father by court order.

*October 23.* We go to Pere village to watch the caulking of our canoe, *Jo po ko ilisi ndrol e yo isati Pere,* which means, "I am coming to Pere to see my canoe." The men taught me to say that and told me what it means. Whether I have "broken up the sounds" correctly to reflect the "words" or morphemes, I do not know at this time. I know that I must record it as I hear it, and in the future, phrases will include similar sounds and the future contexts will tell me which to isolate, and how.

Our sixteen trunks have arrived and Mesian talks to me about her future. Her uncle and aunt have "adopted" her year-old son. Her father promised her in marriage to a man from Baluan whom she does not care about and does not want to marry. She would like to come with us wherever we go. We have already promised Lomot, but will take Mesian anyway.

*October 25.* The *doctor boy* (P.E. young native male trained by the Australians to give medical aid to the village) has gone to Lorengau and — the clinic line-up forms at our house. Margaret has prepared me for this, through all my resistance. "When you can save a baby's life," she assured me, "you will read the medical handbook and you will give the antibiotics."

Chronic respiratory diseases abound. We are dispensing Kaomyecin, cascara, cough medicines, Nivaquine, Chloroquin and aspirin (for malaria in all stages). A close second to respiratory infections is the skin diseases.

I listen to Mesian and others talk to baby Adan. They let him make random vowel sounds first and then they repeat, amplify and mockingly and lovingly give the same sounds back to him. Very different from my style, for I talk to him constantly in an adult fashion. They have just made me aware that I *had* a "style" in communicating with babies.

*October 26.* Clinic again. I keep telling those helping me that spoons used by the sick should not just be rinsed in cold water and thrown in with the rest of our utensils. They will not boil them despite my pleading and reminders.

Another riotous *singsing* tonight and the women ask me to join them dancing. I do so until exhausted. Some Usiai girls send me a message that there will be a *singsing* just for me tomorrow night.

*October 27.* It had to happen! I have a very high fever, difficulty in breathing and severe pain in the bones of arms and legs. The three women in our household throw distant but compassionate glances my way. I make them take out all the silverware and *boil* it. They do it as a performance of a strange ritual. The illness brings me presents: a carved crocodile, a bag of cats eyes, a bottle covered with fine basketry work. The villagers move slowly and silently and are very concerned about my illness, but not so much the illness as the causes. Some think it was because the women urged me to dance at a *singsing* that was culturally foreign to me. Others think it has to do with tensions between people, which is always suspect as the causes of illness here. Off to a hospital by canoe, where the doctor thinks it is typhoid. It isn't, and it slowly subsides in two weeks. Whatever it is, it is responding to chloromycetin. I think it is dengue ("breakbone") fever.

Recuperation at District Commissioner O'Malley's house in Lorengau. Because we are anthropologists Jim gives us books by F.E. Williams, and makes some comments about the nature of justice in the territories. He feels that the intricacies of the law here are used merely to give practice to young barristers, who, along with the judges, conduct cases as though the native litigants are not present.

They do not address them and do not care whether they do or do not understand in this game of trying the wit of the barristers.

Mesian together with a maid to the O'Malleys, wants me to know that Melien, the school teacher from Ndritambat who I so admire, has an illegitimate baby (they call it Buka baby because it is very black and looks like it was fathered by a Solomon Islander, a Buka). The baby is in her village while Melien has a European lover, married and recently fired from his post. Mrs. O'Malley was particularly disturbed by a letter from Melien's native teacher in Goroka congratulating Melien for the qualities she must possess for her ability to seduce a European. They also want me to know that one of my employees is pregnant and "the father" is someone's husband, and that they assume I will fire her. Such events are recounted with glee, and the girls appear maliciously titillated in emphasizing the irony that Melien has the whitest of lovers, but the blackest of babies!

Vere, wife of the District Commissioner, holds a meeting of "the women's club" in her home, and her maid acts as interpreter. She has a large attendance of women who say they will prepare a party for the arrival of Sir Donald and Lady Cleland, and to all her other suggestions she gets a loud and spirited, "yes!" I am to leave this acculturation scene tomorrow, however, to be deposited on the small island of Sori, remote and isolated on the North Coast.

## NOTES

1. Our concerted effort in the Admiralty Islands was to be focused on systems of integration of cultures in one culture area. Based on linguistic models of the syntagmatic and paradigmatic, we sought to learn how various cultural elements could be displaced and "re-environed" from group to group. There was an urgency about the time constraints for such a "transformal ethnography" of an areal culture. Just a few years would witness the death of essential informants; this loss would be accompanied by the irreversible loss of knowledge that would be no longer transmitted. As I write, this has occurred.

*The women's dance: Sori Island.*

*The women's dance: Sori Island.*

# TWO

# Sori, Island of "The Wild"

*November 8.* The Tami, the Manus Administration boat, passes villages along the Coast going North from Lorengau; from Lugos to Bundralis we pass eleven villages, then only bare shoreline for several hours. As the Tami arrives at Sori Island, a canoe comes forth to greet us, then another to help us get our trunks off the boat; the women are lined up to shake hands with me. I am struck by the manner of dress here. Unlike Bunai and Pere, here they all dress in the traditional fashion, exactly as one finds them depicted during the first occupation of Manus by the early German discoverers, who had learned that Sori meant "wild island" (Neverman 1934: 380).[1] They also seem to have what we perceive as the simple grace and trust that characterizes the "man in paradise" native, he who was deceived and made to know shame by the white man, as in the novels, and alas, as in actual historical accounts, all too often.

The old women are bald, as was traditional for the married women of olden times, many uncovered from the waist up. The younger women wear blouses, but, as I later noticed, are bare breasted as they work in the early morning. They wear beaded armbands, about four or five inches apart, on the arm above the elbow, these are very tight and intended to make the arm bulge. Ankle bracelets are similarly placed on the lower leg, but here there is also a black woven band about five inches thick from the ankle to the lower portion of the calf. Every woman I have seen here has considerable tattooing on the face, mostly in the form of diagonal lines,

9

broken down within the lines into small criss-crosses, down on the nose, both cheeks, and the forehead. One sees an occasional child with bleached hair. An old woman has felt obliged to wear a cloth over her bosom since we have been here. It saddens me that she should feel uncomfortable because of our presence. The villagers cannot be too pleased that we have brought "foreign" help from Pere village, but I need girls who know some English and something of European ways for the baby. Lokes knows of the needs of anthropologists and he can communicate about the cooking.

The language seems to me to be rather distinct from that spoken by the Pere Manus. But that for later, I must first attend to setting up house. Water must be brought here from the village tank in buckets. The house is totally native style, on piles, and with no doors. Like the house, our toilet is on stilts, but it is over the ocean, which takes care of flushing; like the house it is made of *saksak* (P.E. sago palm leaves). The island is almost completely circular and its diameter no more than one-quarter mile. All the houses in the village are small and made of *saksak* and are on piles, except for one tin house. The "society store," a co-operative, has louvered windows and is in semi-European style. One sees a group of Sori there always looking over the stock on half-empty shelves. The store has been given a name, "Beripeo" (*stone*, like the name of a nearby island). It is well supplied with hair pomade, featuring photographs of Caucasian belles and beaux of the 1920's on their labels.

There are women here who would like to be employed by us, but we must talk with the chief, Lohai. He tells me that although some married women would like the job, we must not hire them for that would take away time that belongs to their husbands. He will look for a single woman for me. I already have Mesian and Lomot, daughter of Kilepak of Pere, in the house to help me.

At dawn, I watch the women go out to wash clothes in the river, or burdened with the sago-pounder and axes, go looking for sago, all very much like illustrations I had seen in old books on the Admiralties, written by the first European explorers. They speak and are very friendly; the Pere girls Lomot and Mesian are enjoying the prestige of being foreign belles. Lomot gets many concessions from the storekeeper at the society and appears to have enraptured the Tulu schoolteacher, who called on us yesterday. We have been receiving presents of shells, *pawpaws*, fish, and eggs, the latter are considered rare and of value.

A woman called Baripeo calls me to her house; she gives me a crate for an elegant seat, asks me to enjoy the cool breeze and gives

me a large cowrie shell. Baripeo tells me that her name is the same
as the society and the stone, but I am more entranced with her elaborate tattoos, her bracelets, and anklets, the large holes in her earlobes, and the teeth stained from chewing the betel nut. She is very
interested when I tell her what I want to learn about the Sori. Soon
she has a visitor who is dressed in the traditional dance costume:
grass skirt, beads criss-crossed around the breast, bracelets, anklets,
and flowers in these as well as in the hair over the ears. She had
come to ask Baripeo why she missed the *singsing* (P.E. dance and
song fest) at the Sori village that is on the coast off this small island.
It is called Sori *nambatu* (P.E. number two), as opposed to this Sori,
which is *nambawan*, (P.E. number one).

*November 10.* Baripeo had taken me seriously, for on this afternoon she came with eight other women. They wanted to see baby
Adan, for, Lokes tells them he has been named *Pondrilang* in Pere.
He tells me *now* that it means "he who cries." The women tell me
that in the Sori language he would then be called *lau a diregó*. There
is great pleasure in my repeating it and so I do; a chorus of young
boys nearby lets out a wild cheer.

"You see," say the women, "Manus language is so hard and
ours is so easy." They decide that I am going to learn their
language, and what follows is a lesson in language learning which I
had never experienced before. Eight women and thirty youngsters
repeat a word several times, pause for me to repeat it, and when I
do, the children cheer "yay" and we go on to the next word. I ask
for the name of their language. It is *Sa'apoy*.

It is very, very important, they stress, for me to learn that there
is a distinct word for "child" depending on the order of birth. A
first-born male is a *dai*, the next born male is called *papa*, the third
born is *sirip*, and number four is *sapa*. Females also in this fashion:
first-born is *dalu*, then *tata*, then *siwa*, and a number four female is a
*pwepwe*. One of the women dragged me into the ocean to teach me
how to say, "I am going to wash now" and took advantage of the
crying baby to teach me how to say, "now I go look at *lau a diregó*."

After the women leave I recall that Paliau, who came with us on
the Tami, had been hoping to win over these people so that they
might back him as he runs for a seat in the Council in the Territories
of Papau and New Guinea. As President of the South Coast Council, he won every year, but if he won the North Coast too, he would
be legislative representative from Manus in the territory-wide council
in Port Moresby. His adversaries are mainly in those villages mis-
sionized by various Christian churches, but he feels he also has

internal competition. He campaigned a bit, associating himself with us, then went back on the Tami, as he had promised the District Commissioner. His parting remark was that Adan is strong and healthy and that this speaks very well for us, since it means we have not been having sexual congress. He is right on both counts, but the connection escapes me. I thought this not to scoff, but to remind myself to look into such connections and their rationales among the Manus.

*November 11.* Chief Lohai (also the *Kaunsil*) found us another helper. She is not married, her name is Pwepwe, which I recall means girl baby number four, and she is more tattooed than any other female on the island. Why? Because she is the sister of Lohai, and they are "nobles" here. We go to Sori #2. It is smaller than Sori #1, and I get my first view of "a men's house." Called *house boy* (P.E.) it provides sleeping quarters for single men and for married men sometimes, too. Samahong and Arupilai are with me and tell me they are going to teach me how to pole a canoe so that we can get away from *all* the men at Christmas time. Both of these girls have their heads completely shaved. I will remember Arupilai because all her teeth are blackened. Like all other women and children here they giggle incessantly. As I arrive home I find a visitor, a very old woman, who has brought me some miserable shells which I receive gratefully as I give her two sticks of tobacco. I talk and joke with her through an interpreter with my new and poor Pidgin, but we gesture and smile all the while. I tell her I want to learn from her but she replies, "*talk belong me i finish*", for she is too old. She has lost most of her teeth, can't I see, and also she cannot see very well. Several more women arrive to continue with my language lesson. Here when they say they want nothing in return for a gift, it is best you believe it.

I have a neighbor who has four children living of the eight she bore. The very young are fed *pawpaw, kaukau* (P.E. sweet potato, *Ipomea batatus*) and *mami* (a tuber root vegetable, *convolvulaceae discorea spp.*) in addition to her breast milk. Where do the women get a supply of these? From the island of Harenggan.

At night, Lomot strums our guitar with endless variations on chords. Her Manus songs are, for example, about cousins whose elders have fought and split the house, with reproaches for doing this bad thing to their children. There are songs in Fijian and Motu, learned from teachers. And some variations on American folk songs, e.g., "She will wear a yellow *laplap* (P.E. wrap-around skirt) when she comes." And the song they composed for Margaret Mead,

"Goodbye Markreet, we will see you no more — for New York is far away."

*November 12.* My language learning continues now, as I get involved in village activities. The girls and I watch a man making a huge fish net to catch a sea turtle. He made his own rope from the bast of a mangas tree that is used for making ropes for sailing. Pere and Bunai people make fish nets, but they do not go for sea turtles. An old woman chopping wood asks me what I am doing and when I tell her in Pidgin she makes me repeat in the *talk place* (P.E. talk of the place) here, *Sa'apoy.*

I worry about the constructions I am beginning to put on my ethnological observations. People on this island seem sexless to me. Are they? There are no allusions to things sexual, and whatever activity occurs in this area, as it must, is done discreetly and in unseen places. Social settings do not seem to be a context for flirtation, if such exits at all. One is struck by the absence of (even) innuendo. Last night I entertained a group telling them stories about the Mexican Village in which I had done field work (Romanucci-Ross 1973). I said of one man there, "this chap had many women." Fascination turned to consternation and puzzlement, for (I learn later) one simply does not allude, either by word or gesture, to physical attractiveness in others, to sexual affairs (possible or pending or ongoing), or use sexual reference in simile or metaphor to describe other spheres of thought or action.

We want to start recording here, so we play tapes of the *garamuts* (P.E. slit gong drums) of the Iatmul from the big island of New Guinea. That does bring them out and to our place. Baripeo and Lohai and his wife Salai sing a sad, soft, slow song in close harmony, a song about a person who has just died. Then Lohai's father, Simbuom, told three stories about olden times. Two were factual, one of which was about a time when there was no food and the Sori had to eat anything and everything they could find in the bush. Everyone in the room was seriously intent upon his every word, looking very grave indeed. Pranis told three stories about the time of his grandfather. They were of battles in canoes with the Manus. It seemed odd to me to hear him explain that the Manus won because they had better canoes, managed them better, knew how to keep the water out of them with only a *pankal* (P.E. the stem of a palm frond). All were tales of Sori defeats.

Someone told him to "go easy" as there were Manus present. Lokes told me as an aside that the stories were completely factual because he had heard the Manus versions and they were identical.

The one he liked the best was the incident in which some Manus had hidden on a small island; some Sori men went after them and were killed by the Manus. Other Sori men who learned of this saw Manus canoes just idling and went after them. Forty Sori were killed, this being a disastrous depopulation for the Sori people.

After our Sori guests left, Lomot looked haughty and asked me if I did not find the Sori *singsing* "long and tiresome."

***November 13.*** Today I am working on the tapes made last night. I note that when asked why the Sori fought with the Manus, Pranis replied, *"belong tryim strong"* (P.E. a contest of strength). It is of interest that they believe this, but it is also of interest to have an awareness that there is and was much resentment by the coast people of bush people moving down the coast. Bush people or Usiai still cultivate gardens but also have coastal advantages not counterbalanced by new advantages for the Manus coast people. This makes for "uneven" trade markets. For the Matankor groups (such as the Sori) who do both some form of agriculture and some sea-faring, the trading is not strictly necessary. Perceptible or not, previous ecological arrangements are always in a state of flux because of population movements.

We have now collected a workable body of samples for linguistic comparisons and kinship charts, or sets of terms, for about sixteen groups. We work on these, looking for similarities and differences and for language change through time that might reveal linkages to the proto-language of the area. Pwepwe, taking a rest from baby care, is weaving a basket to hold sago for a possible trip on a canoe. Sa'abwen comes out to "sweep" (an excuse for housewives the world over for outside involvement and a legitimate excuse to observe happenings). She speaks to me pleasantly in *Sa'apoy* on the assumption that since I have been writing things down for three days I must surely know the language well by now.

Lohai and Salai's young daughter Julia comes to bring us bananas and *pawpaw* and to tell us that her parents are coming tonight to record some "cries," commemorative songs for the dead). Salai does record two very sad and touching *cries* that she composed on the death of her mother. The other was composed for the death of Lohai's cross-cousin, Luwi. Lohai was impressed that I was touched by these, and goes into an elaborate description of how sad these songs can really be, especially the kind that tell you of the death of a brother or sister or mother. "It will just make one cry whether one feels like crying or not — that is the mark of a good composition," he added.

*Cries* include much information about the deceased and not only flattering events and attributes: for example, the Pere village *cry* for Margaret Mead after her death in 1978 included recollections that she came to learn all about them, wrote books about them that made a great deal of money, but she kept all the money in New York and sent them none of it.

The *cry* for the death of Luwi was composed by Salai. Luwi belonged to a matrisib that has the *manuay* or fish hawk[2] as totem. His other totemic ancestor was the *suru* tree. He died in Rabaul, New Britain, on a visit to some people he knew there. The song is addressed to the deceased, but it is addressed to him as if he were the *manuay* itself. A feather drifted, upon Luwi's death and came to his place here where his ancestors seized it and brought it into the house. Lohai tells me that Salai gave him, Lohai, a gift in writing this song because Luwi is his cross-cousin (Lohai is the son of the sister and Luwi of the brother in a brother-sister pair). Lolau and Ahong, in the *cry*, were relatives through Luwi's mother. With apologies to Salai, I will try to render the poetic words of the *cry* into English:

Oh, *Manuay* you died far away in the long *kunai* grass
Your remains are putrified in a house of *kunai* far away
Your feathers have fallen in a place far from your place
You were done in foully, but you flew close by and your
    *tumbuna* caught some of your feathers here, and
    brought it into the house.

The gentle Southwest wind caught the smell of your
    feathers, *Manuay*, and the smell has caught hold of me
The smell, too, of the small bottles of vaseline from the
    stores of Rabaul in your hair.

Let it remain in Rabaul, the smell of the white man from
    little bottles from the store.
The South wind brings the smell of the fragrant *suru* tree
Lolau ruined this man and Ahong kept him there
Let the foul deeds be covered over by the smell of vaseline
    from the stores of Rabaul.

The South wind brings me the smell of your feathers, and
    the smell of your *suru* tree.
If you were buried here you would smell of the bush.
The men of your father's side have your name, that is all.

Lohai taped a song, that he composed on the occasion of the opening and dedication of the cooperative store, the Beripeo Society, just a few months before my arrival here.

| | |
|---|---|
| *Tape "stua" me 'oh ara* | Put the store on my place |
| *Bwasani dyeo* | Show and teach me |
| *pa moneng bwey* | things are not right here |
| *dyi bowow "karangi" hey* | I walk in an irrational fashion |
| *"gaman" hi mey* | The government comes |
| *Bwasani dyeo pa moneng bwey* | Teach me, things are not right here |
| *"missin" hi mey* | The mission comes |
| *Bwasani dyeo pa moneng bwey* | Teach me, things are not right here |
| *bwatumbu 'oh* | ancestors of my place |
| *me awyunua'* | they must stay behind me |
| *dymange bwatumbum dyam* | I walk now with the ancestors of the white man |
| *bwasani dyeo pa moneng bwey* | Teach me, things are not right here |
| *dyidariu ariseheou* | I am lost in between. |

The words in quotes are *not* in *talk place*. For words such as mission, government, and store, Lohai relied on Pidgin, as well as for "sickly" and "irrational" ("*kranki*" or as he sang it "karangi"). Was Lohai being sarcastic as he sang these words the Administration representatives did not understand, nor cared to understand?

Tonight we meet the very old Tata Tara. (Tara was the name of her father and "Tata," of course, means she is a second-born female.) Most people in the village over thirty years of age have holes in their ears, but Tata has a perforation in her septum also. She tells only one short story and needs to be prodded by Pwepwe to do so.

We have a large audience as we did last night. The women want me to learn how to say "goodnight": *bwo aram.*

**November 14.** We had wanted to go to the village of Lebei today, for it is inland, and a completely Usiai or bush village. But there are no available canoes for the short fifteen-minute trip across the water. Everyone has gone hunting for *lalai* (P.E. trochus shell). I walk around a deserted village making sketches of the houses and notes that I suppose I shall call "socio-economic." It is unpleasant for me to ask people for their names, for they look out at the sea for a long time before they reply. It is as if you are asking them about a secret and they don't want to be rude, but they don't want to give all their power away either. There must be some people at home, but although there are no doorways, one does not ever look into apertures that are "doors" or "windows." I know now that I have more privacy in my Sori house than I've had anywhere. When entering a house there is a silent and circuitous protocol by which those inside are made to know of your presence.

Tata Tara, mother of Salai, will be one of my major informants of the traditional culture. Today I meet Ebei, an old man who will fulfill the same role, and fortunately provide me with the masculine view. He comes bringing six eggs, for which I give him sticks of tobacco. He comes to tell me that the land that this house is on is his, and so are the coconut trees, but that we are welcome to live in it and use the coconuts too. Land ownership is thought of in terms of group ownership, but since he is the oldest member of his group, he can say that it is his. The hunters of *lalai* return weary and disconcerted. Why? Because one only gets sixpence a pound for trochus shell. In the past one got one or even two shillings, but now too many people are hunting trochus shell and selling it. Do I not see how all the boats coming in have big bagfulls? So much diving, so much hard work, and the pay is so small. Lohai's daughter Julia brings us two huge lobsters, for they too had gone *lalai* hunting.

Tonight no one shows up for tape recording. It is because last night we said, "that is enough now, we have finished a tape." I notice that to say anything is to set a precedent. If I say to Lokes, "No tea today," I will never see a pot of tea again unless I request it. If I ask for a grapefruit, everyone in the village will bring grapefruit until I have about 20. I said, "that is enough for awhile," and haven't seen a grapefruit since. How can this be described — perhaps that every contingency creates discontinuity, contrary to our concept that a stated order of things is assumed to have exceptions?

*November 15.* All the villagers are cleaning the flesh out of the trochus shell. The "Beripeo Society" or co-op want to buy it clean. Everywhere I go I say, "You are cleaning *lalai*" which is what I am expected to say. The reply is "Yes I am cleaning *lalai*."

"Hard work."

"Yes, hard work and little pay." These are conversational forms and one follows them. Here it is to ask what people are doing, when you see very well what they are doing. For variation, you tell them what they are doing and they agree. Then one spends quite a bit of time verbally noting exits and entrances. One says, "I go." and the reply is, "You go, I stay."

"Yes, you stay, I go."

Three men come to visit us from the island of Harenggan. They express disappointment that their island was not chosen for this "work," since their island is much better than Sori. For my deprivation they blame the selfishness and conniving of the Sori people. Of course, life in Harenggan is difficult, because in the past they could trade their fish for whatever they needed. Now the bush people keep coming down to the coast to live and all trade is in turmoil. The bush people (Usiai) do not want fish, they want shillings for what they sell. Not only does a man not have vegetables, but he cannot even get a tree to make a canoe unless he has ten pounds in his pocket.

One of these men is the grandson of Angat, mentioned in Pranis' stories of the Pere Manus expansionism. About the time of the coming of the Germans (at the end of the nineteenth century) the conquest of the North Coast by the Manus was imminent. This took the form of frequent sorties against Sori, Harenggan, and Ponam by the redoutable Manus warriors. Angat married a Sori woman, for the Manus don't mind telling you they are, and always have been opportunistic about cross-ethnic marriages. Angat was a Manus man who "made the peace." His son came back to Harenggan to live, and belongs to a clan there.

*November 17, Sunday. Kaunsil* Lohai and his wife Salai come for me to take me to the services at the *house lotu* (P.E. church). It is a six minute walk to the other side of the island and then we will go by small outrigger to the church on Sori #2. I am told that there will be a seat for me there, "on the special side." That turns out to be the side where the men sit. They are first to enter and to leave, and every woman must wait until the last man is out before she arises to go. Mass is performed in Pidgin. The collection plate is passed and emerges almost empty. Contrasts with the *house lotu* in Bunai come to mind. The Bunai Paliau church has a Protestant air about it. It lacks ritual and formality and the close harmony singing that one finds here in this Roman Catholic Sori church. In the Paliau church a person, i.e. a man, can feel free to bring up a subject of social or moral interest. Church doctrine does influence daily decisions and social interactions considerably more than in the Paliau church, so that one is justified in seeing the Paliau church as a Reformation.

*November 19.* Today we photograph the *singsing*, somewhat annoyed that they want to perform in front of the "society store" the only "modern" structure, but we do it to please them anyway. Four women sing, and dance, and the others just dance. I want the names of the women and as I am given each name I have to add the name of the father behind each name, so that for example, Pwepwe is Pwepwe So'osong, and Salai is Salai Balo'ohai. And yet, I am told, the totemic affiliation comes from the mother.

What the photo shows is called a *guhi ahuwep bibihin* (a song and dance performance for and by all the women). I ask a woman spectator there whether there is a meaning to this and she says yes indeed it is about a man who died in battle long ago. It tells of Lalai, a strong, enterprising and greatly-feared Manus warrior who led many sorties against this area when her grandparents were young. Lalai was killed on Sori so the women composed this *singsing* to express the joy that everyone felt over the end of Lalai and the envy of the people of Ponam and Harenggan that the Sori had the honor to finish him off. Suwa Beripeo is regal today, not clowning as usual. As I take her portrait she tells me I needn't think this is what it was really like. How was it different? Well, for one thing, the earpieces and nose rings are missing, even though the rest of the costume is authentic. Only one girl wore a brassiere, not out of modesty, but because it seemed to her to be adding more decor. Lohai apologized for the lack of *garamuts*, but four young men were beating on wood and various sorts of "drums" created for this moment.

I work with Salai to decipher the *singsings* she has recorded. And this provides the occasion to talk about totems. The Sori word for totem is *uwau*, and it means a special relationship between an individual and an animal, bird, or plant, genealogically established. To say that "we are of the same *uwau*" is to say that we belong to the same totemic matrisib. *Narumbwam manuay* means "child of the manuay" or fish hawk, the totem of both Salai and Lohai.

Originally, I am told by Salai, the Sori had no totems. All that they have now came from women who married into Sori from various Usiai groups; as for the *manuay*, she knows it came from the village of Salien. This totem is matrilineal, as they all are here.

These are taboos toward one's totem: to touch, to hold, to eat, to have the misfortune of being in a spot where one has been killed in the past. For these violations of the taboo, (or *tambu* as they say it), a man can become mute ("he will be able to talk only with his hands"), and then will die ("this happened to many in earlier times.") There are no marriage restrictions between members of the same totemic group. (Salai and Lohai are both *manuay*).

A newborn whose parents have violated these taboos will cry all the time. And if the *manuay* or any other totem hovers or cries over the house for a period of time, the child will surely die and "all the medicines and hospitals of the white man will be of no avail." Lohai speaks in dead earnest for he believes this without qualification. But it is Salai who finally gets to the point, and now John, her brother, the storekeeper at the co-op leans forward eagerly to observe what is to ensue. It seems that her mother, Tata Tara, is concerned that Adan cries so much. She wants to cure him. She has always cured babies with this syndrome through her diagnosis and ritual cure. The cure is effected with croton leaves. I said, well, it was alright for her to try to cure him, but I have no totem which means he doesn't have one, and this makes Lohai reflect silently. Then I add, that perhaps I have one but just don't know it. Salai looks wisely at me, but my decision at this time is to leave it at that for if Tata tries and fails (I am certain that nothing will make Adan stop crying since the cost-benefits are too much in his favor), the blame surely will be mine and it will affect my research effort with this wise and knowledgeable old woman. Tata and Ebei are the respective repositories of male and female lore of the traditional culture on this tiny island.

## NOTES

1. See Neverman 1934. The first date we have for the "discovery" of the Admiralties is 1616 and the discoverers: Willem Schouten and Jacob Le Maire. Occasional explorers: Carteret in 1767 and D'Entrecasteaux in 1792. "Formal" visits, with some consequent documentation were begun by the visit of the H.M.S. Challenger in 1875.

2. *Manuay* or fish hawk (*Pandion Haliaetus*) shares certain anatomical features with falcons, but other features link it with the *accipitrine* family of hawks and eagles, old world vultures and Cathartid vultures. Its head and neck are white, throat and breast broadly banded and streaked with cinnamon brown, and its wing configuration exhibits a distinctive "crooked" wing shape. It takes fish or other prey from the surface but more frequently flaps, glides, hovers and dives, creating a shower of spray and emerging with a fish secured by its locked talons and spiny foot pads.

One might speculate on the prevalence of hawks and eagles in myths the world over, from the Amerindians (North and South), and the ancient civilization of Western Asia (Sumeria, Babylonia, Assyria, Egypt, etc). Biblical accounts abound with imagery of bird of prey, so that Moses, for example, heard on Mt. Sinai, "and how I bore you on eagles' wings and brought you unto myself" (Old Testament: Exodus 190:4-6). In the mythopoetry of ancient Greece Prometheus had an eagle eating away at his liver, which grew back every night. Eagles were a symbol of the power of emperors from Belshazzar of Babylon in the sixth century B.C., to the Caesars through the late Austrian empire. (For an interesting review of birds of prey as symbol see Grossman and Hamlet 1964: 42−91).

*Daughter of A'amau of Lebei Village.*

## THREE

# The Usiai Bush People of Lebei Village

During the medical line-up on Sori today I make the acquaintance of the ancient A'amau who had come by canoe from Lebei. He has ugly tropical ulcers on his legs, which fortunately can be easily treated by washing with salt water, then dressing with antibiotics. I take him back to Lebei, where I am greeted by a woman who says she is a Sori who married into this "miserable" inland Usiai village and is sorry about it. She then tells me of her *bisnis* (P.E. *kin*) network on Sori Island. Siwa, who came with us from Sori, then animatedly begins pulling me about and pointing out women who were Sori who had married into Lebei.

The Lebei have their own wondrous "put-downs" of the Sori, e.g., their *garamuts* (slit gongs); it is a simple thing for them to hollow out a tree trunk now and again to make variable sized percussion instruments that produce orchestral sounds. Additionally, they "own" their ritual dramas that tell stories, and their secret myths. As I promise them that their ritual drama will be photographed, one Mwakah offers to tape record one of the very secret myths for a promise to all that I will not play this tape in Sori to be heard by profane and "enemy" ears. Here is a resumé of the myth:

> Pusuuh was an old man, who, with his two companions, flying fox, and mer-man (half-man, half-fish), lived on a mountain top on the spot where the old Lebei group used to be. He did not eat food, he merely ate smoke. One day his companions

23

went to a dance in Ponam disguised as men. Pusuuh warned them that they would regret this and that no good would come out of their pretense of being human. At the dance in Ponam they attracted the attention of the women. After the ball was over, two women followed them and said they would go with them wherever they went, and with great devotion. They told the women to go back, saying, "We are not men. . . ", but the women persisted in their passionate desire. Finally the mer-man began to change into a fish and disappeared into the sea, and the other also became what he really was, a flying fox (a kind of bat), even assuming his upside down position as he flew. The women were desperate; they had come such a long distance from their village of Ponam and. . . no husbands. As they continued their journey they fell upon old Pusuuh, with his bellyfull of smoke. They told him what had happened, and they then lived with Pusuuh.

One day the women suggested they go fishing. As Pusuuh bent over to spear a fish, one of them pushed a spear into his anus, releasing all the smoke. Then they began to feed him. The first two times he vomited the food, but the third time he held it down. They had now taken the first step towards making him human. One night as he slept, one of them put him on top of the other woman. He awakened and told them this was odd, he felt peculiar, and furthermore he had to urinate. "Well, go ahead and urinate," they said, "and then we will have a baby." This was the beginning of the Lebei people. Then the first generation created the next incestuously, i.e., brothers and sisters mated.

Pusuuh was the progenitor of the line to which Mwakah's mother belongs. The name of the line is Motokow, and these people lived at a place called Buta;isiliming. Then the Lebei discovered the ocean, which was "wet" and surrounded by a "different kind of ground" which was, as they learned later, white sand. These Lebei men in the beginning took it back to show the others and they thought it was good. The place of the sea and the sand was the place where the Motokow had settled, but the Lebei had a plan for getting this place for themselves.

They made their spears and put the parinarium nut paste on the obsidian and bamboo. They got ready for war and killed all the Motokow, and this is how they did it. The Motokow were more numerous than the Lebei and had been very successful in wars, so one of the big men of Lebei started a house of prostitution. For the cause of putting an end to the Motokow, *all* of the women were recruited for the service. First a pair of Motokow came and could hardly believe it, but they were finally convinced that the Lebei were really offering them the delights of the *house pamok* (P.E. brothel). Then came five, then came ten, and they took the good news back to the other Motokow. The Lebei felt secure in knowing that all the Motokow really believed in their generosity and so arranged for a large party one night. All the Lebei women and men, old and young were alerted by the war leader to keep a strict vigil all night, to keep each other awake by holding hands, until all of the Motokow were slain. A very large number of Motokow were killed (he says 1000, but that just means "a lot"). Three survived, and this was because of two old women. All the men who passed by asked the women for betel nut and leaf and they refused all of them except these three young Motokow who were the last to come. The women wanted the three to return the betel nut and leaf, and this delay saved their lives. Mwakah makes the point that all of the Motokow who were killed had availed themselves of the *pamok* pleasures that night.

Then the Lebei took over the place on the beach. The Lebei had descended from four men: Sosopah, Tondrih, Pamuh and Liuh, who came from the South Coast where the Manus Tru are now. They brought their names to this place and gave those names to the patrilines.

Mwakah tells of an incident during which an old man of Sori was killed. They cut off his legs and placed them near Managayeheu, so that later the Sori thought it was the Ndrehet or the Motokow who killed him. The Sori took their revenge. The Lebei had done this intentionally to destroy both the Motokow and the Ndrehet. Then the Lebei came to the beach and took the place.

Since the time Mwakah was a baby, he had the following food taboos: eel, pig, and several kinds of fruit that grow in the bush: breadfruit (family *moraceae, autocarpus integra*), a kind of large red banana, and other fruits of the bush. Mwakah tells me that they do not pay attention to taboos anymore, but I note that they do.

Although taboos are inherited from the mother, they vary according to sex and birth order. The first born will be tabooed with foods that his younger siblings can eat. Totem, called *uawu* by the Sori, is called *kuwoh* by the Lebei. Mwakah says the totem can break your arm or your leg. Another person here says that his totems are the *soholeh* tree and the flying fox, and that he got these from ghosts and ancestors. The other speaker says he got his tree totem from his father and his flying fox totem from his mother, who is a Sori. Another says there are two trees that he cannot use for firewood.

Harm would come to him even if only food were cooked on the wood from these trees unbeknownst to him.

Although I have now much interesting Usiai linguistic and cultural material, I am nonetheless relieved to leave Lebei and go back to "my" village, Sori. Lebei people stand around one and stare and keep moving in closer and closer. Even though they are extremely respectful, I feel more at ease in Sori. (Am I beginning "to buy" the Sori view of their Lebei Usiai neighbors?) We must, they say in parting, come to film their *singsings*, (P.E. songs and dances) for the Sori *singsing* is nothing compared to theirs; their *singsings* have men and real slit gongs, and their dogs' teeth are of better quality.

*November 20.* We arrive in Lebei with two large boxes of equipment; we have to wait two hours before we can begin filming. The men had spent the previous day in the bush collecting large leaves to be used for decoration but the women are only just beginning to cut them up. The children are blowing triton shells and imitating the women by cutting up smaller leaves in play. Finally we put the drama on tape and film; here is the sketch of the plot:

A Lebei woman goes into the bush. She throws a stone and inadvertently kills the baby of a *marsalai* (P.E. bush spirit, usually spiteful and malevolent). The *marsalai* are infuriated and declare war on the village. *Marsalai* are afraid to go out at night and when they come to the village in the daytime, all the people are hiding in their houses. The Lebei outwit the *marsalai* by food-gathering and water-collecting at night. Eventually the warriors defeat the *marsalai*. The movements are "danced" and the choreography is complex and interesting. The dialogues are sung by four in close harmony. The women sigh with relief and appear to be happy that I am enjoying this. Our Sori crew make derogatory remarks about the slit gong performance saying that it wasn't all that great.

Mesian and I return to Sori in a small canoe with A'amau of Lebei and BoBoyang of Sori. Midpoint between the mainland and the island we are caught in a tremendous downpour and gale. A'amau yelps continuously as though crying for help, shouting *"tambung,"* which in Lebei means "we sink." Mesian continues to bail out the water but the small aged canoe is being pulled away from our destination. I am tempted to jump out and swim to shore just to get away from A'amau and his *"tambungs,"* but I recall that that is what Michael Rockefeller did, so I concentrate on keeping my notebooks dry and on what I will do when I get home (*if* we get to Sori) to avoid getting pneumonia or something equally deadly here. I think I now know why all the Manus and Matankor have chronic bronchitis and respiratory infections. We do arrive, after an hour or so of terror, and I expect Pwepwe and Lomot to be concerned about our soaked and frozen appearance. They look frightened, sharing some inner dread, but not from concern about our perilous adventure. Actually, the wind had terrified them out of their wits and they cringed in fear that the roof would blow off the house. After hot baths and hot tea, a young girl called Shwausif, her twin brothers and her little sister pay a visit. They want to make a present to Adan of a very old ladle, made by her grandfather. As she hands it to me she tells me that she would like me to know her "real" name. It is Teresia. Some will tell you their Catholic names first and then give you their "real" names which are the original traditional names. Now this has become the focus of each new introduction. Someone will give you a Catholic name while their friends shout their native names, or vice versa. This is followed by loud arguments about which name each person there is sure that I want to know.

Today the boat named the Sunam is arriving loaded with copra from various villages; the copra will be taken in to Lorengau to the Society. Ted will board the Sunam, and he will then spend the next six months on the big island of New Guinea. Salai is teaching her baby nephew to say *"dong"* which means canoe. The women joke with me, make comic gestures about how I will be poling canoes in the future and they say to me in *talk place*, "Now you are one of us, the woman who must stay on Sori Island, alone."

*November 23.* This morning (is it because I am alone now?) the medical line-up is rather long. There is a young girl with a vermillion tropical ulcer that has eaten one-half inch into her leg. A teacher from another village brings his little girl who looks at me and screams! (Otherworldly creatures, both good and evil, are sometimes described as white-skinned. Is this how it feels to have the "wrong" skin color?) There are others with symptoms of malaria and headaches and other pains. All day people in the village reassure me that they will take care of me and the baby Adan, for now I am *theirs*. The wife of John the store man tells me that she and I have much in common: she is from Harenggan and I am from America. Is Adan Catholic, and what is his Catholic name? "Antony," I reply. And this is greeted by a group of children shouting "yay," as they did all day as various persons said that I was now theirs to have and to hold and to care for. Now that I am one of them I find it a pleasure to observe leisurely as Beripeo cooks a small, scrawny stale-looking fish in her outdoor kitchen on an old piece of metal fence. Other women are beating the trochus shell and cooking the meat from it. One of the women, who has a small baby hanging on her pendulous breast as she beats out the trochus shell meat, reminds me that Adan and I now belong to Sori. A young girl is scraping coconuts on a roughened corrugated extension to the stool upon which she sits. As I admire and as we discuss her fault-less and productive twists, a small boy runs up to scoop a handful of coconut flakes and pops it all in his mouth. We all laugh at her feigned anger, but they watch me closely as if they do not want to be mocked about my true feelings about any occurrence, no matter how minor. I am studying them, but they study me no less.

I begin to work with some of the older men to elicit information on photographs of old artifacts housed in the museums of Bremen and Stuttgart. As we work, Ebei (the old man who told me that while the land and coconut trees are his, I am welcome to them) "takes over," and the others are silent. It is a pattern seen over and over again — the hierarchy of deference. Pwepwe defers to her older brother Lohai, even though she is a better informant. Salai expects her husband Lohai to defer to her and he does. If he inter-rupts she will not speak at all until he is absolutely quiet, then she will be sullen and taciturn until he begs her to continue the explana-tion. So it is with Ebei that I work the rest of the morning.

We are interrupted only by the advent of Fathers Kopunek and Freeh from the Catholic Mission of Bundralis. They want to hear my radio and display "shock" when I tell them I have none. They announce that President Kennedy has been assassinated; that is all they heard before their radio "died." They are nice clean cut Western Pennsylvania types, who are off on a jolly crocodile hunt before they go back to Bundralis.

The Sori, having learned from the Fathers that the *number one man belong America he die finish*, are busy discussing with each other that *their* American is very emotionally upset over the death of her president and find it really touching that this could be so. I may become ill, what can they do for me? Perhaps a *singsing* will make me cry, release the tears so that nothing will get *bugger-up* (P.E. ruined) inside of me?

*Making <u>saksak</u> (sago) on Sori Island.*

*Women of Sori making shell money (sawung).*

FOUR

# On Learning To Love the Stranger

## Possessions of the Dispossessed: Sawung and the Cloud

As life becomes a bit routinized, I hope that my house will not turn into a dispensary, but of course it already has and the dubious reward of "medical successes" is more patients, but that is *not* why I am here. On more than one occasion my question, "and when did you first notice this horrible stomach pain?" elicited the reply, "just after I swallowed the pills (anti-malarials) you gave me." From tending the wound on the head of a young schoolboy severely beaten by a teacher, I learn that his mother is my silent neighbor, that her name is Sa'abwen, that she is sister to my friend Siwa, that they are both daughters of A'amau from Lebei now of *dong tambung* ("the canoe sinks") fame. The story that brings hilarious laughter of how he thought his small canoe was sinking will die only with him, or perhaps survive him. He is now referred to as *dong tambung*, and no longer A'amau. As Sa'abwen brings me pumpkins to be cooked for Adan, I go to the tobacco box to find only one stick where I was sure there should have been twelve or more. As I apologize for giving her one stick she tells me that my Manus help steal. Everyone knows that the Manus from the South Coast steal, don't I know it yet? Besides, Lomot is definitely a *meri belong hambak* (P.E. playful and promiscuous woman), and I should fire her.

At the same time, as I go back home, Pwepwe tells me that it is time I learn about the village scandal. I shouldn't be so friendly to Siwa because she is a seductress who "married Pamaleo, a man with a wife and six children, three of them very small." A young girl named Sangan enters, and Pwepwe has readied her for this meeting. Sangan, Pwepwe avers, has a sad life for a young girl. She has to work very hard alongside her mother to support the three small children of her father Pamaleo and her mother Sambuwarei, because they were all abandoned, in Pwepwe's words, to *stop nothing* (P.E. remain with no resources or support). Sambuwarei is very ashamed of all this, and that is why she avoids looking at me and why she has not come to my house yet. Indeed the entire village is deeply ashamed of this, and Pwepwe has been commissioned to tell me of it. Pamaleo had married Sambuwarei in church which he no longer attends, and the church *Padre* (*in absentia*) had even then conveyed his disapproval. So, here is the reason that Siwa has no friends in the village even though she is a delightful extroverted creature, and why she has worked so hard at getting close to me and making friends with the Manus girls in my house. Village sentiment does not approve the fact that a young girl should assume the heavy burden of the father role, chopping wood and fishing with her mother, while Pamaleo has allowed his head to be turned by a woman younger and more attractive than his wife. Sambuwarei has shaved off all her hair and wears drab, worn and torn *laplaps*, in stark contrast to her replacement's bright colors and other items of ornamentation.

Bernard is an expert in preparing food for babies. He comes in the afternoon to show me how to add sugar to the pumpkin, and some canned milk. Adan and I have an audience of 25 watching this event and my feeding him the Bernard pumpkin. When he is finished the children in the group let out a wild chorus of "yays." They then go off to spear *apwie* (a fruit) from trees, bring me some and ask me how I like their "fish." They show Adan the five pronged spear and jokingly tell him that if he were a fish they would spear and eat him. It amazes me how much cannibalism remains in the humor. Ebei and Tata still recall eating human flesh, and Ebei has on occasion indicated which parts of my body would have been particularly succulant and has added that the baby, of course, would have been considered choice. Pwepwe, still concerned about the assassination of President Kennedy wants me to write my government to say that after they hang the assassin, the body should be sent to the Sori, who will cut it up in little pieces and eat it. I am not comfortable with this humor. (What are they *really* trying to say? Do even they know? )

The afternoon has been spent with Sa'absing, aged female. I

guess I have been doing ethnographic archaeology today. In the evening, as I listen to the giggles of a group of girls night-fishing with a lantern off the shore, I am visited by Beripeo who brings me a woman whose hair has been shaved off. Beripeo asks me what I would call this, in *talk place*, please. "*Lamibatum nya' apweng*," I reply. With a lusty shout of approval, Beripeo goes on to explain that the woman shaved her head because her brother died. Now the woman looks familiar to me, and Beripeo affirms what I have been thinking, that this woman is none other than the deserted wife Sambuwarei, and that the real purpose of this visit is to bring me firmly down on the right side of morality that will have me ignore Siwa, the seductress. Just as Beripeo tells me that everything Pamaleo earns goes to Siwa and not one bit of it to the mother of his six children or to his children, who enters but my neighbor Sa'abwen, sister of Siwa, who came to stand silently so that Beripeo might be quiet. And I further learn that Sambuwarei is the sister of the dead Luwi of the recorded *cry*, so of course, Salai, Pwepwe, Lohai, Tata, i.e., those with whom I work most closely, are pressuring me to ostracize the woman who is an insult to their relative. One is forced to cut off access, so that one does not lose access — that is one of the difficulties of doing research in human societies that does not plague colleagues in other fields.

*November 26.* And then there is our Pere girl, Lomot, a "native" never encountered in the anthropological literature anywhere. She hears a plane and tells me that it is an American plane. I ask, "How do you know?"

"Because it is loud, like Americans, who are all loud." As she asks me for a cigarette I tell her to stop "bumming" cigarettes as I need them for people who are kind enough to work with me so that I might record their culture. "Yes," she replies good naturedly, "I have noticed how, with one cigarette, you open their hearts." Yet there is a way in which I am very fond of Lomot.

Today I am made a gift of *sawung*, the shell money for which the Sori are famous throughout the archipelago.[1] Pwepwe, who is present, says that she hates the *sawung* and vows she will never work for it. It is too hard. So much standing in the hot sun in the attempt to get the *sawung*. Furthermore, she recalls her childhood, when her mother and the other women left the children to "cook in the sun" under a hot pandanus mat or put them to sleep on a rock in the sun, while the women thought of nothing but their *sawung* work. Pwepwe thinks it was incredibly cruel to children, all this concern about getting and working the *sawung*.

In Sori the story of the *sawung* and the story of the cloud are always told together, an artifact and an event that are of essential significance to the Sori. Tata wanted me to know the story of the cloud first, before we did *any* work together:

"In the earliest times when there was nothing on our island but us, our people had nothing and no knowledge. A huge cloud was above the island and came down very low. It was so low it covered the houses. Alright, our men took an obsidian spearhead and put it on a pole for poling canoes. It was thrown up in the air to shoot at the cloud, which then dispersed. Those of us who came behind had no water and no food and we went about hungry. We searched and searched, we left the island, we died in numbers doing that. But some went back to our home island, and they had children, they perdured, they survived. Now there were four men: one was called Sindrayeng, one was called Bwaso', one was called Bwa'ubwehay, one was called Bwasi. They went to the sea to find fish, they saw movement and thought it was fish, but they threw a stone at it and saw that it went down. It was *tambu*, it was the *sawung*. They picked it up with bailers, then they worked it with stone. They had a big feast with this, a big ceremonial exchange with this *sawung*. They sent out the word to other groups that there would be a big feast, and the passing of time was marked by putting ten white ovalis shells on sticks. With the passing of each season, one white shell would be taken off the stick; one shell removed at the end of the monsoon, one shell removed at the end of the good weather season. That is how we told time then. These white shells were the same kind used for the penis shell dances we had then. During this big feast, they made a great deal of noise and once more threw the spear with the obsidian point up to the cloud. The noise and the spear made the cloud go away, and the *sawung* made the Sori famous in the area as the sole manufacturers of *sawung* as money and the bride price. Sindrayeng had a son named Anruhi, his son was named So'ahem, his son Mana'ahem, then Luhai, who was the father of my husband Balo'ohay, and that is why I am known as nyauBalo'ohay (widow of Balo'ohay). His son is Sapalona that some people call John the store-man. His son is Adan's new friend Cristop Ahen.

By the time of the big feast they dug a hole and put a stone with some *sawung* in it to mark who owned the *sawung*. It would be the generations to follow Sindrayeng, and Yapiyop, and Pasok and Kupweray. Later the Germans, the white man came to our big island and everything was turned topsy turvy. We lost our island, our place, our first *sawung*, our original *sawung* but our rights are still marked there, inside the stone, inside the coral.''

# The Observer Observed

The ''clinician'' aspect of my role playing is becoming troublesome. The headaches are easy and aspirin tablets are viewed as dispensed eucharistic miracles, but when I tell them that I do not know something, or that I cannot cure something, they do not believe me and find such modesty truly gracious as they smile.  Not only do they think I can cure anything, if only I *want* to, which is dreadful in its implications, but anything I say immediately becomes part of village verbal archives and living mythology.  Because I was on the canoe with A'amau, that poor old man is now known as *dong tambung* (the sinking canoe).  Because I once jokingly called a young man *bwatumbu* (ancestor) he is now known as *bwatumbu* by everyone, which has strange implications for his everyday presentation of self here.  The children cheering with every short speech I manage to complete in *Sa'apoy* is beginning to unnerve me a bit, also.  Time to read a novel that has nothing to do with the Admiralties, and to open cans of *paté de foie* and artichokes, for gustatory escapes from the present.  Also, I am beginning to learn of my shortcomings here.  Everyone on this island sees specks of sails in the horizon about twenty minutes before I do.  And I cannot seem to learn to pole a canoe, or scrape a coconut, or fish.  A typewriter will be of no help in survival here.  Still, for whatever they feel my presence is worth, I seem to be involved in exchanges constantly:  fish, pumpkins, sweet potatoes, a kind of spinach, eggs, shells, and carvings.  I give what they want:  tobacco, or sometimes tinned Australian bully beef.

Our Manus girls have been taught sewing by ''girl guides'' down on the South Coast, and they are teaching some of the women here. Although they are taught measurements, they cut by viewing the fabric and viewing the body it is to fit, then they sew with a fine stitch and inevitably the garment is too small.  They will not baste, though they have been taught that, preferring rather to use a razor to painstakingly rip seams.  Lokes will not let me teach him how to make an omelet.

In the yearly time cycle, these people are Christmas-oriented; in linear distance, they are Bundralis-oriented.  A child's age is expressed as so many Christmases, and Bundralis is where the *padre* has his seat, where one goes for Christmas and where one goes for "exams." Economic orientation is towards the bush on the mainland for sago and wood, toward the co-op in Lorengau for money, toward the sea, their reef, and old Sori for trochus shell and fish. For kinship and exchanges they look to the island of Harenngan.

# Sori Prolegomenas on Language and Culture

*December 4.* The acquisition of language is a major concern of the Sori. I had been struck by their emphases on the difficulty of the Manus language compared to the Sori language (which has no basis in fact whatsoever). Now it appears that all of Adan's attempts at making sounds (he is five months old) result in sounds that happen to be Sori words, a fact that is constantly brought to my attention by someone or other in the village. The first time it happened Beripeo said, "Ohoh, *Sori talk i kamap nau*" (P.E. Oh, oh, the Sori language is now emerging). A sample: *ma'a* (stone), *bwa* (mouth), *meh'* (he is coming), *bwey* (not), *da'* (sea), *gum* (house). Somehow Adan incorporates glottal stops, too (which I indicate by the apostrophe). His stops sound very natural and are not labored, as mine are at this juncture in my language learning.

Explanations abound for this phenomenon of Adan's *talk place*. (They curiously parallel the theories of professional linguists, though not as abstrusely worded). Some say, "you see, *Misis*, we told you that our language was easy," others use it to prove that Adan does belong to this island. Still others, now growing in number, are reaching the conclusion that this proves that the Sori language is as old as man, since a baby from a far away place has proven that it is the first language that comes to a human being naturally when that human being doesn't have his cultural language thrust upon him. To them, Adan is talking, not babbling, as he is to me, and they refuse to see it as a fortuitous coincidence. Then there are other explanations: mothers here think he is too large a baby for the five months that I claim he is; therefore I don't really know that he is older than I think! For it is a rare occasion on which one hears a Sori or Lebei baby make a sound; mothers do talk to their babies but they do not seem responsive. Teresia talks to her son, but it does not arouse the slightest bit of attention from him. I am told by Sa'abwen that if I had Adan at the breast day and night, which is where he should be, he would not cry. (And I think that probably he would also have no cause to speak.)  Thus I am told once again by Admiralty Islanders that American and Australian women do terrible things to their babies by allowing them to cry at all.

I keep working on linguistics, hoping to get more and more material in the *talk place* myself.  It is evident that in using an interpreter, usually Pwepwe, much is lost in translation from *Sa'apoy* to *Pidgin*.  Pwepwe is incredibly intelligent, she knows what I am looking for, has a good sense of boundaries in words, phrases, and sounds, as she translates for me, and she beams with approval when she feels that I have understood and doesn't wait for me to say I don't need the translation into *Pidgin*.

Kaseo and his wife Landai are ready to work on the sago palm that they felled yesterday and tell me that I may photograph the process.  Like everyone else here they are gracious about it.  I have yet to see anyone angry or sullen.  They seem to live in an Aurelian tranquility, everything in their known universe being a source of potential delight to them.  Except Bau.  He walks about, one leg thinner than the other, like the dethroned nephew in a Greek tragedy, and resentful of the chief Lohai and his family.  Still, even he is able to forget this brooding and rally a quick smile.

Kaseo tells me that *saksak* (P.E. sago) is their main staple food.  It is particularly "their" food.  They have a clear-cut notion of the uniqueness of their culture and often stress that uniqueness, overlooking similarities to other groups in the Admiralties.  I ask him if there is a "story" connected to sago and its use.  Yes.  Their ancestors did not have *saksak*, but they went to the mainland and got the seed and now they have it.  But only the Lebei know (read "own") and can tell the origin of the sago palm.  If you ask the Lebei for the "story" of anything, you get a long, involved origin myth.  Sori ancestors had cultivated *saksak*, but mostly on the mainland nearby.  Here and there on this tiny island of pounded coral one can find very small clumps of sugar cane and little gardens of a native spinach, and a red fruit that grows in a tightly knit cluster called *ayang*.

Kaseo tears off the bark with a sharp stick.  Landai is waiting at the conveyor (one-half of the lower part of a huge palm tree), the stakes and legs of which are also of palm branches or stalks of young trees.  It slants downward so that the sago falls into a dugout canoe used for receiving it.  Coconut fiber cloth is attached at the end of the conveyor to act as a sieve.  Landai gets buckets of rainwater from a hole in the ground which she throws over the shred of the fiber that is inside the sago palm.  She works it with her hands and a sort of powdery liquid goes through the *ba'a* (coconut fiber sieve).  This later settles, the water is thrown out and the powder that remains is *saksak*. Landai's apron is a large water resistant leaf.

More of Adan's Sori talk; that is, the early stages of Adan's babblings, which they are all cataloguing as proof that the Sori language was the first on the earth (this is the theory that has won over all the others). He is saying *mbu'* (banana), *'ana* (it or he/she comes to me), and *'a'a* (coconut fiber). Landai stops by to tell me she is still washing the sago palm fibers, but also wants me to know that her father married three times and now it is finished for him because he is an old man, but do I not find it ridiculous that she is taking care of a child born of her father's third marriage? This is said with much laughter, and also it is added that her brother is on his second wife, because the first one died. I ask why women die off faster than men. *Sick belong ground tasol* (P.E. illness and diseases that go with the place, that is all), was her reply. It was only much later that I was to learn that her death had to do with witchcraft that defies the cures of Western scientific medicine. Landai isn't keen on continuing the conversation about why these women die, so I gently let her go by saying that I have to go back to work. Later, as I question Pwepwe about magic, she is not willing to discuss it.

But Lomot, who was reticent about magic in Bunai, is very eager to talk about this magic, since here she treats these people as good-natured *kanaka* (P.E. a derogatory word for native). She takes me to Ebei's house to show me the *tanket* (P.E. croton leaves)[2] and how they are tied together to work magic on a man or a woman. She demonstrates how they chew pepper leaf and spit toward the person they want to kill. The intended victim does not know it; she or he thinks that a person near them is simply chewing the leaf with betel (areca nut) and lime,[3] for this is a frequent diurnal custom here. "The difference is," says Lomot with a leer, "that the leaf is very hot, and — you are busy killing someone."

Today the tape recorder is broken down and I work with Ebei, but just copying what he says in my notebook. The linguistic product is slightly different when I work in this manner. My "informant" tends to speak more clearly and repeats sounds with greater distinctiveness when I ask for a differentiation. Pwepwe sits nearby rolling her eyes to the skies as she listens to Ebei; she tells me from time to time that his *Sa'apoy* or Sori talk is not in the best classic form. I tell her, of course, that, as she knows, no one else can tell me the stories that are Ebei's "property." She agrees it has to be done this way, but is reluctant to feel satisfied with the custom. Today he gives me a story about sea turtles and two stories about thefts of canoes. These things happened before the English brought the "courts," which they think a most wonderful invention. The Germans did not have courts here, and Ebei did not like the Germans. Why? Because they threw the Sori people off Big Sori. I say I had read in the German books that the island had been purchased. Not at all, says Ebei, and everyone else within earshot. The Germans are liars. "They didn't buy it, they just threw out the *kanaka*!"

Salai comes by; I know she is going to be my best informant. For this reason I have not been pursuing her, but have played a waiting game until she came to me. She has a really interesting story, "the assassination of President Kennedy." Well! I have no news of this at all, and I write down what she tells me as she expects. The President became "John here," and the assassin was "man on top" (this is because, as she explained, in this America they build houses on top of each other and he was in a house on top.) He shot. John was dying and one can imagine, she dramatized, the feeling of a wife whose husband is dying next to her. When the man on top shot John, he said, "You, John, wherever you have been there was war." Unlike Pwepwe, she did not offer me condolences because my president had died, but felt she had given me something useful "a real story" that her husband Lohai had heard in Lorengau.

But I want to get her to talk about what in her eyes is a lesser thing: tattooing. First she dismisses a nine year old boy sitting near us, "be off with you, what business do you have sitting around with women?" The little boy darts off just in time to avoid the stick that Julia, Salai's daughter has hurled at him. He is properly frightened and there is great laughter among the females. Salai looks at me intently, and there is sudden silence. She begins,

"When a girl begins her sickness, her face is marked so that all may know that she can get married now. It is time for this." With her as with others there was a terrible bloodletting; Salai almost choked on her blood. Even with Sa'amang who is only 16 and has only a small tattoo on the center of her forehead, an infection developed and she became very ill. Salai does not want Julia to be tattooed and added, "anyway, this isn't done anymore." What is the equivalent rite of passage for boys? Salai looks at Lomot and laughingly says, "When the Misis learns that she can tell me, too." This form of not knowing what one is not to know is rigidly adhered to, but she did then venture to say that boys go sleep in the *house boy* (P.E. men's house), so all the secrets are kept there, and that is where I must go to find them. This is accompanied by a sly mock-wicked smile.

I close my notebook, but Salai is not about to end the session. Why, she wants to know, do I bathe my baby only once a day? Is it a custom of America, or do I fear he will become sick? Yes, I could say it is an American custom to bathe a baby once a day.

"Aha," she said, "that is the trouble with Adan. A baby must be washed four or five or even six times a day. He must be bathed after he eats, he must be bathed after he sleeps. . . how can he sleep covered with the sweat of the mother's arms and body." Salai feels very good about having taught me something, and I thank her. Then she adds that little Julia brushes her hair down all day because she wants to have her hair straight and flat like mine. Her last "story" for me was that of a Lebei woman who came to *Kaunsil* Lohai (Lebei village does not have a government-sponsored representative known as *Kaunsil*). Her husband had dragged her out of the house in the nude, without her *laplap*, and beat her up rather brutally in front of a group of men. Lohai will now arrange to have this case brought before the Australian Administration. Quite a contrast to the not too distant past, in several histories of adultery as I have learned from Ebei. In one instance a man and his single friend went hunting in the bush, but the single man returned to sleep with his married friend's wife. The husband came back with a knife and killed both of them. The adulteries of "time belong before" that I am told of by the Sori are all of Lebei village, however.

*Sunday, December 8.* Ebei comes to call on me, and he wants to take me to see the sea turtles that are kept at Sori #2. He had given me all the information about sea turtles in *talk place Sa'apoy*, and it was entitled *Boy ma hu'ungop Hi'inang* (Twenty turtles of my patri-clan *Hi-inang*). These were being held for a large feast to be given by his clan, but they broke the fence and got away. As women screamed and ran around the beach and into the water, the men recovered the turtles. The story itself does not appear of earthshaking significance. But such stories always contain the names of participants and the entire genealogies of those involved, as well as the "place" of each in the present society. Movements are precisely described and places are very carefully designated. A tale provides the occasion for asking questions and one can learn, for example, that the Sori still hunt for sea turtles anytime the weather permits, but I would never have known it, because they are not brought to the village unless it is for a feast. If they are to be sold or exchanged they may be kept near the house of the visiting patrol officer but not in the village. Why? Because villagers would die if sea turtles came into the village.  Why?  No one remembers why, but that is what they were told by those who went before them and they act accordingly.  All the turtles in the "passage" still belong to the Hi'inang clan and if anyone else takes them, Ebei can take them to court. Only men make the nets which are made in Ebei's house and must be completed in one night.  During the manufacture, there must be complete silence in the village, any noise at all is *tambu* (forbidden). One baby's cry can mean no turtles in the hunt, or a tragedy for the hunters.  I cringe with fear and guilt as I also learn that some in Sori fear my baby's crying for this very reason.

Ebei had promised me a special treat:  he goes out of the house and returns shortly with his "exhibits":  a coil of the rope with which the net is made, a wooden fish model made by him, a stone tied about with rattan cane, and a piece of wood hewn into a sort of handle that could be held by two or three men.  The net, which I am to imagine, comes from the island of Andra.  One half the net is still there and the other half of the net is in Sori in Ebei's house.  Ebei added, "When we go hunting for sea turtles, the two halves are joined.  Now this fish (here he shows me the wooden model) goes in the middle between the two halves.  It is taboo, and as you see, charred black by fire before it is fastened between the two halves of the net.  Taboo it is because the fish takes care of the net for us.  It remains with me and only I can put the fish between the two halves of the net.  Once another man performed that task and he died. Because it is taboo."

The fish must be placed in a special position with the head down and the tail up.  In this position it is called *ba'o*, otherwise it is called *ni*.  (*Ba'o* means place, or center, or origin, as, for example, the name of one's original patriclan ancestor is called one's *lo ba'o*, and it was translated for me in that manner — the locus of one's beginning.)  Ebei demonstrates how he weaves the rope.  The larger strand he calls *tineng* (mother of it) and the smaller strand he calls *narung* (child of it).  As he pulls them tightly together with each "stitch" he says, "*tineng, narung, tineng, narung,*" etc.  Of the utmost importance in fishing for sea turtle is to know how to "turn the talk."  Things must not be called by their real names,  that is, their usual names. They have their special or taboo names for the occasion.  For example, canoes are not called *dong*, they are called *eyyam*, the dugong or sea-cow is not called *hou*, but must be called *bwasa'o*.  The small fish *ni* are called *nimondrong*, and the *barey* (sail) must be called *loukako*. The crocodile must be called *sahay*, and not *mbuey*.  So too for the shark and the stingray, and other creatures of the deep: they must not be called by their "real names" during the sea hunt. If this taboo is not strictly observed while the net is in the water, there will be no catch. The net is put together the night before the sea hunt. There is also a taboo against yawning. The men begin to work on the net at six in the evening, and must be finished by six the following morning, with no yawns. Pregnant women, as well as mothers of small children who might cry must go to the other side of the island. The husbands of pregnant women must also go to the other side of the island, because "it is about something new," and these men also cannot join the hunt for the sea turtles. The first turtle caught must be killed by an ax in the net. His blood must run in the net, and this will insure that more turtles will be caught. The subsequent catch, however, is kept alive and these will be kept in a fenced area on #2 Sori on the mainland. Each time a turtle is caught the *garamut*, the slit gong that is brought along for such an occasion, is beaten. When the fishermen come back to the island, both men and women join in the cooking.

Today Pwepwe is especially annoyed with Ebei's tale. She repeats phrases in *Sa'apoy* at my request (an aged informant with a persistent cough and missing teeth is not ideal for linguistic analyses). She sends for Tata, who upstages Ebei, though Pwepwe has to repeat her phrases very loudly so that I can hear them. She brushes aside the turtle story as true but insignificant (only later will I learn that the Hi'inang and Luhai clans vie and have vied for ascendancy for generations). Tata wants me to write about the first contact of the Germans with the Sori people, and of a great cannibal feast that the Lindrow people had at the expense of some of the Germans. At this point a Sori named Lukas interrupts Tata, "get to the end please, I have something to say about the Germans." I ask him please not to interrupt us now, but Tata is miffed, gets up to leave and tells me we will continue another day for she must tell me about the Germans and the seven ships.

Lukas is upset because he heard that in a book I read, written by the Germans, they said that they bought old Sori Island. No, they did not buy it. Would I please write that down? They threw out the *kanaka*; they stole it. Oh yes, they gave the *kanaka* a box of cloth and glass beads, but could they really think anyone would sell their home, their land, for such trifles? The Sori accepted these trifles because one does not refuse a gift. They were just being decent to let the Germans *use* some land to plant coconut trees, land that no one else was using at the time. Salai interrupts Lukas to say that I must not keep paying everyone in the village for every egg and every piece of fruit and every little favor; it was a bad example for the children.  Couldn't I just accept things as a gift?  (One is expected to make return gifts, I suppose I am just repaying gifts too fast.)

Lukas takes the floor again.  Do I know that everyone loved the American soldiers here, and that he worked with them, not on Sori, but on the South Coast of Manus?  They were generous and paid natives very well.  But the Japanese!  They killed, they stole, they looked down on the native.  "Do you think," Lukas continues, "that the Japanese would ever come and write about us and ask us questions like you do, or like that *bikpela meri* (P.E. important woman — i.e., Margaret Mead) did for the Pere?  No, they don't care.  I helped win the war, but no I didn't kill any," he added with great shame.  "But I helped the Americans carry things — they wouldn't give me weapons."

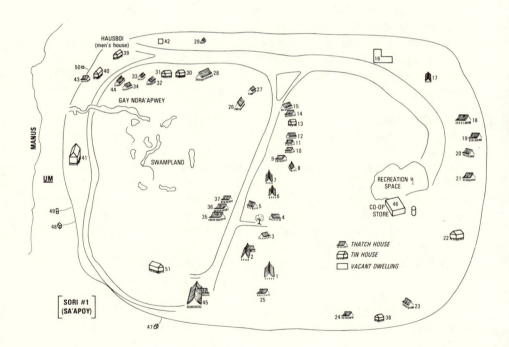

# Some Rain Must Fall

*December 9.* Blue Monday. It has poured and continues to pour rain, torrentially, and the wind blows and has blown all day, tempestuously, without respite. Not a soul in sight. I work on texts all day.

I fall through a rotten board in the floor. This brings a sudden visit from *kaunsil* Lohai, and four men ripping out the rotten boards to replace them. Among them Pwayyam, who is grateful for the opportunity to repay me for what he considers the saving of his leg from an intractable infection. Today there were elections for *kaunsil* and Lohai won again and will continue in his position. The balloting was handled in this manner: An administration official came from Lorengau to supervise the putting of pieces of paper into the tins that were labeled with pictures of coconuts for Lohai, and pictures of fish for Damian of #2 Sori, who lost. Several men mentioned to me during the day that they found this choice rather odd — they liked both fish and coconuts. When I tried to explain the symbolism for the candidates they said that they also needed both men to run the village, and they added, "It is just as stupid as choosing between fish and coconuts."

*December 10.* The baby has had sores in his mouth for several days, and none of the medications that I have are of any use. He cannot eat and his cries are becoming more and more feeble. At times like these, I wonder what motivated me to come to this outpost of former empires to poke into the secret museums of human culture. I am overcome by guilt and shame; what kind of a mother am I? It is the season of the Northwest monsoons which they call *dyapay*, and no one sails. But we are not alone and forgotten on this tiny island, for on this afternoon two Catholic brothers who "simply never stop on Sori Island" just happen to do so today. After they introduce themselves saying that no one had sent them, I said, "You are wrong, Saint Anthony sent you, let us be off." And so with Father Kelly and Brother Ryan we are off to the Catholic Mission at Bundralis in a 19 foot sailboat with an outboard motor not meant for this vessel. We suffer a terrible two hours, with both Mesian and Pwepwe white with fear as the boat is tossed on immense waves which I had never even imagined possible. The little boat is turned at precarious 45 degree angles with unforeseeable rapidity as we work furiously with buckets and bailers to keep the hull from filling with water.

I keep punctuating the long silences by pronouncements such as, "This is it!" which annoys Brother Ryan, who keeps assuring me that once we are inside the reef we will be safe because the boat has a keel. Only later does he tell me he was sure it was the end. Only later do I learn that the "captain" kept swearing in his *talk place* of Bundralis that if we sank he would bring this matter to court, that he had never been in such rough seas and that only a madman would set forth in them.

Bundralis has been a seat of the Catholic Mission on the North Coast of Manus for about forty years. When Father Kopunek came here circa 1957 there were only shells of buildings riddled with bullets from World War II. But a school, a plantation and some surplus trucks from the Australian Navy has turned this into a Mecca for the Catholics of North Coast villages.

There were a certain number of Sori people there who had come for the upcoming holidays, and they gave us a rousing welcome. All our movements were accompanied by hordes of children shouting, "Adan, Adan, Adan First Class, Adan Number One." Adan has "thrush" and I am given dequadin paint for it by Dr. Kila Wari, a native from New Guinea trained in medicine in Fiji. An Anglo-Indian doctor is here also, and he is to accompany Dr. Kila Wari to the North Coast to investigate incidences of tuberculoid leprosy. Some cases have been found there, particularly in the village of Lessau. These patients will be sent to Port Moresby, then to the island of Analawa for isolation and cure.

*December 11.* From Bundralis to Lorengau, where I stay with the O'Malleys, pick up copies of Time magazine, and my daughter Deborah, who has come in from the Ascham School for girls in Sydney to Christmas vacation with me. I wait for a boat that might be going to the North Coast but since there is none I look up Reverend Norman Dietsch of the Lutheran Missions to rent the Talatala, which seems to me to be an engine with a minimal boat-like shell around it.

O'Malley's maid wants Mesian to tell me the latest news about my "beloved" Melien the Dritambat schoolteacher. (I will never be forgiven for having said she was charming). It will be recalled that in addition to her illegitimate "black Buka" baby she had a Caucasian lover and that he had been relieved of his post because of it. *But*, now I should know that Melien would be in for a surprise. Said lover was to have been sent to Goroka, but instead will be sent to Australia. She will not find him there, and when she returns she will be told that she no longer has a job in the Manus schools. As I checked this out with my "European" friends here (all whites are called Europeans), I commented that it was a bit too cruel. Yet both European and native think her "cheeky" to have an affair with a white, and consider him to have behaved in very bad taste. Many think his age (fortyish) made him lose his head. Another Australian who has taken up the fine sport of being seductive with native girls is considered merely contemptible, and all feel sorry for his wife who works at a Chinese trading post in Lorengau.

*December 15.* Norman Dietsch is not going to charge me for the Talatala because he is taking back 15 North Coast inhabitants anyway, but he wants me to lend him a book or two to read. The trip is noisy and miserable, and I am relieved to arrive, but puzzled by the fact that only one canoe with two small boys and another with people I don't know from the village are there to take us to shore. Pwepwe turns her face away in shame, Lohai tells me that he would have come to get me, but he was asleep. Something is wrong, but how will I know what and how should I conduct myself?

*December 16.* Only Beripeo stops by the house. The rains are torrential. She had just been to Ndrehet, looking for food. She has none, there is none on the island and her son "America" comes home from Bundralis today. She found only a bit of sago and so I give her a pumpkin and ask Lomot to give her some of my rice for a meal for her family. Lomot gives her what must be seven pounds of rice. Angered, I say nothing until Beripeo leaves. Then I tell Lomot that it is not possible to give one person in a starving village seven pounds of rice, and to give nothing to anyone else in the village. This can only lead to one friend and many non-friends, not to mention the total injustice of it. Then she shows me a large sack of rice that is ¾ gone, saying that Lokes, the cook and Pwepwe gave it all to certain people in the village, and that these "certain persons" also received tinned beef and tinned fish from these two. Lokes always like to play village chief with the supplies of people he works for, and I suppose that it makes sense to him. What is so damaging about the episode is that those who accepted rice from Lokes are so ashamed that they cannot even look at me. The Sori are proud and do not want "something for nothing," as I have noted on many occasions. Shocked by bad manners, discourtesy and appropriation of the property of others, they must have been in dire need to have accepted handouts from Lokes. These people would have gladly promised to work for food received, and he has damaged my excellent rapport with them. Today, then, I send 3 lbs of rice to Tata, with the message that this was to thank her for all her marvelous stories.

It is a bad *dyapay* this year, there is no fishing, and virtually no food on this island save for the coconuts. It must have been the same in old Sori, for many of the historic recountings abound with reports of no food and "we were spent, totally weakened, we had to leave."

Tata and Pwepwe decide they want to help me with some difficulties I have been having with the texts Tata dictated. In addition, she offers to give me two more stories, which here seems to mean recountings of historical events. It seems that when the English came to Sori to claim the island, they put black cloths around the trees to mark their possessions. A neighboring group came to steal the cloths and were massacred by the Sori, and their corpses were sent to the Tulu, as a gift for a meal or two. The old people of Sori speak with utmost candor about cannibalism, and this candor is deplored by the young and the middle aged. Tata witnessed this incident herself, and went to hide in the bush when the fighting got ugly. As we work, we are surrounded by children who listen with attention and who occasionally break up an utterance for me so that I "will be able to write it better." They appear to look for cues, a wrinkled brow, a pained expression of mine, and then they come to my immediate aid. My appreciation is not shared by the adults, who growl at them to remind them that they are not "in their places" by doing this.

*December 19.* I begin to work with a young man named Takaray from Lebei. The language is very different from the Sori. Most of the Lebei do not want to come here to work since they think I should have anchored in their village. Beripeo's son "America" comes bearing eight coconuts and several small fish, to repay the rice that I gave them several days back. The lack of food is creating a problem, still it underlines the basic integrity of these people. I cannot seem to dispose of articles that are no longer useful. A pencil that will not write or a broken thermometer will be returned to me. Talk of shillings causes embarrassment, though they will accept tobacco. Hard times are reflected in the fact that everyone goes out everyday into the bush for sago, or stands for hours trying to catch tiny fish which they don't find at all tasty. They are graceful figures, standing in the sea, looking much like a French painter might imagine women and children fishing in the South Pacific. When I photograph them they turn toward the camera with charming smiles. Several men have remarked that the most extraordinary thing about Adan is that he knows how to behave when he is being photographed. Yet my inquiries yield the inconsonant information that only one or two of the men and none of the women have ever seen photographs of themselves!

Pwepwe's father is Simbuom, aged and ill, but he wants to work with me anyway.  He is so grateful for the miracles of aspirin and particularly the suppositories.  Like most of the other elders, he can recall and recite eight generations, though some can go back as far as ten or twelve.  After that, like all the others, he gives the totem animal or bird as the progenitor of the furtherest generation he can recite.  His patriline members are well memorized, but he doesn't know who his grandmother is on his mother's side.  Reluctantly, after my prodding, he will release the name of a woman in the father's lineage, adding, "but she married a Ponam man."  Marrying out into another group spells the end of her for family reckoning. No one in Simbuom's family is quite certain of the names of her children, exactly.

After Simbuom, I thought it fun to do Ebei's genealogy in depth since his *Hi'inang* clan was the "other half" of the island's largest groupings (in the classical anthropological moiety pattern).  Ebei begins by asking me if I want to know how God made all the families first and perhaps made even God's family, though he is not sure about that.  He is relieved when I say that we can dispense with that part, since I already know it; let us just begin with his family.  This took many hours of description and explanation, but I did understand why the *Luhai* clan claims that Ebei's people "run all around inside the *Luhai* clan."  Ebei's little grandson is the last survivor of the *Hi'inang*.  Ebei shrugs as he says this and adds, "The *Hi'inang* women have made plenty people come up inside the *Luhai* clan."

But Ebei much prefers recounting historical events about thefts, lies, adulteries, and cannibalism.  Whatever I may have heard, he warns, in the interest of accuracy I must know that the Sori did more than their share of eating other people.  But not the *one-talks* (P.E. those who speak the same or closely related language).  They only ate people whose languages were unintelligible.  If they understood the language, these cadavers were sent to trading partners so that *they* might eat them.  In this version of the story of the early meetings of the Sori with the Germans, not unlike the others, he also tells of how these two groups could only communicate with gestures, but it was friendly.

When there was hunger on the island, the Germans and some Sori men went to the Lindrow further up the North Coast for sago, but they were themselves killed and eaten.  The Sori were shocked to be ousted from their original big Sori island by the Germans, and they felt certain that when they returned merely to ask for some food during hard times, they would be lent food. Instead their return was greeted by a hail of bullets.

*December 21.*   Clinic time is too busy, there is much fever, many headaches and a great deal of *deygay* (diarrhea). I feel like an ancient Egyptian doctor treating only symptoms, but I do not dare to do otherwise. Kaseo has split his foot open with an ax and is deathly white with fear. All assure him that the Misis can take care of anything, which makes me uncomfortable. A man who got a severe case of *deygay* "after the aspirin" I "gave him," got a long lecture from me on valid inference. Whether he understood or not cannot be known, but like the others here, he responded very well to being scolded.

*December 23.*   Christmas time. The Manus people in my house asked and got my permission to go to the South Coast for the holidays. Lokes has found me his replacement as cook and general caretaker, and Pwepwe will have Adan all to herself. Lomot, Mesian and Lokes are going off in a canoe as far as Lorengau. Adan is greeted hourly by someone or other who shouts joyously, "Oh, Adan, your Manus girls are leaving you." I lend our canoe to Lohai and others that they might sail to Bundralis. All of their canoes are much too small for the open seas in this monsoon season. Of course, for our *lakatoy* (large sea-going canoe of the Manus Tru of Pere) one needs a sizeable crew, and after recruiting in both Sori #1, and #2, all Lohai comes up with in the way of crew is four women, including his own wife and daughter. He then asks if he might borrow my sails only; a sail the size of mine on a canoe a quarter of the size would do wonders for a trip. As he unfurls the sail, he repeats with tenderness and fondness, "Oh, what magnificent sails." This is said to Adan, of course. When the Sori express any emotion they do it to the baby, never to me. And when Ted was here, no emotions were ever expressed in his presence. The beach in front of my house is crowded with those leaving and those wishing them a good journey and giving them small things like tobacco or fruit.

I am working with Tata, and those who hear us express disapproval of her use of a word *a'en*, which they tell me is not Sori talk. Since this non-Sori object was "on his arms and on his legs as he was put in a jail" I decided it had to be a re-phonemecized English word, "irons." My departing helpers shout their approval of my agreeing with them, and explaining it. As they hear the "*ho langa*" (sail is going up now) announcement of departure they scream with delight as I reply to their questions in *talk place*, and in proper form.

*December 24.* I had asked Lohai if I could be *kaunsil* while he was gone, and he had said, "Yes, *kaunsil* of Pwepwe and Sirip (a young boy)" Pwepwe added, "and Adan shall be *kaunsil* of Lebei." No one ever forgot this and it seemed hilariously appropriate that the Lebei Bushmen should have for a *kaunsil* a baby with a ludicrous sunhat, a chin stained by gentian violet medication, who dribbled and put anything in his mouth. Pwepwe now calls him *kaunsil* of Lebei each time she changes his diapers, and when she takes him for a walk and shows him the *Um* side of the island that faces the Lebei village she will say, "*Kaunsil*, behold your people," while all the Sori within earshot laugh loud and long.

*December 25.* All have gone to the *house lotu*, and I am here alone with Adan and Deborah, who is busy making a neat copy of my map of the village. It is a pleasant sunlit morning and hosts of birds appear. Four of my "patients" arrive, however, but they are all doing well and leave to go back to Lebei. Deborah sighs that the children have no Christmas gifts and I ask her to notice that they do not feel deprived because of it. She constantly wonders how they can have "nothing to play with" and yet appear to have so much fun. They are delighted with their own games of hide and seek in the swamps and in the huge clumps of grass, and no game of "kick-ball" was ever played more enthusiastically than theirs with one old deteriorated ball.

After *lotu*, Lukas comes to visit and brings me a polished oyster shell and wants to ask me something, if I have time. How did the war end? He wanted to know if it was true that the Americans dropped one big bomb over Japan and killed all the Japanese. I felt very ill at ease telling him about Hiroshima and Nagasaki, but Lukas' reactions were not expected. He said it was fine; Americans were good, they would win all future wars.

*December 26.* Alas, not everyone is a good informant. Some will tell you what is wrong with the original version of something, but they do not know it, nor do they know any version. Some cannot give you their genealogies. Some give you series of unrelated explanations, but Pwepwe knows everything. As I notice quite a few *nyau* before names, I learn that it means widow, and that both men and women assume the names of their dead spouses as long as they honor their memory. But one can lose "their right to it." Beripeo used to be called NyauLoniu (widow of Loniu) but after she had a lover, a teacher from Ponam whose intentions were not respectable, her deceased husband's sisters made a public request that she be called by her own name. Beripeo is ostracized in other ways; she may not get on canoes when everyone else does but must join the canoe later in a lonely spot, after everyone else is on it. Small children are not brought to her house, for they may become ill. Two unions are frowned upon in this village; Siwa, mentioned earlier, and her "husband," and Dzoppa and Nupepa. The latter left his legal wife for Dzoppa with whom he has had four children. They are not avoided on village paths, but no one goes into their homes. These ostracized women were quick to make friends with my Manus Lomot and Mesian, putting the Manus girls out of favor with the village. And, of course, the Sori do not like the fact that the Manus girls are not Catholic but members of the Paliau church. Village wisdom has it that the Southcoast Paliau church approves of such godless unions; that is why these girls befriend Siwa and Dzoppa. Pwepwe asks me, for the villagers want to know, is it true that America abounds with divorced people and insane people? I tell her we have a goodly share of both and she replied, "That is because you have too many people in your country."

# On Sori Identity

Tata gives me a "story" of the dispersion of the totemic matrilines, which to me recalls the Diaspora. It is not an arbitrary choice, for I see much similarity between the Sori fountainhead of morality and that of the Ancient Jews: loss of the Big Island (their homeland) and the long historical wandering. It is this loss and this wandering that gives them a sense that they are superior to those who have not been thus deprived, that is to say, "chosen." And to this end, genealogy is crucial to identity in satisfying requirements for group membership. For this reason they also scorn adulterers, prevaricators, and the eschewing of Puritanism in any form.

As they depend mostly on the random game strategies of the ocean for survival, they scorn "Bush people," here in the solid flesh as their neighbors, the Lebei; for Bush people have a steady food supply, and even those large trees for canoes, for which the Sori have to bargain and trade. They heap scorn on the Lebei myths while they rejoice in the agony and poignancy of their own *real* history. They have been truly hungry, and in this they see their validated moral strength and superiority.

They see their language as pristine and pure. Not only were phonemic comparisons constantly drawn for me between Sori purity of sound compared with the "cumbersome" Bush languages, but I was also urged to note the finer /l/ to the cruder /r/ shifts as one went from the Sori tongue to the closely related language of the islanders of Harenggan.

In the cloud story, aside from the interesting feature shared by other cultures of the world, e.g., the dispersion of a cloud (or other intrusive dystonic occurrences) by a loud noise and pointed objects, Tata brought to my attention the bases of social structure in naturally occurring events. The year is divided into two seasons, the *Duupwiy* ("good weather, clear water") and the *Dyapay* (the Northwest monsoon season). Each period lasts about six months. The passage of time was noted, for ceremonial purposes only, by erecting posts on which white shells were placed and then removed with the passage of each season. These were only for feasts, dances and songfests that led to the *lapang*, or "the feast of the important man," celebrated after the tenth shell was removed. The *lapang* is the only festival that depends on a period of time and not on the marking of time through rite of passage in the life of an individual.

Basic to social structure is the manner in which the island is divided conceptually, and this is based on the directions of the winds, which, in part, bring the seasons:

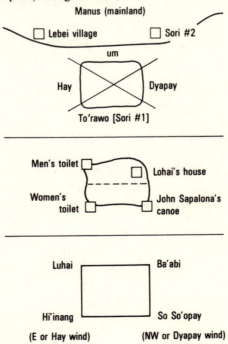

Manus (mainland)

☐ Lebei village          ☐ Sori #2

um

Hay          Dyapay

To'rawo [Sori #1]

Men's toilet ☐          ☐ Lohai's house

Women's          John Sapalona's
toilet ☐          ☐ canoe

Luhai          Ba'abi

Hi'inang          So So'opay

(E or Hay wind)          (NW or Dyapay wind)

The above "concepts" of Sori are superimposed. Each of the four patriclans is identified with a wind direction. Hi'inang and So So'opay were regarded as the closest of kin which (I am told) is why they were given the "winds" that are "theirs" and which mark the part of the island they may live on.

When I ask which lines are the most distinguished I am told that *all* the patrilines are *lapan* (of important men) and no one is *narubweyey* ("not son" or commoner). Ebei gets particularly infuriated to even think of such folk, if they were here at all, "Such people have nothing. They are rubbish and would resort to stealing. We have no such here in Sori." Of course, he wants me to know, many left Sori during the time of the famine that followed the cloud episode, taking whole families with them and leaving lines so impoverished that they then became extinct.

In the past, a *Loba'oh* (patriline) had its own men's house, called an *amang. Amang sayyem* referred to those who belonged to one men's house. In Sori, all men, both married and single used to sleep in the men's house, leaving the family house (*gum*) to be slept in by only women and children. Men must always be ready for a raid or a fight and that is why they slept in one place, so it is said. They used to visit their families and sleep with their wives "but not very often" (About once a week?) No, not that often. Men had to be ready for attacks from enemies. Women used to cook food in their *gum* and bring it to the men's house to their husbands and sons. The *amang* (men's house) contained carvings of snakes, birds, and human figures, carved in secrecy and brought to the dancing platform. There were also four posts carved as men, two each guarding the two doors to the *amang*. (When the Americans stopped there for a short while they used the posts for target practice. This distressed all considerably since they thought that in all other ways the Americans were very very kind and good.)

A boy's initiation to the men's house consisted of nose-boring (making a hole in the septum), performed by the mother's brother, who would suffer social censure for not observing the proper ritual in this regard. Foodstuffs were brought and a cut ear of a pig was thrown on the roof of the boy's father's men's house. A boy was then isolated with a wall of pandanus mats (made from a tree of the family *pandaceae*) until his nose was healed. The feast for this event was called the *anay dari*, which means, the "food of the boring." The child was named by the women of the patriline after an ancestor of his.

One has to show nothing but great respect for his or her *giriye'* (woman of the patriline). If you do not, you will get sick, your bones will loosen from the flesh, you will get sores, you will die. The *giriye'* have cursing power. ("They can throw one down, they can destroy one.") The verbalization of this cursing power is called *tutuhu*, and it is, "probably the worst taboo one can break amongst us."[4]

Cross-cousins may joke with each other; Lohai wanted to emphasize that here it is only between cross-cousins of the same sex, for only these may joke. I note once more that since I have been here I have seen or heard no nuance of any relationship between the male and female sexes.

My Lebei "texts" are interesting not only because the language is very diverse from the Sori, but because rather than focusing on historical events the Lebei accounts are characterized by having those elements common to many myths in other parts of the world. It would delight Levi-Strauss to find his structural elements of "the high and the low," "the inside and the outside," and the web of kinship in every plot (Levi-Strauss 1969). In the interstices we find a bit of fornication, a great deal of flatulence, noises counterbalanced by deep silence, and messages made explicit by covering objects with faeces. Deborah finds their "stories" (her words), "psychotic," but I find them fascinating and one might say "primordial."

*December 27.* My new caretaker is (not to my surprise) Lohai's younger brother. He cannot do anything except prepare seafood and he has done marvels with a large number of river oysters that I have received as a present. Lukas comes by with a finger so severely cut so that it is almost detached. I stop the bleeding, bandage it, and revive him with a double Scotch, as he smiles with pleasure. There was a sizeable audience for this small miracle as people gathered to await the arrival of those returning from Bundralis.

How is this night different from other nights? Having been up since before dawn I decide to go to bed early, exhausted from working on Lebei material. As I put out the Coleman lamp, there is a small explosion and I note that I am ablaze! It occurs to me that *I* can set the house on fire, the baby on fire, as well as the girls, and Deborah, and my field notes. I run out (an error!) through the kitchen so that I can alert the girls to keep their eyes on the baby and the house and the lamp. Pwepwe and Mesian take one long look at me and began to scream and to weep. I continue to beat the flames and try to rub them off my clothing, but pain put an end to that. Leaping down the rickety "stairs" and looking at the shore I think I know the solution. Lomot alone keeps her head; she jumps down the stairs and douses me with a bucket of water she herself had filled, as the others wailed. Throwing sand on the flames, she puts me down on the sand and rolls me over in it. The others are still weeping and it is up to Lomot to go into the house and put out the blazing lamp before it engages the thatched roof in a bonfire.

I am badly burned and out of medication for burns. (People get burned frequently here while cooking or using fire for other domestic purposes.) The entire village has come to the house, some inside and others outside, and all stand about as in mourning. Lohai wants me to be taken to Lessau by canoe, but with no wind I feel I would just as soon take my chances in the morning, if there are any chances then. Lohai imperiously orders seven men into a canoe (*lau ehetarop ila dong*), and suddenly I realize that I finally understand the *talk place*! Now John Sapalona (the "storeman") steps forth to place the blame for this travesty. He commands, "Let me see that lamp!" and then he announces to all, "This lamp is ruined. It was filled up too much, and that is why the Misis is in there suffering." The people gathered about then begin to say that the Manus man, Lokes, trying to play Big *Lapan* (important man) had lent the lamp to men to go night fishing while I was in Bundralis and Lorengau, and that is when it was ruined, and that Lokes also chose as his replacement Sirip, telling me he had worked for Europeans when everyone knew that he never had. So, although "the Manus" Lokes and his pretensions were the immediate cause, there ensues much discussion about other *real* fundamental causes, for they stay outside my house for most of the night. Their voices and phrases carry connotations of a collective guilt: why did this happen? They had promised they would take care of me. But since to them what is contiguous in time and space is causal they conclude that it was something "no good" on this island to which the Germans had condemned them that caused this evil.

The pain begins to subside somewhat around 4:00 a.m., and the baby has to be nursed, pain and agony notwithstanding. I begin to worry only when I ask why my hands are bandaged so tightly and am told that they are not bandaged. The swelling and color of my hands, arms, body and thighs are horrendous, so I look no more, but gaze at the indifferent moon over a sea that now seems to rise vertically creating prison walls, and I ask myself once more what drove me here, and why does a force within me prevent my using this minor (or major?) tragedy to leave this isolated and difficult island, that should have remained in the imagination of scriptwriters and novelists.

## NOTES

1. *Sawung* is a small cone shell found on the reef of "big Sori" Island from which these people were ousted by the Germans. In color and shape it is like the Virgin Cone (*Conus Virgo Linné*) found in Indo-Pacific Bays, except that it is extremely small measuring under one-half inch from tip to tip and in diameter measuring under one quarter inch at the widest point.

The tips of this cone are chopped off with a sharp-edged stone and the resulting "beads" strung together. In other instances, *sawung* refers to belts made from these shell beads. Some of these are cut to an approximate size so that they can be placed in a stone with rounded out depressions in it, then they are polished off with a flat stone. The resulting "beads" of shell are then strung together and pulled through grooves in a rock that has been prepared for that purpose. They are pulled through these grooves repeatedly until they become smooth.

2. *Tanket:* (*Taetsia fruticosa* of the *liliaceae* family). Leaves may be purple, pink, green or yellow and sometimes white-spotted. The plant may attain a height of ten feet. It is widely used in the territory for ceremonies or magic.

3. The betel nut is the nut of the areca palm (*Areca Catechu*); it produces noticeable physiological effects, and contains a narcotic that relieves fatigue and hunger and induces a state of well-being. Betel nut, as will be seen in this narrative, is an important ingredient in many facets of social interaction, both casual and formal. It can be a message to ask another group for help in a war. It is also associated with ritual and magic, as one can see by perusing the myths included here.

Lime is produced by burning either coral or shells. The specifics were given to me and will be found later in the text.

4. The parallel among the Manus Tru of the South Coast is the *tendri-teniteni*. See Fortune 1935:78.

*A Sori widow in proper attire.*

# FIVE

# Further Usiai Encounters and "Home" Again

## Among the Lindrow, with Reflections on Christian Missions and "Primitive" Thinking

*December 28.* The Reverend H. K., Lutheran Minister and Missionary arrives at 6:30 a.m. to take me to Lessau, having been summoned by the men who sailed from Sori. He removes the liquid from the huge blisters of fluid with a syringe, provisionally dresses the burns, while villagers look on in wonder and horror. Then we go: I, Pwepwe, Lomot, and Adan, while Deborah and Mesian remain in Sori. The Reverend Hans is annoyed that the canoe is not ready, while Lohai stands about speechless, looking miserable and penitent. Later the Reverend is annoyed that the crew would rather be pulled by a little wind than row and he reprimands them. In his annoyance he tells me that natives are like this about sickness, even with their own families, although one cannot beat the South Coast Manus for being particularly lazy, proud and stubborn. According to Hans, the North Coast people are much better. Nevertheless he generalizes, "You cannot tell them anything, they know it all. You can't even tell them what is wrong with motors, about which they know nothing." On such occasions, Hans himself had been given "lectures by the Manus on motors." On one occasion, he said, after six hours a young man was still trying to get a motor started, but Hans was so impressed by the lecture the young man had given him on motors that Hans decided not to help him, although he could have.

"Now watch" says Hans, and what he predicts occurs precisely. The crew of nine from Sori scream at the wind, the rocks, and at each other. "Take down that sail," screams Hans, but they do not, as we come dangerously close to the huge rocks on which the German Mission had placed a huge cross. Hans commands that they "scoop up the sail and direct the wind." This they do (they might have done it of their own accord and of their own judgement) and we miss crashing into the rocks by a hair. The Sori crewmen murmur to me as we disembark that the Mastah might know something about the sea, but they know more, for they, Manus, don't crash into rocks, do they? (They refer to themselves in this context as "the Manus" rather than Sori!)

Receiving excellent care and collecting linguistic samples and myths and historical accounts from the Lindrow is an unexpected bonus. I do not even have to work for rapport, for Hans brings me the best and most knowledgeable informants and tells them that they must tell me what I want to learn. They do so openly, willingly and with great generosity, for "archival" materials do not arouse too much anxiety — either in the informant or in the investigator.

*January 1, 1964.* I learn that a young man, So'ong, who had gone with others to search for opossum in the bush on the mainland had been lost. Men had set forth daily from the village to look for him, returning at night but to no avail. A witch in Lebei had been consulted, and he said that So'ong was dead of hunger and bush spirits. When they were told that the Lebei witch Ndrayawin said he was dead, they gave up the search. And it was on that very day, four days after he was lost, that So'ong appeared on the beach, exhausted and practically starved. The beach, that is, on the mainland. Baripeo saw him as he raised his arm and rubbed his stomach with the other. She rounded up some men who went to get him with a canoe. Too weak to walk or talk, he was carried and fed immediately. (I wonder what this will do for the witch Ndrayawin's professional future. It will probably give more business to the other Lebei witch until *he* makes a gross error and the error of Ndrayawin will have been forgotten as clients then rush to him. It will certainly prove the superiority of Sori Purity over the Bush Devils of the mainland.)

*January 2.* I have re-read all of the New Testament, not only to please the Reverend Hans and repay his kindness, but because that is the only literature available here. I am well enough to go to the house of the missionaries for dinner and we discuss the systematic theology of St. Paul in the Epistles. We discuss whether and when Christ is or is not in history. He enjoys these talks and says he will use them to think about sermons he will give in Germany.

The Lutheran Evangelical Mission is also called Liebenzall Mission of USA, Inc. It has been in New Guinea since 1914. Actually it is Protestant interdenominational but leans toward Lutheran and Methodist. In the Admiralties they have bases at Lessau, at Lugos, and at Loniu. (Most of the financing for these mission activities comes from Germany, but some also comes from America.) There was one donation from a tiny village in the black forest for the Manus Mission: 65 very poor people gave $75.00. According to Hans, almost one-fifth, about 4000, of the Manus are Lutheran. Of these, he would call one-half of them Christian and one-half of them "followers." Lessau features an infant welfare center, where people do bring their babies to be checked and weighed, to get vitamins and inoculations and vaccinations. They also come from several other nearby villages and islands. The Reverend Hans does not like the Catholics who are based at Bundralis, Bipi, Patu, and Papitalai. He thinks that they teach the natives not Christianity but Idolatry. But he really despises the Seventh Day Adventists, whom he refers to as "spiritual pests." The Catholics, according to Hans, used to build their churches like men's houses, for added allure. He said that in 1959, the Catholics began a rumor, coming from four points of the compass in Manus, that the Day of Judgement was coming and only Catholics would be saved. This was a clever imitation of cargo cult behavior, Hans felt.

Cargo cults are types of millenial movements which predict the day of the return of the ancestors, who will bring all the goods and privileges of the white man for the native. To receive this, elements of the traditional culture have to be destroyed and moral rectitude has to be observed by all. Failure of the day of reckoning has been explained always by the moral failure of some person or persons to abide by the prescribed behavior: confession of sins and purity of motive.[1] Hans adds that his own native teachers were inclined to believe in cargo cult promises but threatened some sort of reprisal when the Day came and nothing happened. As he begins to excoriate the intelligence of the "natives" again, I tell him about a cargo cult featuring flying saucers and judgment day in Michigan, U.S.A.

*January 6.* Sister Traute puts me back to bed for days, saying that I have been working too hard and I am "worsened." I have been working with a very good informant called Bogandi, who finally told me his "real" name, So'opon. The myth of Lapalokoyan is a real find. He will not tell me their precious myth, that of Busibati, because that belongs to an old man and can be told only by him. My Lindrow informants are surprised that I know some words in their language and I tell them that there are similarities there to both the Sori and Lebei languages. "Yes," I am told, "Ours was the first language, and it was later given to the Sori and the Lebei, but neither group was able to learn it correctly."

Bogandi had not wanted to tell me the story of Lapalokoyan, the founder of his patriline. A pity to waste such a good story on a woman. I insisted, saying that white men would hear it if I now wrote it down on paper. The Reverend and his wife also convinced him that he was wrong to consider me less than a man, for in our country it was not so. Reverend Hans remains to be be sure I get the real version, and to provide a male audience to avoid expurgation of texts. It is difficult to write with both hands bandaged, but my persistence is appealing to Bogandi, who first "gets trapped," and finally caught up in the Lapalokoyan story:

> "His head is that of a man, his body is snake. His name is Lokoyan and all my *tumbuna* derive from him. He didn't sleep in a house, he slept in a tree. He slept coiled around the tree putting his head to rest on top. His mother slept in her house on top of the mountain. He could do nothing but fish. He didn't eat food, he ate betel nut, that is all. In the afternoon he would ask his mother to fetch his small canoe, his line, his *karuga* (P.E. "raincoat" of pandanus leaves), the betel, lime and leaf and he would go "hook." By dawn, having caught many fish, he would dock his canoe on the beach while his mother would take the fish, smoke them and eat them. He would then ask her to bring betel nut for him.
>
> Now it was the time of the Big Northwest (monsoon); a big tree that had been uprooted drifted to the shore. Lokoyan heard the noise of the tree knocking against the beach. He came out, and sitting on his usual stone he asked, 'Where did you drift from?' The tree stood up. It was not shaking anymore from having been rocked by the sea. Lokoyan went for a love charm from his own tree where he sleeps. He asked the tree to bring this to a girl named Botohusini'in who was about to be married to a man. He told the tree to split open and as he placed the love charm into it, he ordered it to go to Salien. The tree drifted to the place that was the drinking water source of all the Salien people. The women used to come there to fill their receptacles with water. The tree opened up and the scent of the love charm escaped. The girls asked as they inhaled the fragrance, 'Where is that wonderful young man that we smell?' They found the tree which had drifted ashore. All of the girls came to wash in the water where the tree was standing and rubbed themselves against the tree but they did not tell the men anything about it.

Now it was the wedding day of Botohusini'in. She was itchy and overly warm and got her father's permission to go bathe in the cool waters around the big tree. Excusing herself from her friends who had accompanied her she sneaked away to the bushes to the tree itself, straddled it, and the tree went off as if propelled by a motor. The girls squealed, 'Oh, look, the tree took the bride away.' Men of Salien took to the pursuit in a canoe, but lost sight of the tree, which went all the way to Sori, to Sopasopa, to Harenggan and then came back to the snake on the stone in Lessau. Now the sun had gone down. It was Lokoyan's mother who got the girl and took her into the house to look after her. She put the girl on the table, as in the traditional ceremony for a bride to be, a table with a special carved ornamentation on the sides. But Lokoyan said to his mother, 'Oh, I cannot marry her, I am a snake, how can we have children?' Now Lokoyan's mother did not have trouble taking care of the girl, because all she had to do was think of something and it would appear. The girl was usually astounded to see food suddenly appear for her to eat. Well, the men in Salien had not given up pursuit of the girl and they finally found her. Upon being questioned Lokoyan said, 'I found her on the tree, and feeling sorry for her I took care of her. Before you take her back, come into my house and eat, and rest.' Because of the mother, there was no problem with the food for all. The next day as they planned to take her back, the girl cried and said she could not go, because she had stayed here. The men knew that she was right and also they did not want to offend Lapalokoyan and his mother. So Lokoyan and his mother paid the dogs' teeth and shell beads as a bride price and sent it to the former groom's family. There was so much of it that they could not carry it all. But Lokoyan's mother was able to get it all in one small basket for them and it was not heavy. They went back to Salien and told this story to all the people.

The Salien people were astonished: who could possibly eat all this food and possess all these goods? The food was distributed. All the things that had come from the groom's family previously were returned to them, and they got more, and the bride's parents had enough to keep for themselves. All the ceremonial obligations had been met and then some, and the girl was Lapalokoyan's with right.

Meanwhile, Lokoyan went fishing every day and ate betel nut, just as he did before, for that was all he could do. The bride stayed home with his mother but longed for his company. 'Why doesn't he stay with me, why doesn't he talk to me, why?' Once when he returned from fishing and coiled around his tree to sleep, she made a fence of coconut leaves around the tree. Later that night she put fire to the dry coconut leaves and burned everything. The flames were consuming him and he could not be helped. He was burned to a heap of charred remains and these were put in a basket by his wife. She fastened the basket to the rocks and left it for two weeks to be washed by the surf. One morning she noted that the remains had swollen and become human. She took this human form into the house and put it over the fireplace to be smoked and dried out. She put leaves on the shelf and kept turning him over every day, from front to back, from back to side, and back to front again, until he was smoked dry. Then he sat down and said he was hungry. She gave him food. Now he was truly a man. Now, whenever he wanted anything, all he had to do was ask, and it appeared. When they needed food, all he had to do was ask for it. He gave up fishing and stayed with his mother and his wife. He threw all his gear out — the hook and fishing line were picked up by the Japanese. The tree was given to the Europeans, and that is why they have big ships."

What I find remarkable about this myth is that it contains descriptions of marriage "exchanges" and procedures for corpses that were practiced until recently; some still are. The sudden "appearance" of food and wealth by someone willing it is a fundamental belief of the cargo cultists, even now, while the "mythical" elements should delight Freudian psychoanalysts and structuralists alike. To Bogandi, it is true history and cultural prescription.

Late in the night, Lomot comes to awaken me to tell me that the moon has disappeared and that Pwepwe is frightened to death. Lomot always ascribes to others any of her own sentiments that she views as weak. I say it is probably hidden by a cloud. "No," she says, "worse than that." I should not take it lightly, the moon has disappeared, and will I please call the Reverend. It is an eclipse, but Hans does not explain it to all gathered about. He jokes that Bogandi has stolen the moon and taken it to the Bush, and asks men to get lanterns to search for Bogandi and retrieve the moon! They do not do so, but await in silent dread for the passing of the eclipse, and he laughs (rather madly, I think). The Lindrow don't know what to make of Hans, but they respect his efficiency, his caring for them, and in more sober moments, they do exactly as he says.

*January 10.*  Back to Sori on the Talatala. Too tired to work, but enough energy to re-read *Les Fonctions Mentales dans les Sociétés Inférieures* (Lévy-Bruhl) occasioned by the Reverend Hans' personal variations on this theme.

I think Europeans have defined what we mean by "concrete" and "abstract": a simplistic dualistic view of how we ourselves experience the world. What we call concrete is what "primitives" sense and codify, whereas the Western mind apparently is able (in its own view) to scale heights of abstraction undreamed of by our primitive contemporaries and predecessors. I am finding that these "primitives" have an ability for abstraction that we cannot comprehend; more of that later. I cannot interest them in novels, because they are constantly observing inescapable "novels" unfold all about them daily, and their own lives *are* unfolding "novels" with so much that is unpredictable. We Europeans live with our time fragments and our safe alternative actions, so we are intrigued by the novelist who gives us continuity over lifetimes and generations. Nor do we find it necessary to "develop" characters in the discontinuous compartment of time and space in which we lead our lives, so we enjoy having a writer show us that it can happen sometimes.

One might understand Lévy-Bruhl in these terms: for him empiricism *replaces* (instead of complementing, as it should) symbolic logic. When such an assumption is put into practice, fieldwork, for anthropologists, replaces thinking. There has been very little fieldwork done on "how natives think," but somehow it is all supposed to "add up" after one has read how they build houses and canoes, evolve basketry, how they group socially and address their kinfolk, and how the perception of the fieldworker has separated notions of form from notions of function in a particular society. It doesn't "add up," of course, but then researchers hope that the reader doesn't notice, or perhaps the researcher hasn't noticed. My frustration at my physical handicap that makes it impossible for me to work sees me to the close of another day.

Because of my infant son, I see many a sunrise. The canoes look desolate in the sand before the tide comes in, their outriggers are mournful appendages. I can do nothing with my hands yet; how far can I travel on this tiny island?

Back to Lévy-Bruhl. He is too repetitive, as are most writers who are not primarily writers. His notion of the abstract is insufficiently transcendental. Had he come here, he might have learned that because a group does not have the word "hard" it does not mean that they do not have an abstract notion of "hardness." Why was it so difficult for L-B to make *his own abstractions* about the uses of language? Did Lévy-Bruhl, Mauss and Durkheim create false antinomies between "primitive thought" and our "evolved thought?'' From their assumptions, many still continue a dialectic. What Lévy-Bruhl reserves for the ''primitive'' is a ''talent for the practical,'' which Lévi-Strauss later calls ''the science of the con- crete,'' adding to the fine architectonic of an illusion of knowing other cultures. How these illusions germinate and grow, aided and abetted by ''European'' intellectual *kula* ring exchanges and self- congratulations in commentaries and counter-commentaries!

I learn that John Sapalona, who had taken his son Cristop Ahen to Lorengau for his swollen glands, returned with the sick child and called Makah, the witch doctor from Lebei who works with leaves and incantations. He will not tell anyone what Makah says, but John swears that only he was able to cure Ahen. ''Makah worked all night and in the morning Ahen was well,'' says John, who is by far the most acculturated person in the village.

# Back Home in Sori, Further Rejoinders to Lindrow and Other Usiai Experiences

My dearest and oldest informant on Sori, Tata Tara, has heard from Pwepwe that I was given the story of Lapalokoyan in Lessau. She comes to visit me (in my invalid state) since I am recuperating, bringing a group of people with her, and telling Pwepwe, as she draws a circle and speaking furiously fast, that Bogandi doesn't even *know* the story of *Mwa' Busu'* (The Snake of Busu') which he ignorantly calls the story of Lapalokoyan. Busu', as she indicates by a spot on the circle, is the hilltop above the shoreline where the stone and tree of Lokoyan still stand. The girl of the story was from Apwopway, which is near Busu'. The three islands mentioned in the story are Pabimbu, Baranyara, and Barua. (As in other myths and folktales, the very existence of these places and the fact that one has seen them is proof that a story is true.) This is in fact, Tata stresses as she looks at me for my total attention, the story of a girl who was instructed by her ancestors of her father's side to marry the snake of Busu'. She did not like the snake, but the snake had a human brother and she plots with the mother of these two to marry the man instead. They discuss their plans while cutting firewood, because the mother didn't like her snake son either. They planned an elopement and this was wrong because the girl's ancestors had already put the red clay paint on their heads. (In this case it was the father's sisters and father's father's sisters, i.e., all the ''women on the father's side".) This meant that the person she was to marry had been officially designated. Well, snake had been hiding in the bush while his mother and his intended schemed, so he made plans of his own. As the eloping pair went off in a canoe, snake talked to his betel nut, which whisked him off to the canoe. The human brother then cut the snake to pieces with a knife while his head was eaten by a shark, but the shark also ate the human brother and the head of the snake inside the shark also ate the human brother.

Tata and Pwepwe both want to emphasize that all this trouble happened because a girl disobeyed her *tumbuna* who knew more than she did. She was foolish. If she would only have married the snake! It was wrong to have scorned him, for he would probably have turned into a man, as Lokoyan did turn into a man after all. Apparently *that* part of Bogandi's story was acceptable to Tata as a probable, if not historically accurate, ending.

Takaray of Lebei replied to my note by coming to work with me in Sori. He tells me of the wedding of a boy from his village and a girl from Sori #2 that I had the misfortune to miss. Takaray was one of the musicians, playing the banjo, and it seems that my daughter Deborah obliged the villages of Sori #1 and Sori #2 and Lebei by doing the Stomp, the Twist, the Charleston and a South Coast dance borrowed from Polynesia that Mesian had taught her. According to Takaray the entire native audience laughed hysterically and urged her to dance on and on into the night. Now I know what a woman of Sori #2 meant when she had told me that my *dalu* (first born female child) had given them a good time, such as they had never had before. So the only other details I got of the wedding were what Takaray thought mildly important: that the groom got intoxicated, that the bride, as in old traditional style, did not participate in any of the ceremonies but stayed indoors.

Working with Takaray, contrary to my expectations, is slow and tedious. Although very valuable because he knows some English, this actually detracts from him as an informant. He insists on finding the English expression for a word, whereas Melanesian languages translate perfectly into Pidgin in a very literal way, and it will be only in knowing both cultures well that I will be able to translate conceptually into English. He keeps inventing verb tenses. Still, when he leaves for Rabaul in New Britain for the Mission High School, there will be a gap that will not be filled.

*January 17.* Sori village is puzzled. Mohe came from another part of the North Coast to talk about six men who will be running for political office and all must vote for one of them "who will be the head of Manus and go to Port Moresby.'' These are Paliau Moloat (religious, political and former ''cargo cult'' leader), Cholai, Mohe, Pomaija, Joseph, and Peter, all of whom had to come up with 25 pounds each. Villagers were equally puzzled to hear that they ought to be buying Savings Certificates so that the Government can use the money to build roads, bridges, and pay them ''interest.'' I was still immobilized and unable to go to their meeting but this is what was reported to me by Lomot and others.

*January 17.* Lokes is sad and wants to discuss Mesian with me. He talked with her father over the Christmas holidays, of his fears that she will become pregnant again, and would I take things in hand and act *in loco parentis* and stop the *hambak* (P.E. in this case, sexual horseplay). Her playmate, and it seems that I am the last to know, is John Polai, teacher at St. Martin's school in Sori #2. Ideally, an anthropologist should never intervene, but her parents consider me an employer who has taken her away from home, and therefore it is my duty to act in their stead, I am told by Lokes.

My first interview with John reveals unequivocally the fact that he has no intention of marrying Mesian, a South Coast Manus girl, and will not marry her even if she does become pregnant. I regret to say to him, however, that since his intentions are not honorable, I must insist that he stop seeing her every night. Her father was promised that I would look after her ''as if she were my own daughter,'' and that is what I think Mesian's father understood the meaning to be in this case. Lokes and I add that if Mesian becomes pregnant, he should be prepared to be responsible. Father Kopunek might force a wedding, and Mr. Jensen of the Administration, who is ''fed up with immoral examples of school teachers,'' would probably fire him. Lokes rather enjoyed this encounter, but I did not.

Adan, ever the joy of Sori is now known as *lamibatum na'heya* (P.E. *grass belong head belong em i kamap now*, or his hair is growing). Prior to this he was known as *lamibatum bwey* (P.E. hair, not). Now that he says ''momma,'' everyone in the village has learned to say ''momma.'' Every new word he learns in English is passed from mouth to mouth in the village and repeated to him while they learn the referent. All of this is done with exuberance and glee.

There is still much concern in the village as to the cause of my burns. Lohai comes to tell me that he still weeps at night over the suffering that I went through. Others come to tell me that it was the bush spirits that whoosh up from the trees in the forests around Lebei to cause mischief and damage in Sori; that is why Ahen got that terrible fever and why Makah of Lebei had to be called. Hopes are expressed that if Adan becomes ill again I will call Makah, because all the medicines in my patrol box would be of no avail against the bush devils now that we are Sori folk.

*January 21.* Her name is Arup amana'asumbung, and she and Sa'absing, both elderly, brought me some fruit, and wanted to sit in my house and visit until the rains passed. She wanted to "story" about the Big War between Sori and Andra a long time ago that left her a widow.

The two women begin to joke with Adan telling him they are going to eat him. Sa'absing tells me that she did once attend a feast but did not participate in the eating of a man called Drasileh from Li'indrow. He was killed by the father of Owa' of this village, and the Lebei were also invited to eat. She described for me in detail how they cut him into little pieces and cooked these pieces which were then mixed up with sago. She heard all say that it was quite good. "Yes Misis," one sadly comments, "No matter who wants to lie about it in this village, we the Sori, not too long ago did eat human beings."

*January 22.* Working with Takaray on Lebei language again. Lebei has at least three separate numeration systems for flat objects, round objects, and long objects. But I haven't cracked the code for attributes other than those listed yet. At first I thought all animate things were members of a set, only to discover that crocodiles and chickens come under different systems of numbering. Houses have a numbering system that applies only to houses, and so do knives. I thought I might get a clue by asking about special attributes of knives, so I asked, "Why do knives have a numbering system all of their own?" The reply was swift and conclusive, "Because they are knives." Anthropologists working in societies like these don't expect to get answers to "why," but I find the answers interesting anyway, so I keep asking. (In my Mexican fieldwork, my main informant would invariably respond, in Spanish, "Because that is the way it is." She and I performed that little codicilic episodic interchange, after long sessions, for three years.)

But Takaray holds the knife up to me so that I can see for myself that such an article needs a numeration all of its own (See Appendix I). Sometimes I am glad that he insists on finding English equivalents rather than *Pidgin* because *Pidgin* words carry such heavy semantic loads that they strain and creak under the burden. For example, in *Pidgin* one can say that hair is *strong* (kinky, difficult to manage), sleep is *strong* (sound and deep), a look is *strong* (intense), language can be *strong* (difficult to learn), you tie something *strong* (tightly), you walk *strong* (at a good pace), and this by no means exhausts the examples of the *"strong"* semantic spectrum of meanings.

A myth or history that has gained a reputation for delighting me will soon elicit many others of the same genre. Today Takaray wants to tell me of *Pok Loku*. Like other stories, this one revolves around a kinship node, a boy, his mother's brother, and his father's mother. The boy makes a hole in a seed and being transported in it finds his way to the two sisters he wants to marry. This, of course, has elements of the two previous snake tales.

I am sent a note by the Administration that the village is going to be sent a "Doctor Boy." His name is Steven of Powat and I welcome him, as he will lift a great burden from me, the responsibility for the medical problems of Sori #1 and Sori #2 and Lebei. I have run out of antibiotics and have only anti-malarials to dispense.

Simbuom, Pwepwe's father, stops by almost in tears to tell me that he is sick but that the Doctor Boy told him he is not sick. Do I believe he is sick? Yes, I do. Then he tells me again that he is sick because of the eight anti-malarial pills I gave him! Did he take them all at once as everyone says he did? No, he took four in the afternoon and four at night. According to my medical books that should not make him ill, and besides everyone here either has had or has or will have malaria. The village is not misrepresenting when they say he took them all at one time; what they mean is, that he took them in the span of time between the time he received them and the time they talked to him. But of course, the pills made him ill, what else? If the bush spirits wanted to make him ill, they could have done so any time and would not have chosen the time he was taking pills, since they want it *known* that they can cause illness. And, since he was in bed he could not have done anything to have broken any of his taboos.

*January 26.* A bright full moon last night. The village children run and play all night long on the exposed beach, which, due to the low tide, unites Sori island with the mainland. Their shouts ring out with exhilaration and sense of freedom as they are no longer confined to this small island. They play run and catch and don't stop until dawn, knowing that tomorrow they will be walled in again, by the sea. The moonlight is so brilliant that it appears to be suffused daylight.

Steven is very pleased that I refer patients to him, and tell villagers that he knows about medicine. And I am pleased that he tells me everything about his encounters that will be of ethnographic interest to me. Bo-Bo, who was very sick with bronchial pneumonia confidentially wanted Steven to help him call the *tamberan*[2] from Sori #2. Now that is news to me, for the Sori always joke about the *tamberan* men of Lebei, but somehow have neglected to tell me that they have one of their very own.

Steven cures a child with an injection for his very high fever, and in the morning the grandmother comes to him and says, "You can tell me, you are posing as a doctor, but you are really a *tamberan* man".

Lomot runs in breathlessly after church. What she wants me to know, as she gulps for air overcome by the excitement, is that a girl of Sori #2 is "prenganent" and that it is a great scandal. There is going to be a "court" in which the girl is planning to accuse two young men from Lebei who are already vigorously denying paternity. This has happened before and the last time she accused three men. The *Committee* (P.E. one man who is also a government sponsored village representative along with the *Kaunsil*, second in command) has told her before and is telling her now that she cannot be helped as long as she accuses more than one man. She is considered somewhat "crazy." Pwepwe sniffs, "And she must be really crazy to tell people how many possible men could be the father." Reactions appeared all too rational and as I will learn later, one needs a great deal of information to interpret correctly such a simple straightforward interchange here.

*January 27.*   Steven, it seems, is a ventriloquist, a Hawaiian guitarist and a singer of Lutheran hymns as well as Doctor Boy. He appears to be quite intelligent, but suffers from Barber-of-Sevillism. There is nothing on which he is not an authority. He tells me that I should write my *talk place* on one side of my notebook and the translation into *Pidgin* on the other because my habit of writing one line of text above and the translation below is very confusing to him as he reads over my shoulder. He doesn't like the cover picture of Margaret Mead's *New Lives for Old* and says it will mislead the reader into thinking that the Manus are really catching up with the twentieth century when actually they *"tamberan* everything they touch, even me."  I tell him that it is a book about the South Coast Manus, which he says are indeed very different from this lostlorn place but not as she thinks. Now take the girls. Steven just doesn't like the North Coast girls at all.

It is a hot afternoon on the wind side of the island, and as we sit here trying to cool off in the breeze, Teresia and Lomot sing this song in *Pidgin* to Adan:

*Adan Adan Liklik manki*
*i go waswas long draiwara*
*pukpuk i ron i go*
*i kisim em long wanpela leg*
*Na mama i no sabe*
*i tink sem i dai finis*
*nogat sori i no dai yet*
*tupela sumbung belong em i sanap.*

(Roughly: Adan, Adan, little boy, goes to wash on the beach at low tide, a crocodile runs and grabs him by one "leg." Now his mother doesn't know this; she thinks he is dead, oh no, sorry about that he is not dead, two breasts emerge on him now). The girls giggled endlessly because it took me so long to understand this crocodile-induced transsexual operation.

*January 28.* The village has been sent notice that the small trading ship, the *Sunam*, will stop by here in two or three days to pick up copra.

For the past year income from copra has amounted to 1063 pounds and trochus shell has brought in 105 pounds. This is for all the villages in the co-operative: Sori #1 and #2, Lebei, Lessau, Jowan, Ndrehet, Sapandruan, Little Jowan, Harenggan, and Nihon. John Sapalona, "storeman" here, is the accountant, no doubt accounting for his great allure for the young ladies. The villages in the co-op do not all share similar religious affiliations.

As we begin the vigil for the coming of the *Sunam*, on this sultry afternoon I find Siwa, her brother Pwayyam and John the storeman flanked by a watchful Pwepwe playing a game of cards called *Pokomus*. The stakes are bits of tobacco twist. Siwa is masculine in stance and aggressiveness, and also in the sense that she plays this game at all, and *with men*. But then, her brother is there and her excuse is that the women do not talk to her. Pamaleo later has to walk by this place and stares deeply into the ground, speaking to no one. This is an exceedingly small place to be constantly trying unsuccessfully to avoid one's abandoned wife and five abandoned children among a group of people who disapprove of such abandonments.

How do Siwa and Pamaleo tolerate the contumely of the villagers? They have been together for seven years and they seem to get along very well. But Siwa laughs loudly and too long at all manner of trifling events; she sings much too loudly as she paddles her canoe across the passage. Pamaleo looks absolutely miserable all the time. He speaks to me in a most friendly fashion only when no one in the village is about. He and Siwa invite my South Coast Manus household of Lomot, Lokes, and Mesian to eat sago with them with great frequency.

*January 31.* I work with Tata on taboos and totems and social organization and I feel like Alice going into the looking glass, back in time; my luck in finding the classics, still alive and breathing, seems too good to be true. Steven the doctor boy bursts into my house (as no Sori would venture to do) to announce to me that he will be going on a speaking tour in these environs to talk on hygiene and condemn *tamberanism* and will I assume his patient load? I am not pleased to play physician again, having been liberated of the responsibility.

Tonight I also meet an old friend from Mexico, the Virgin of Guadalupe. It seems that Father Kopunek of Bundralis shows pictures and tells stories of the poverty-stricken and dark-skinned Indian Juan Diego, a shepherd visited by the Virgin Mary long ago. He tells also of the miracle of the robe and the portrait on it and the roses she left with him so that he could show proof to the Bishop. And the robe can still be viewed after all these years in a huge cathedral in Mexico City. How do the Sori and Lebei react to this story? They are entranced by it. I tell some here that I have seen this robe, which only confirms their belief that the story is true. No point in adding anything about the nature of proof and inference, as I tried to do, and I recall that in this magical and mystical island, to see with your eyes or hold with your hand a tangible object said to be connected with an event, is proof that the event occurred.

*February 1.* The *Sunam* does not come, but that hardly matters, for the anticipation of it makes the occasion. Waiting for a small ship here is the event of the season, for we are then all assured that there is a world out there that has "cargo," is involved in business, has people in it who are not running into each other every five minutes throughout every day. John Sapalona, who now calls me "Lola," tells me that the crew of the *Sunam* are not meticulous about schedules and that every time he talks to them they are clearly drunk. "Europeans" give them whiskey and they indulge in this heavenly experience anytime it suits their fancy.

The villages around here are pleased that Father Kopunek has chosen six of his Bundralis graduates to go to Rabaul to pursue further studies, and that all of them are boys. Although children are valued, what is not valued is a young lady who has been sent off to school and comes home pregnant, father unknown. This means there will be no exchanges between families, no ceremony, no obligations and privileges exchanged between patrilines or clans over the marriage and birth of a baby. Lokes tells me in this context that Benedikta's twelve year old daughter in Pere has just given birth to twins, father unknown to all including the child-mother. It matters not the context, it is difficult to get information about pregnancy from anyone. It was laborious even to get Mesian to finally tell me that during her pregnancy she was told not to eat sago, for the baby would be tiny, nor to eat fat drippings, or the baby would be greasy. Lomot wants her boyfriend So'ong to ask my permission for him to marry her, while So'ong is busy getting a transfer. All this is distracting from the concentration required for working with Ebei on genealogies.

Pwepwe who is sitting by us feeding Adan his baby food from little jars imported from Australia, dares Ebei to tell me the story about the sea turtles and *bekbek* (P.E. faeces), but Ebei demures. I become insistent and Pwepwe finally says, "OK you old Ebei, I will tell the Misis the story and if I am wrong you correct me." Ebei consents and this is the story from Pwepwe:

> "I was yet a little girl and did not wear a laplap yet. Now it was the time of the big war when America and Australia were fighting Japan and here in Manus too. Now at this time Sori was having fight after fight with Ponam. Why? Because of the sea turtles. The Sori used to go to Tulu and stop there fishing for turtles, but the Ponam men used to say that it wasn't right because Ponam was much closer to Tulu and Sori was going out of its way to deprive them of sea turtles. Neither had real rights there but the Ponam said they were close and the Sori insisted they had as much right as anyone. They had fights over this. It really makes me laugh to think of Sori and Ponam fighting over turtles when there was really a big war going on. Well, there were people hurt over these fights, though. For certain there were two Ponam men who died from head wounds; they were beaten with heavy sticks. The Sori were not brought to court in Lorengau because of the confusion here due to the big war.
>
> One time the Sori had been told that the Ponam were coming to fight them. They prepared and waited. The Ponam did not come. The Sori went to Bundralis and lit a big fire, hoping to call the Ponam to come and fight. But the Ponam did not come. The Sori then went to the house for visiting Ponam men in Bundralis. The Sori took the saucepans of the Ponam house and defecated in them. Then they lit fires under the pans and cooked the *bekbek*."

*February 4.* I try to begin to learn about leaf remedies and beliefs about illness. I am thinking out loud about which elderly ladies to begin with and the daughter of Sa'absing tells me that Tata Tara exaggerates what she knows about curing. The only cure she knows is to take the sap of a tree called *sibana*, which is put into the liquid of a young coconut that still has soft meat. Drinking this relieves one of constipation. Then she runs off to bring me her mother. Sa'absing tells me that children get sick because the father or mother steal something from someone, or if either of them gets angry with someone. A sick child used to be cured if an old man put his hand on the child's head, hands, legs, or chest. A child would recover if it were a good child. A bad child would not get well. If it died that meant it would not have turned out to be good if it had lived. Bush devils *also* make babies sick.

I ask, "Why is it that a woman might not bear a child?" Sa'absing replied, "The mother breaks a taboo of her totem and then when she gets married there are now no children."

*Ka'awar* is a small leaf used medicinally in earlier times, but now it is used in harmful magic if chewed along with betel nut and lime. The victory leaf, alluded to earlier, also is used to harm another. The person using the magic ties two of the victory leaves together and points to the house of the person he wants to affect.

*February 4.* Giving up on the *Sunam*, the young boys are taking a canoe to Bundralis, as all cry tearfully on the beach. When anyone leaves, for places not known to the village, the expectation is that they will never be seen again. Another canoe leaves with a group that is going to Harenggan for the funerary rites of a relative. The women take sago, rice and *golo* (a large round bottle of coconut oil) for the feast after the ceremony. Pwepwe gets very talkative when everyone is gone. She is happy, for she is to cook for John Sapalona since his wife must go to Harenggan. She decides that my constant indigestion is due to the tinned food and wants to cook for me a meal completely "fashion belong before," an old-time Sori meal. Sitting on the small bench used for scraping out the meat from coconuts, she tells me the different names for coconuts in varied stages of maturation. The scrapings of the coconut are passed through a screen. To this liquid she adds cut up bananas and then boils this for a time; it becomes a tasty soup. It is only the old coconuts that are used for cooking or put into rice and sago. Sa'apa completes the old-time meal for me by bringing Pwepwe a small fish shot with a "gun," the barrel of which is a small pipe; it has a rod of thick wire and a trigger with three pieces of an automobile inner tube for the triggering and releasing action. He said he got the parts from Lorengau and that men in the Philippines have this kind of "shoot."

Lukas comes today for an unexpected ethnographic session. He has written what he wants to tell me in a notebook, both in *talk place* and in Pidgin. It was a bit annoying, however, to have him check everything *I* wrote in my notebook. Explanation of the apostrophe I use for the Sori glottal stop develops into a short lecture on descriptive linguistics and universals of language, which he finds fascinating. Pwepwe interrupts to express her opinion of his use of the word *sonay* instead of *hiyu* for the verb of action on the canoe, "When you were in Bundralis the canoe was not on the shore so you did not *sonay* (throw it in), you merely *hiyu* (moved it by paddle in the water).

"Well, how do you like that," said Lukas, "a fellow can't even talk about a war in which he took part."

Pwepwe counters that there is only one way the Misis is to write the Sori language, and that is the correct way. The session comes to an end when Lomot bursts into the house having just got off a canoe. She saw someone in Lorengau and he is very sick. He is sick because he stole our things when he accompanied Ted to the large island, and he knows it and she knows it too. He even asked Lomot whether I talked about the things he stole. Yes, Lomot told him, and they want the things returned. She said he looked sicker than ever when he promised he would come to Sori to return them.

*Friday, February 7.* During my post-prandial break, sitting on the windward side of this tiny island, I have made a discovery. I, too, can spot a speck in the distance and know that it is not a cloud, not a wave, but a *sail*. It is not due to 20/20 vision which my eyes barely achieve corrected by lenses, but a question of attention. Here, where I feel walled in by endless leagues of ocean that seem to shift from horizontal to vertical walls as time goes by, my expectations lie on a spot between the sea and the sky where something will appear that is the harbinger of a letter, or a visitor, or a lost colleague who escaped the pygmies after all, or even just a person from the Administration to look into malaria control or the co-op store. The shades of blue and white become so familiar that the slightest speck that "doesn't fit" is immediately a stimulus for conjecture. The sail I see is quickly perceived also by Mesian, and we play the game of "what might it be," discarding guesses with each length of sea covered that eliminates classes of possible crafts or ships. It proves to be the group returning from the funeral in Harenggan, very tired and very hungry, but laden with *Kaukau* and *pawpaw*.

Ebei figures that I am in a generous mood and asks to borrow 10 shillings to buy kerosene. He says the land this house is on used to belong to his family and he will repay me. I just give him the kerosene as a gift and ask why he wants the money. Someone takes advantage of this exchange to tell me that the village is sick of Ebei living in the past (a boon to my research), that he is a liar and a braggart, that he never captured 200 sea turtles as he claims. Pwepwe goes beyond her usual nastiness to him tonight. He comes to tell me that his new grandson, now called Dai, or first-born male, will be called Ebei when he is given his real name. "He will not," snaps Pwepwe, "He will be called Ndrawahla." Old Ebei is stunned into silence. Elders are not always respected here, nor children indulged. Nor are mothers as outwardly affectionate here as they seem to me to be in Pere and Bunai. My next door neighbor routinely clouts her children on the neck with an old thong. They cringe, look ashamed and stalk away. These same mothers are very tender with very small children however, and the worst punishments are meted to those of about eight or nine years of age who are even slightly remiss in taking totally dependable care of the younger children while parents are working.

# The Universality of "Soap Operas."

*February 8.* Today Lohai had to go to "court" in Sori #2, to "try" the case of the girl who is about to give birth and has slapped paternity blame on two young Lebei men, who deny it. She has lately been saying that it is not those two at all, but rather Pwayyam from Sori #1. Perhaps she was swayed by all those who counselled her to give the name of only one man. Her version now seems to be that Pwayyam, knowing she desired a young man from Lebei, sent her a message, as if it were from the Lebei man, to go to the copra house that night where he would meet her. She went to meet the boy of her dreams and did not find it unpleasant to be thrown down on the ground and seduced. But it was very dark and she did not know that it was not the Lebei lover of her fantasies. Then Pwayyam sent her another message as though it was from the other Lebei man she liked, and the same drama occurred, only this time he got careless, finding her so compliant that perhaps he thought it would make no difference to her if he walked her out into the moonlight. She greeted her discovery with horror. Pwayyam denies it all, but he will be forced to go to "court" this morning.

Pwepwe turns to me as the canoe drifts off toward the mainland, "That girl is really stupid. In the first court hearing she said that this baby is coming up with only two sexual encounters and the committee said to her, 'Do you think we are so stupid that we are going to believe that only two sessions of sex is enough to make a baby?' Isn't she silly to try to put that one over on her judges?" It is believed here that it takes many sessions of sexual intercourse to complete the making of a baby. And I learn today also, in further questioning of many others, that the reason the girl was told to name only one putative "father" is because the Australians have this naive belief that you can make a baby with only one man and, in fact, with only one time. The mother-to-be was counselled that if she wanted the Australians to see to it that she got child support she had better give information in a manner that would indicate that she had the same simple-minded beliefs as the Australians about how babies are "made."

Steven the doctor boy comes to put acriflavin on the last remnants of my wounds. He talks work and salaries, annoyed that he receives only 6 pounds a month with no rations, and he has a certificate! He listens to me for quite a while, but I soon perceive that he wants to talk to me of something else. He begins, "Mesian is very good with your baby, but she is no good. Do you know where she slept last night? It seems she slept with Polai in Polai's sister's house." I tell Steven that the sexual bantering of my Manus girls is beginning to weary me but I do not want to intervene, and that I have discharged my obligation to her father by talking to John Polai earlier. Steven wants me to fire her. At this juncture Lokes bursts in from the kitchen indignantly adding that Mesian and Polai have broken a big *tambu* in the village because they slept in the house of a married couple when the male of the house wasn't there. Now Lohai is angry and will call a "court" about it and furthermore he is sure there is a government law against it and what do I plan to do about it?

The following afternoon a "court" is held in my house. Bau, the "committee," sits on the floor, has nothing to say and no opinions. We all wait until Mesian is finished feeding Adan. He goes through several tins of baby food one after the other to our utter amazement and Mesian begins to open another, hoping he will keep on eating. But the case begins.

Lohai appears embarrassed and says that the Misis wants something straightened out about last night. I beg his pardon, and I say that I was under the impression that the *village* wanted this case discussed because a village *tambu* had been broken.

Lohai and I realize that we have both been tricked by Lokes into thinking the other wanted this case tried. But he nevertheless summarizes the main points of litigation here. There isn't a rule against two single people using the house of a married person to sleep together if they have the permission of one of the married persons, either the man or woman. Polai wants to know who brought this matter up. Lokes proudly says that he did it because of his promise to her father, along with the fact that he is "committee" in his village of Bunai, and because Mesian went to school in Lorengau and had an illegitimate baby and it "buggered up" her career, and because she left this child "as though it were a pig or a dog" in her village, and here she is ready to do it again. Mesian gives me a helpless look, the last stand of an animal that knows it is cornered and about to perish. John Polai looks astonished as he hears this for the first time, surely. I am ready to escort Mesian out of the room but Lokes continues, "and her mother has TB and Mesian is really no good, and if the Misis doesn't *raus* her and send her back to Bunai, I will." He contrasts Mesian's behavior with Lomot's behavior, Lomot having done things right, by first asking him for permission to marry So'ong, then asking permission from her father and uncle. (The only fact Lokes leaves out is that So'ong never asked Lomot to marry him and asked for a transfer when things got too thick). Lokes becomes articulate and rhetorical; Lohai is kind and soft-spoken. Polai cracks his knuckles and throws me desperate looks hoping I will remember that he told me he had no intention of marrying Mesian.

Lohai asks them both to talk, but Polai remains silent and looks down at the floor. He then breaks the silence: this had been a trick by Steven who had feigned to want to help the young lovers, and had asked Ayeng for his house. He told Mesian that Polai was at the house waiting for her, but Mesian went there to find Steven who twisted her wrists and kept asking, "What do you want with Polai, I love you too." Mesian struggled, escaped and ran to look for Polai, and the rest of the tale was one of tenderness and sympathy to the lovers, a felicitous rendezvous at the time.

Lohai gently reprimands Mesian for lying to me about her activities of the evening and the night, which absolves me completely as she agrees she had lied. Then the talk takes a strange turn; one gets the impression that love is legislated between village *kaunsils*. Lohai asks Mesian why she loves Polai. She says she doesn't know, she just loves him, "And what do you know about love?" shouts Lokes. She says she loves him enough to marry him.

"In that case," Lohai decrees, "It must be cleared with your *kaunsil*." But he becomes clearly annoyed, "If I tell you that I love the Misis here, I can tell you *why* I love the Misis." But despite all prodding, Mesian can not explain why she loves John Polai which proves conclusively to the men of the "court" that this love is "something-nothing." Lohai now says that he will handle the case from Polai's side since he is Polai's *kaunsil* and Mesian will have to work it out with her *kaunsil* (her uncle in Bunai on the South Coast!). I am sure the two young people are as genuinely confused as I am, though Lohai assures me that it is because I do not yet know all about Manus customs.

Later Lokes tells me that Paliau is a wonderful orator and that no one can best him in a "court." Paliau once won a case for him even though he was in the wrong (Lokes' wife had brought Lokes to trial because he was "befriending" another woman, which was true).

Pwepwe later tells me that if those two wanted to act like pigs or dogs they could go into the bush; the village of Sori will tolerate no fornicating fun that is "something belong play and that's all."

Still, the way I can help Mesian now is to compliment Lokes on his skillful and forceful oratory, and ask him which of us has not sinned. And I get him to agree that Lohai has summed up the situation perfectly and that probably, owing to this, Mesian will sin no more. Lohai had said, after Mesian described her love as strong enough to marry Polai, "You are acting as though something you wished were true were true. It is not. You would like to be married but you are not married. You are here in Sori not because you are married to John Polai but because you are working for the Misis. So last night instead of helping the Misis you went to bed with your husband who is not your husband. This is a lie, you are living a lie and it is not right. When you lived this lie in the middle of the village you made it a problem for the village to solve. Before that it was not our affair."

So this is love in the South Seas!

# Of Totems, Kin and Affines in Sori

At the present time, the island is "divided" into two parts. The "line" runs through the middle, the markers are the men's toilet and Lohai's house on one side, and the women's toilet and John Sapalona's canoe on the other side. If you ask someone for his or her *loba'oh* (origin) he will give you the name of his patriline. Old Sori had four major divisions or "company": Hi'inang, So'opay, Luhai, and Babing. There is only one Hi'inang patriclan here on the island, Ebei and his family. The major "company" here is Luhai. The other Hi'inang, and the So'opay and Babing settled in Sori #2. Another way of designating a lineage, useful for purpose of designating proprietorship (as, for example, of the previously discussed shell money), is to name an ancestor two or three generations back (let us say Simbuhem) and then his descendants will be called NaSimbuhem. *Na* is "particle" of *narung* which means "his children."

So, all of the residential family units on this island are Luhai with the exception of four structures that house the Hi'ianang.

There are ten *loba'oh* (patrilines) of Sori people: of the Hi'inang there are three — NaSo'are, NaLohey, and NaSa'apo'. In the Luhai "company" we find the patriclans of NaSipoha', NaNdruhi', NaLuwi, NaDyawo, NaSomwa, NaBasawa and NaSimbuhen.

These are the totems or *uawu* in the village of Sori #1:

| | | |
|---|---|---|
| *baringe* | - | or the flying fox. One does not eat this if it is your totem animal, but the Sori don't eat flying foxes anyway, although the Lebei do. |
| *mwa'* | - | or snake. As above the Sori do not eat snakes in any case. |
| *mbu'* | - | or banana. Those who must observe a *tambu* toward the banana may eat two of the three varieties on the island that are not their totem. |
| *sipi* | - | a type of parrot called *koki* in Pidgin. |
| *dyang* | - | a fish; also the sun. |

| | | |
|---|---|---|
| *nangai* | - | called *welpato* in Pidgin (wild duck). |
| *mbusi* | - | a bird. |
| *u'usi* | - | pussycat (relatively recent; a loan word). |
| *mwi* | - | dog. |
| *manuay* | - | sea hawk. |

Some people have several totems that are passed along matrilines. Baripeo's totem is *dyang* (the sun). But *dyang* is also the name of a fish. Baripeo therefore has a two-in-one totem (a word play totem!) and so the *tambu* applies to both objects. She must not eat either. Now in the case of the sun, she told me this means that at all cost she must avoid the sun's rays falling on the saucepan.

The consequences of eating a food that is *tambu* or any other violation of one's totem is usually illness, complicated by paralysis, a speech defect or insanity. If a member of an *uawu* eats his/her totem the teeth would fall out immediately, or he/she might lose the power of speech.

For one week after Baripeo's baby was born, neither she nor the baby could go out into the sun or their skin would be ruined, and there would be no milk for the baby. After one week she washed the baby in the sea, for the *tambu* was over and the danger past. She could marry some one who belonged to the same totemic group, although she reminds me again that males have the membership but it is passed on generationally *only* through the women. Males are recipients of, but not givers of, totemic membership. Baripeo will not speak to me of the totems of others and claims she doesn't know.

Tata Tara is able, all of the Luhai clan assure me, to cure children who have the *manuay* sickness, characterized by high fever and convulsions. (The mother who breaks a *manuay* taboo while she is carrying the child will cause the illness.) One does not always know that one has broken a taboo, for to walk or go by canoe over a spot where a *manuay* died cannot always be known and avoided. What does Tata do?

First, the mother has to cook sago with water and coconut oil. Tata and other members of her kin group, also *manuay* of course, go to this woman's house at a very special hour, when everyone is asleep, at an hour sufficiently past most of the night but enough before dawn so that no one is stirring. The women will be there, waiting, with the sago. The *manuay* people sit around in a circle with some sago placed before each person. Tata places a *karuga* (P.E. pandanus raincoat) over the mother's head and then she places a victory leaf on top of the *karuga*. She says something (but will not tell me the words because she said I would not understand them, as no one does). After the ceremony the *manuay* kin quietly eat sago. Now the child will be alright.

There is a warning to the mother that the illness will come if the child hears the cry of the *manuay* very distinctly. There is nothing she can do, it is already too late. But Tata will come to cure it if she is called.

I ask if everyone calls Tata and I am told by Pwepwe and Tata, unfortunately no. "As you know Misis, since you did the drawings on paper of all Ebei's family, you know that he has three dead children that belonged to his son Uweh. Well, one had the *manuay* sickness really bad, but they didn't want to call Tata, calling instead a *tamberan* from Lebei. Just sinful too because Uweh's wife is a *manuay*. The trouble started because she broke a taboo when she was pregnant. Of course, she could not go against her husband's wishes and especially not against that old fool of her father-in-law, Ebei. Two of her children who had died had the *manuay* sickness, but two were lost while they were sick in a dreadful fashion. All because Ebei broke his taboo against his totem, a fish called the *bai-manuay*. Now these two sons of Uweh, son of Ebei, were on a canoe in the ocean and they disappeared in the mouth of a *bai-Manuay*. Ebei had broken his *tambu* because he once caught, cooked and ate one of these. Now when you asked him if he had a totem he told you, 'oh no misis, if my mother had one I don't know about it.' That was his lie to you so that you would not know the story of his crime, but now you know."

The *manuay* can also dry up a mother's milk, but Tata can cure that too. Tata can also set arms and legs, and once she set old Ebei's leg when it was broken through in two places, "ask him." (I asked Tata if there was anything she could not do and she laughed, "Yes, I cannot cure the pain in my own knee, a pain that will be the end of me.")

Another totemic cleansing is called the *mpurupau* and it is performed for a child who is born in a location other than Sori and is coming home for the first time. It is also performed for one who has been in a hospital or visiting another place and is coming home. The *mpurupau* is an invocation of the totem or totems of a child to protect it: the child or adult is placed on dry coconuts with sago and a *laplap* placed around it. Pandanus raingear is placed over the head of the individual and a coconut is broken over the it. This is done by an older family member, either male or female, who also directs speech to the totem:

*Manang ire lo Ponam, Manang ire lo Nauna*

or, "the eye of *it* go inside Ponam, the eye of it go inside Nauna," etc., or wherever the person has traveled. The officiator sings the name of the totems. After each totem is invoked the assembled group responds in a chorus call, e.g.,

officiator:   *mwa', mwa', mwa'* (snake)
group:            *Wuu - uu - uu*
officiator:   *ehe, ehe, ehe,* (small parrot)
group:            *Wuu - uu - uu*

After this there is joking behavior. If a young granddaughter of Tata were being "cleansed" one might say, "Tata *uriang tinang*" (Tata of the big belly). Then the group would shout: "Ha ha ha yey i yoy yohoy" and the ceremony would end.

A person in Sori belongs to the larger division, now called "company." He/she belongs to the patriclan, a group defined by relationships reckoned by descent through the men on his or her father's side. But a person in Sori also belongs to a matriline, descent reckoned through the mother, and this identification is symbolized by the totemic ancestor. I have mentioned the totemic ancestors for Sori above, for the village Lebei one finds the crocodile, and several varieties of small birds and the breadfruit tree.

To get to the origin of these totemic lines is not an easy task, for Tata, the only authority, does not say she knows something if she is not "entitled" to say it. Once long ago, it seems, a woman of Salien married a man named Barep and had four daughters. She knows their names and she knows who they married and the names of their offspring for five generations. She does not know how these women came into totemic relationship with the *manuay* (fish hawk), and tells me that there was an old man in Salien named *BwaManuay* who did know but that he is now dead. She does know for certain that if you are in these "fish hawk" lines and break a taboo, certain terrible things will happen. She recounts them once more and gives me an example of a small boy whose father took a *manuay* for a pet when it was small. He fed it and took care of it and when it died he buried it but first cut off a foot of it and hung it in his house. One time the boy fell asleep under this foot. He never learned to talk.

The several old women listening to me and Tata look shocked and frightened, and imitate for me the attempts of this young child to talk. They all assure me that any person on this island who is not deaf-mute, nor barren, whose child has never been sick, who has never been paralyzed — those are the only persons, you can be sure, who have never violated a *tambu*.

Salai records a *cry* for me about Tata's story of the female lines. The *cry* has an interesting feature. True, the only information about the totem is that it comes from "a place from where the East Wind has passed," and it mentions So'owey and Bipi as two places where the carriers of *manuay* women stopped to begin lines of *manuay* totems. Totemic lines were also started at Sou, Nya'aKik (a place in the bush on the mainland), and other islands. But it is brought to my attention in this song-poem of Salai's that some words are substituted by other words in formal speech appropriate to occasions treating of totem and taboo. In the *cry*, for example, the word for woman (*bi'ibing*) becomes *pihi*; the word for mother's mother (*nyabarip*) becomes *mbelip*; the word for mother's sister (*Tiney*) becomes *yunay*; the word for East (*Hay*) becomes *Ray*.

Salai's *cry* about these women in four founding places of the totemic lines describes the routes of the spread of the totem *manuay* throughout various small islands as the women "married out" of Sori, but says nothing of origin and meaning. What is one to make of totemism here?

In the literature of anthropology one finds theories of totemism, all of which, it seems to me, can be reduced to three types of explanation:

1)   Totemism as the erstwhile mystical fountainhead of religion: it represents primitive peoples in the early stages of relating their group to the entirety of creatures and creation in the world.

2)   Totemism as an aspect of structuralism, such as that put forth by Lévi-Strauss: people think with what they have to think with, and animals and trees and fish serve as excellent symbolic indices. Group A is to crocodile as group B

is to fish hawk, etc. From this, people can create an "alge-
bra" of groups relating to each other and generate rules of
exchange and interaction (Lévi-Strauss 1962a).

3)   Related to the above, and also espoused by Lévi-Strauss,
      totemism as emblematic and contributing to  personal and
      group identity (Schwartz 1982).

Of the above, only 2 and 3 seem to obtain where the Sori are
concerned. They are very "matter of fact" about their totems, and
mainly put forth their totemic affiliations to explain rules of conduct
and avoidance in some important areas of behavior (Romanucci-Ross
1978; see also de Vos and Romanucci-Ross 1982).

# On Marriage and Other Forms of the Exchange of Women

People think with what they have to think with; they also exchange
whatever they have to exchange that others consider of value and
will pay for. If we speak of the exchange of women, then we must
look at the structure of the exchange mechanism and the ceremoni-
als involved. To begin simply, consider the following: △ means
male; ◯ means female; ⎯ indicates a sibling relationship;
| indicates descent.

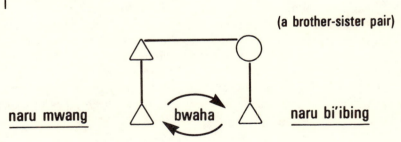

**(a brother-sister pair)**

**naru mwang**          **bwaha**          **naru bi'ibing**

The brother-sister pair in the above diagram each have a son.
All the the descendants of the brother are called "side of the man"
and the descendants of the sister are called "side of the woman."
*Naru bi'ibing* (child of the "woman") here means a child of the side
of the woman in the brother-sister pair. This person can ask, or
demand of the *naru mwang* (child of the brother of this pair) a wife
for his male children. That is to say, the female side can claim back
a female from the male "side" two generations later. Thus far the

above is similar to descriptions by Fortune (1933) and Mead (1934), although both of them wrote only of the Manus Tru of Pere. Here in Sori, however, the cross-cousin of the female line may ask his *bwaha* for a male also, if that is what is needed. (Lohai tells me to note very carefully that in this respect they differ from the Manus Tru!) Lohai has not read Lévi-Strauss, but seems to know the Sori had an "*échange generalisé.*" According to Tata, the male needing a wife may indicate to his father or uncle which particular girl he likes, and the request is sent along with betel nut and leaf ("the native whiskey," as Lukas explained it, "As if you people would send a bottle of whiskey when you ask a favor.") The parents of the boy ask the parents of the girl, who in turn consult with all the relatives who decide whether they want to go into this exchange with the other group. If they do, it means they take the girl to the family of the intended groom, who then cover her with dogs' teeth and shell money to indicate what the side of the bride will receive. (For example, in 1945 Lohai "bought" Salai for 600 dogs' teeth and four belts of *sawung* (shell money).) Sori #2 and the island of Harenggan usually provide the women for Sori #1.

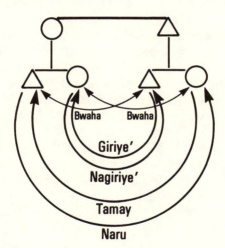

The side of the bride brings coconut oil and dried coconuts and *saksak* (now also rice). But here again, unlike the earlier descriptions of the South Coast Manus, those on the "side of the man" *also* send oil of coconut and pigs and tobacco as well as the valuables of dogs' teeth and shell money. There follow a series of feasts and exchanges until a date is set for the wedding.

The decoration of the bride is done by the girl's family, both her mother and her father's side participating. First they place on her head the stem and leaf of the betel nut palm, and on top of this the *laplap* (P.E. material for loin cloths); then the decorations: dogs' teeth around the head as well as dangling from the ears, and a decorative piece through the perforated nasal septum (Baripeo takes my pencil and puts it through her perforated septum to show me!. . . . the young girls howl with laughter as I look aghast!). Arm bracelets are placed on the upper arm and their complement placed on the legs. Ten men carry the bride to the *eyau* (P.E. wedding table). Then there is a feast for which the groom's family provides food and tobacco.

I ask Baripeo about her wedding. She says with some bitterness that no one consulted her as to whether she liked the man Loniu, whom they had chosen for her. The proper kin arranged it all, the side of the man of her family sent tobacco and dogs' teeth to "make the road" (formalize beginning of arrangements), and then Loniu's kin of the poorer sort, as they told me, sent sea turtles, then her kin sent back oil of coconuts, sago and other edibles. The men of her kin group carried her from the wedding table to the house Loniu had built for her.

Prior to marriage arrangements, how is a girl prepared for this? At the time of the first appearance of her menses and after she is tattooed, there is an *anay a'abo*, a menstruation feast. During her menstrual periods, rain and the ocean are taboo to a girl; she can bathe only with water from a hole in the ground. She may eat only from her own dishes; if not, her flesh will not form properly. In earlier times, she used to sleep in a menstrual hut during these *tambu* days, but now sleeps at home. The rest of the time, always carefully watched, she stays in her mother's house. At her initiation feast, a huge wooden bowl containing a coconut with a shoot on it is placed before her. The women of her totem will still ceremonially call upon the totem to take care of her. If this were not done her arms and legs would be paralyzed.

Many girls and women tell me of the terrible pain caused by the tattooing, when the face is cut with obsidian or a sharp rock, and more recently sometimes with cut glass. Ashes are then rubbed into the wounds. The bleeding is profuse and the more decorative lines a girl has on her face, the more it says about her rank and ability to withstand pain. Pwepwe is the most tattooed girl in Sori, and she has already explained to me that she was happy to have been able to endure the pain since it would have reflected badly on the Luhai clan and the long line of male leaders in her family had she given in to the pain and told the tattooers to stop. It is well that one can say of her, "*hi bi'ibing la be'etong*" (this woman is strong).

The tattoo markings remain as though they were etched in dark blue ink. There are some women who specialize in doing these markings, and no special kinship relationship is involved. Some children are tattooed, and this has to do with their having been ill, and is not related to puberty. It was explained in these cases as a "mark" of sickness. Tattooing makes the blood run and the sickness is released from the head and face.

During labor a woman's abdomen is rubbed with a leaf called *lawueyeng*. They tell me there isn't anything else one can do, for the woman "just cries and screams and says that she is going to die" and "everyone does the same thing every time." A woman who wants to abort ties a rope very tightly about her middle, as tight as she can stand it. Then she sets about carrying heavy trees or rocks. It is quickly added that this is wrong, but some do it. They say they know of no abortifacient other than this. To overcome sterility, Tata heats a leaf from a tree called the *lau'a* and rubs the girl's abdomen with it.

When the first baby is born, there is "a feast for a new person." "Side of the man" brings the food to be consumed and the red paint to be placed near the baby. There is no circumcision.

Divorces were traditionally granted and still are. Reasons given are the laziness of the woman or her inability to have children, or the woman herself feels mistreated and wants to go back to the home of her father. Of course, the dogs' teeth and shell money have to be returned to the side of the man in the case of divorce, as they are in the event a marriage is cancelled. But the reciprocity and exchanges continue over a marriage that links two groups. One is not through paying for the woman at the wedding. Seven or eight years after a wedding there is a payment called *supusop*. The next payment is the *apé* or the first haircutting for the child. All the males called "mother's brother" come to bring food, dogs' teeth, and shell money for the ceremonial haircutting. This is to pay back the *supusop*. The *masap* is a further payment for the woman, seven or eight years later to pay back the *apé*.

Most of the people who work with me on marriage customs are politely informative but some tell me later they found it all rather pedestrian and boring. Both men and women urge me to ask the old women about the *gum parapalei* and the women who inhabited it, the *saparapalei*. Now *there*, they say, I will find something to tell people back home that is *really* interesting. *Gum parapalei* is what is called *house pamok* (P.E. house of prostitution).

Women taken in a "war" with another group were put in the *house pamok*. In the past, they had "wars" with Harenggan, Ponam, Bipi, and many other places. (Were women from Sori ever put into the *haus pamok*?) Yes, if a woman did not have the proper kin to arrange a marriage for her then she would be placed there, or if a marriage was arranged for her and she absolutely refused to marry, that would be her fate.

What happened to them there? They would stay there until they were old, then they would have to go out and procure food for themselves, those that lived through such an experience, that is. This *gum parapalei* or *haus pamok* was, however, a variation on an ancient custom called the *Mati-No*. To get the facts on the *Mati-No* several people run to get Sa'absing to tell me about it.

"It was a house," Sa'absing began as she lit up her tobacco twist rolled in a bit of an old newspaper she found on my table, "and to inaugurate it there was a huge feast, and when all this was done, this was a place where all men slept with all women." All the members of my usual audience to these ethnographic sessions lean forward and strain for every soft-spoken word from Sa'absing's almost toothless mouth. She relates that not only the Sori, but people from surrounding villages came to sleep with partners. The women who participated were only single women and some widows. After their evening meal, women were lined up and each man chose his sleeping partner. (Did the women ever get to choose a sleeping partner?) *"Bwey, bwey,"* (no, no) where did you ever get *that* idea?" she laughs.

After the choosing, and after all had prepared for going to sleep, a man was assigned to walk around all night with a torch of coconut husk, to make sure that no one did "something improper." I suppose I still did not understand that when the Sori say "sleep" it is *not* a euphemism for something else, for when I asked, "What would become of the children of such unions?" Sa'absing assured me that no children resulted from the *Mati-No* experience. Did I think they depended only on the man walking around all night with the torch? No indeed, both the men and the women were bound with the bark of a tree (for in those days there were no *laplaps*); tree bark that had been worked with clamshells. The men had their private parts bound against the body; the women were sort of diapered. Baripeo, always the mime in order to guarantee that I understand Sori words, jumps up and down as she performs a charade of diapering herself.

"*Em, em,*" laughs old Sa'absing, meaning "that's it."

The *Mati-No*, terminated by the Mission, was a form of court-ship: it was hoped that couples would like each other. It was also used to kill the invited men from other villages, as the women held them in an embrace. Tonight I learn that among the Sori many think there is a problem in getting the girls to even begin to like to consider the idea of marriage. I share their amazement at this, but they do not seem to think this has been a perennial problem, as the Mati-No might suggest.

*February 9.* I inquire about the procedure for requesting a bride. For this purpose there is a very formal statement that must be made. The *bwaha* (cross-cousin) asks his *bwaha* (cross-cousin) for a female child to go back as wife, or a male child to go back as husband. As I look at this diagrammatically, I think it is time to summarize what I have learned about Sori kinship terminology thus far. (See Appendix II for kinship terminology and for the census to village map.) Today I also learn that personal names in this village have meanings, literal meanings, as perhaps names from more complex civilized societies had in their early beginnings. Here are some examples:

| | |
|---|---|
| *Bweyaiyai* | *bwe* = 2nd son + *yaiyai* = swimming |
| *Suwalomburoh* | *Suwa* = third born girl + *lo mburoh* = in the long grass |
| *Boboyang* | *Bobo* = a man who talks a great deal |
| *Saiyop* | *Sa* = woman + *iyop* = running |
| *Sangam* | *Sa* = woman + *ngam* = evil spirit of the bush |
| *Nyausuwalang* | *nyau* = *widow* + *suwa* = third born girl + *lang* = wind |
| *SaBo'ohang* | *Sa* + *Bo'ohang* = "woman who stinks" |
| *Suwagumso* | *suwa* = third born girl + *gum* = house + *so* = hungry |

*Sapalodyang*          *Sapa* = fourth born male + *lo* = inside
                       + *dyang* = sun

*Sa'absing*            *Sa* + *apising* = "a no good
                       woman"

I ask about the occasional pejorative names that people bear, and am told that *Sa'absing* is a case in point. Under what circumstances does a child receive such an uncomplimentary name? It seems that Sa'absing's father's sister had a quarrel with another woman and the woman called her a *sa'apising*, or a "no good woman." Now when such a name is given to you in anger, and is not true, it is too much to bear. So the father's sister in this case named her brother's daughter Sa'absing. This is to show that you reject this name that was given to you in anger and that it is not true of you. Although, here, the father's sister (*giriye'*) may curse her brother's children, it seems that to do something like this is *not* considered doing the child any harm. (In Sori it is the *giriye'* group, or the women of the father's line, who name the child, and usually the father's sister. This is in contrast to the South Coast Manus where it is the mother's brother who names a child.)

Some names are commemorative. *Kaunsil* Lohai, for example: *Lohai* is the Sori name for a small yellow fish (Garibaldi or Moorish Idol, *Zanclus cornutus*). During one of the bloody fights with the Manus who raided the North Coast, Simbuom's father's brother was murdered by the Manus. His corpse was found floating near the shore, surrounded by these small yellow fish "who had not abandoned him and kept watch until he came home."

Tata has been observing me, with sometimes evident pleasure. She likes the fact that I nurse the baby on schedule even if it means working the tape recorder at the same time — this usually brings me the benign smile of the ancient grandmother. She is usually pleased when I pass the linguistic tests that the Sori are fond of giving me: "And what, Misis, would you say So'ong did when he came in that canoe for Lomot?"

"*Gisihini*," I reply, which indicates to Tata that I have gone beyond translating directly from Pidgin, and appear to have learned that there are one-word "sentences" in the *Sa'apoy* language. This word means "I have come with a canoe to get someone, and to take said person, or persons, home."

So Tata decides that it is time that she give me her unexpurgated version of the story of the "place," i.e, what has been referred to earlier as the story of the cloud and the *sawung*. She had determined that I had to learn first about "lines" (social organization). As in the previous account, this fuller version explains that the heavy cloud which hovered over Old Sori Island for a long time was finally dispersed by the throwing of an obsidian point spear and by the *sound* of the slit gongs. What she adds, however, is that there was a special slit gong, made of bamboo known only to the Sori. This version adds that when the cloud had cleared away and the Sori were faint with hunger, they went among the *Usiai* (bush people of which the Lebei are members), who refused to give them food. So they subsisted poorly on seed fruit on the mainland. Some began to steal coconuts from each other and were severely punished by severance of the stealing hand. The hand was then hung with a vine of rattan, and left in the hot sun along with its previous owner "without food and water," to die. There was much dispersion and death.

Members of patriclans (Luhai vs. Hi'inang and Luhai vs. So'opay) fought with and killed each other and sent the dead to such places as Tulu, where the cadavers would be eaten (we mentioned before that the Sori did not eat people who spoke the same or similar language). Thus began "exchanges," for to have sent such "food" meant that the Tulu would send something in return, such as sago or coconuts. Exchanges of women were begun with Sou and Mokerang to be followed by the exchanges of consumables and durables that occur over the years when two families become allies in a marriage.

"Now things began to get good," says Tata. They learned (through culture contacts) to extract oil from coconuts for cooking, to make baskets with coils of rope, and to make *kasta* (P.E. paste) from a nut (*parinari laurini*). The shell is grated and also used to caulk canoes or gum spearheads. They learned how to make *laplaps*; they began to fasten hair with slender vines, so that it didn't snarl and give the appearance of "wildmen." From the Mokerang, they received the first pigs. Luhai was the first patriclan to give the big feast of important men (*lapang*). They were the *first*, and they invited the other three patriclans and the people of Andra, as well as their guests. The line that gives the big feast, of course, as in other parts of Manus, demonstrates its superiority and ascendancy over those invited as guests. All went very well for awhile, but then the four patriclans of Sori began killing each other again. Down on the South Coast, the Mbuke began killing the Manus Tru, and the Pitilu started killing too. There was killing all over Manus, through small, continuous and fierce "wars." Tata shook her head, "They were killing now just to kill, and then, just at that time, the Germans came. Then came the English, then the Australians, putting up a house for the visits of the *kiap* (P.E. District Officer) and then the churches came, and then the society store and now that flag up there, a Co-op flag. Now we dry the coconuts, and we get money for the copra from the society. And *lalai* (P.E. trochus shell) too. Oh yes, I forgot about Japan. Japan came and got cross with the *Ningili* (English). The Americans came to help the English and Japan had to leave. This time, however, unlike the time of the Germans, no one threw us off this island. Americans put up airplanes, and towers and cement on other parts of Manus but not here on the North Coast. For awhile we were given back old Sori, but we didn't have enough men to work there, so it was given to a company (i.e., used as a plantation), and we were not paid for our island, the company took it for nothing."

Pwepwe's father, with help from Pwepwe, also tells the following history of the fights between the Manus of the South Coast and of the North Coast Sori during a time just before the Germans came in 1880, when the Manus were in an "expansionist phase." The Manus came to Sori and killed a man of Hi'inang; the Sori sought revenge. They set out in two canoes and stopped near Mbuke. A man of the Sori called Isi'ini, grandfather of Lukas, threw a spear and with the obsidian point cut the rope of the sail of a Mbuke canoe, making it an easy task to take it and its human cargo. The Mbuke canoe and the four men and one woman in it were brought to Sori Island. To the accompanying rhythm of slit gong drummings, and the "tattoo" of sounds from it, the mast of their canoe was put in the middle of the men's house and the five were made to sit in front of the men's house. (If the mast were put in the men's house it meant the captives would be eaten; if the captives had been given baskets as they were made to sit down they would have been adopted into the Sori group.) Three men were eaten (with sago) and the woman was given to the Bipi for whatever uses they had in mind, possibly for prostitution. The other man was spared so that he might go back to this people to tell them what the Sori did to people who chose to fight with them. The man was forced to relinquish his wife so that the Sori could give her to the people of Hus. He was given safe escort to Mbuke so that he could describe the events to his people and the other South Coast Manus.

I ask if they had any other encounters of a less hostile nature with other Manus, or inhabitants of surrounding islands. Not really, but their very close kin of Harenggan told them of the kinds of behaviors one can expect from strangers, and that is enough for the Sori to know that it does not pay to venture beyond one's own reef for human companionship. This elicits a recounting of the Harenggan culture contact experience which I summarize:

Awesaang, son of Bariah went fishing and drifted very far out to sea. A bird alighted on the bed of his canoe. The bird had bits of coconut husk fibers in his mouth, and so Awesaang knew that land must be somewhere nearby. He observed the bird in flight, and he and his crew took the direction of the bird. This is how they discovered the island of Luf.

They were graciously received and well treated. First they were fed, and then invited to sleep with the women of the place. They liked it so well that they stayed for two months and then came back to Harenggan, where everyone had thought they had died at sea.

Later, the Luf returned the visit, but were surprised that the Harenggan idea of hospitality did not include the offer of women as sex partners for the guests. The Luf were offended and muttered sullen reminders that their hospitality had been more generous (nor had this generosity with women been spurned). The Luf offended their hosts further by spearing a certain kind of fish that the Harenggan catch only by ritual and magic. It was all too much to bear for everyone, and since the Luf do not usually opt to give vent to their anger by fighting, they left for home and the Harenggan were glad. Both decided that in the future they would consider the deep ocean that separated them a felicitous barrier.

There were places that one went to for marketing, of course, mainly to exchange fish for sago. Such were Ndrehet, Lebei, Oharo, Tulu, Lindrow and Su'uhi. Market exchange places, often on rivers, were especially good places to surprise another group, to kill and eat them. The Tulu, it seems from Sori histories, did this from time to time to the Ndrehet. The Sori had only one minor "war" with the Tulu, but it is possible (my speculation) that the frequent "wars" in which the Sori killed others and sent the bodies to the Tulu for consumption provided a "pay off."

# Sori Death

Broken taboos and the souls of the dead could cause illness in others. To counteract this, one employed a *lelei*, an old woman who could see these spirits and knew what they were doing to the sick. *Sarum* (the talk with the ghosts) could get to the causes of illness. In addition, the *lelei* was the expert for the laying of hands on affected parts and laying of heated leaf on areas of pain or pathology.

The *lelei* communicated with the ghosts through whistles. The spirits that were busy killing a man had already put his soul in the hole of a tree; the "familiar" of the *lelei* (i.e. the medium) would be working to extricate the soul as the *lelei* concentrated on getting the patient well.

A cause of serious illness emanated from a large stone on Old Sori Island. This stone is thought to contain a spirit, a force that is called *Indrey* — the stone is called *Ba'Indrey* (stone of Indrey). It is the very same stone in which the first shell money had been placed.

Illness is conceptualized as a dislocation somewhere in the mind-body-person-family-community-universe system; both cause and remedy are sought in connectivities which most of the Western World today would not consider relevant (Romanucci-Ross 1969, 1979, 1983).

Information about mortuary rites comes at the end of a *cry* that Salai wants registered on the tape recorder, so that they can hear it again and again. Her mother's older sister, the eldest female in Tata's family, had come to Sori to live with Tata when she was old and sick. Salai had to take care of her. This *cry* is a reproach to her relatives who were obligated by kinship rules to assume the caretaker role, but did not do so. Salai's song tells of her resentment at the being caretaker by default, and how it was inconsiderate of mother's older sister to come to Sori. It was shameful for her to have "followed the road belong her mama rather than the road belong her papa" which is what was indicated here. (She and Tata were born of the same mother but different fathers which is why, according to the rules, her "road" for asking help should never have been to Sori Island. In any case, Salai *did* take care of her when she was old and sick.) When she died Salai washed her, covered her up and lay her on the bed. At daybreak she went into an adjoining room and composed a *cry*: "*Awehu wo la tiney Awehu wo la tiney*" (you go to the mother ). The rest of the *cry* expresses her sentiments.

After the composition of the *cry*, Salai prepared for the burial, which wasn't the traditional kind. She assured me however, that the *cry* was exceedingly traditional, for each *cry* is unique in its expressive content. A person will put into such a composition personal and individual feeling, not necessarily complimentary. It is not meant to be performed by others, yet people in Sori do call on Salai to compose their *cries* for them, particularly those who do not feel that they have the poetic gifts to rise to the occasion. Though performance is not the purpose of a *cry*, it is performed and the audience is always moved, at times profoundly.

This afternoon that I play this *cry* for Salai and an audience, she really has to push back her tears to help me translate it correctly into Pidgin. Her mother Tata weeps copiously and insists on reminiscing some of the old *cry* she had written in her day, much to Salai's annoyance at the interruption. Pwepwe cries shamelessly and Lokes, our Manus cook, goes off weeping with emotion into Salai's house, not to be seen weeping with women.

I ask Salai if she remembers funerary rites before the church forbade them and she relates the following, with frequent nods of approval from Tata and some other old persons there:

"When a man died, the first thing they did was dress him up in paint so that it would seem that he was not dead but dressed up in finery and ready to accomplish something. Then they put him on a bed. When the skin would swell up and break, the spot would be covered with red paint. The corpse stayed and stank and stayed and stank and stank increasingly." (Salai expresses revulsion, brought on by her own description.) "Everyone however, was obliged to eat and have the smell of their food mingle with the smell of the rotting corpse. Here is the body, here we are, here is the food, and there is the stink all around, as we have to eat this way day after day. Then there were the women who began to wash the corpse, all the women in the father's line, but not before the worms had begun to feast on the decomposing flesh. When only the bones were left, more or less, these were put out in the sun to dry." (Salai is now over her disgust and speaks with more equanimity.) "When the bones were dry they were hung up in the doorway between two rooms. The head was put into a large wooden bowl around which there was a huge feast provided by the males in the matriline of the deceased."

Tata assures me that this is exactly as she had seen it done many times. There were some variations, however. Ebei and Lukas say that some people would smoke the dead, "just like you smoke copra," by having a fire near it, the smoke then escaping from a hole in the roof of the house. In the time of the Northwest monsoon, the corpse would be kept out in the rain for about two months so that the rains would clean the bones, and then the sun would dry them. The bones and sand from the place where the corpse had lain were thrown into the passage so that the fish would be frightened and leave. It was not thought a good thing that people should be happy about catching fish so close to the island so soon after a death. People who had acquired something new would take it to the mainland after a death for fear that the dead would be jealous of the new things and see to their destruction. Although the Sori had heard that the South Coast Manus invoked the ghost of the dead skull in a house to protect the family members from illness and death, they themselves did not follow such a custom.

Tata not only shakes her head vigorously as an *imprimatur* to everything that Salai has said, but then adds a personal experience of her own. She had been invited to Ndrehet to mourn over a relative of her husband. She was shocked to have arrived late in the affair, for his skin had been peeled off, red paint by now all over his flesh, his arms and legs tied and appended to a body horrendously swollen. She remained, however, for the time of the cleaning of the bones, putting them in a basket and placing the skull in the large wooden bowl. A small leaf with a strong sweet smell which I judged to be akin to the anise plant was placed in the nasal orifices in the skull. The women of the father's side of the deceased decorated themselves with the bones of the dead man and walked about the place in mourning. The new widow, accompanied by two other widows and viewed by no man, went to wash in the ocean thirty nights after the death. This was followed by a sago-eating ceremony. They worked magic with ginger root on the way to the ritual cleansing. The following day, other women accompanied the new widow to the low tide to catch fish. This completed the cleansing rites and she could once more be a member of the community. Her normal life resumed, but she would not re-marry unless she was very poor and could not get family help to raise her children.

## NOTES

1. For a complete description and analysis of the Manus Tru cargo cult, (based on his thorough research), see Schwartz 1962. Mead also writes of it in *New Lives for Old* (Mead 1975).

2. *Tamberan* is a term that denotes a "mystery," a cult, a sense of traditional community. It also refers to masks, ghostly presences, power to heal or render ill, spirits of the ancestors, sources of strength. Men's houses were often repositories of things *tamberan*. In Sori it is a term said to "belong" to the Bush people, Usiai.

*Tata Tara and Sori children.*

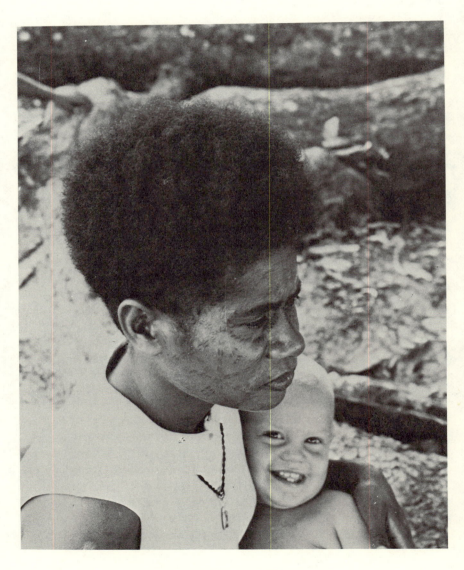

*Pwepwe of Sori and Adan.*

# SIX

# Across a Narrow Strait

## The Polygamist and General MacArthur

I borrow Ebei's canoe to give me an excuse to give him three shillings, then taking the baby, Mesian and Lomot, I go to Lebei and Sori #2. The sea is getting roughed up a bit by a strong wind, so it is a nice bit of exercise for me to paddle across the passage with Mesian (and also to paddle astern). We go through the mangrove swamp, for I do not like the looks of the sky nor the feel of the wind, but my Manus girls assure me that there is nothing to fear, that it will not rain. I have noticed that their weather predictions are no better than mine, however.

Lebei villagers come to tell me about their aches and sores, and also that rather than seeing Steven they have been a-*tamberaning*. Soon there are swarms of children about us, but I clear the ground by asking that someone go get Tuam for me and they *all* do. One woman calls out to me, ''NyaSupik,'' my new name in Lebei, which means ''widow of the Sepik.'' They are all certain that Ted has died there. Tuam is Takaray's mother's brother, and he is going to tape some of the Lebei histories that I had taken from him with paper and pencil. He notes that this is a good time for me to see and photograph him with General MacArthur (''number one man belong America belong fight, name belong em Makato''). Later, Tuam walks with me to Sori #2, mainly to tell me that if Takaray fails to pass school in Rabaul he can come to work with me so that his English will not be wasted. Tuam is energetic and affable, and I recall now that he was the most enthusiastic actor, killing *marsalai* all

101

about him when the village put on a ritual drama for filming. I can
see that only Tuam would have the energy for three families; he is
currently the only polygamist in Lebei village, although it is permitted. His stories contain the mythical and historical justification for
polygamy. Here is the "prestigious" story as Tuam gave it to the
tape recorder, and as I translate it from his language. It is called
*Sisye Pwa'apwep*:

"One man married two wives and both wives had a child at the
same time. His relatives gathered in a house and talked about
him. They said, 'How is it now? All good men have two wives
or more, one can have a child but for the other it is possible to
wait awhile. But this man, two of his wives have a child each at
the same time?'

He was standing at the back of the house and heard what
they said. When they were through he entered, but they talked
about other things. He stayed awhile and returned to his house
thinking that all his relatives had talked about him. In the evening he told his wives, 'Tomorrow morning you fry some sago
for me and put it in a basket.' He took this sago and paddled
up a small river and put his canoe at the estuary of Sanoh. He
left his canoe there and walked up to LepePapei, man of
Pwa'apwep. They greeted each other and Lepe asked him to
come into the house and sit on the bed. He went into the
house and sat on the place where fires are made, which is not
good for visitors. They argued about this, as Lepe pointed out
that he had wanted him to sit on the bed. Lepe then told his
wife to make sago and oil for his visitor and when he returned
with the food he said, 'Brother, you come sit on the bed and
have this *saksak*. So he sat on the bed, had his meal, drank
some water, and asked that the residues of the dinner be put
into his basket. Then Lepe-Papei said, 'Alright, brother, now
you can tell me your news.'

'I hear you have many eels.'

'Yes', said Lepe, 'What do you want an eel for?'

'I'd like it for a feast.'

So they went to the place of the eels and Lepe commanded
all the eels to emerge. As they floated upward, the visitor chose
the largest one. Lepe told the eel, 'If I send you to him you
must in no way harm him.' The eel let Lepe know by his movements that he would do no harm to the man. The eel returned
with him, going under the canoe. That night the man's wives
went to catch fish with their bamboo nets, and there they found
the eel. The man and his wives tried to spear the eel, but each

time the spear broke, so they got disheartened and returned home. The eel went back to its hiding place. The next night the three brought a group of people with them to try to spear the eel. For a long time no one could do it, but finally they got it out of its hiding place and killed it.

They put it on a carrying bed, blew the conch shell and sang songs and beat the slit gong drums while both men and women danced. Then they cut it up. The meat of the eel they distributed to every house; only the head was put into a big dish and placed under a hibiscus. All the meat was cooked by all who had received it at the men's house, and everyone ate a part of the eel. Then everyone went to sleep. In the morning, everyone was dead. Everyone had died, no one survived. The man who planned this heard the silence in the village and knew that his trick had worked. Everyone had died, the place was silent. He said, in the village, to all the dead, 'Before you said that I am not one of the good men to live among you.' He got the intestine of the eel and threw it into a stream called Korok. He spoke against all of the people there until he had finished, then he went home to his wives and said, 'Let us be off to a new village,' and they went off to a distant place.

His wives stayed in their new home in the new village, but he went back to see the old village once more. He discovered that the head of the eel, inside a dish, sang songs. He took the jaw and put it around his arm. The man and the jaw then started to sing a song. That is how the Lebei people became the singers of songs around this part of Manus.''

This is only one of several stories of mass poisonings to punish what most here in Manus consider mild infractions.

Although polygamy is approved and practiced, it is not considered good form to have more than one wife pregnant at any one time. It is wrong, in fact, because the others have to help the woman who is carrying a child and then nursing a child. For this reason it is curious that the hero of the above story kills everyone for rightly criticizing him. The Sori and other groups about here find Lebei stories and the Lebei themselves rather bizarre.

Approval of polygamy does nothing to mitigate feelings that adultery is wrong. In a story called "Drayah's War," the protagonist finds that his wife is unfaithful and that her lover, Drayah, has committed adultery against every "house" of Puuh. The Puuh group lines discussed it and then decided what to do. The plot was to get Drayah to commit adultery against his own "house" of Yunuh. Drayah did not disappoint them. The betrayed husband then followed Drayah to the men's house and killed him. Those sleeping in the men's house said he should not have done it, but now he might as well kill Drayah's wife too. Sooniang, his wife, unfortunately was a Sori. She was injured by his attempts to kill her and her brothers came from Sori and took her home. Now the Puuh people escaped and hid in the bush for they feared the Sori, who were very angry about the injuries sustained by one of their women. The Sori came across the passage and burned the entire village and everything in it. This is remembered as "the war of the 100 obsidian spears." Scenes of the victorious Sori smearing themselves with the blood of the slaughtered as they rejoiced, are recalled with horror. The Sori were joined by the Lindrow, who killed 40 Lebei for a cannibal feast.

The Lebei are not only singers of songs, but bards and myth-makers as well. Several weeks after So'ong from Sori got lost in the bush, as recounted earlier, the Lebei had a version of the tale: So'ong, lured by bush devils for three days and three nights, was promised a huge store of betel nuts. That is how he got lost. He struggled against Satan knowing it was wrong to listen to him and so his feet began to find their way back to the beach from where he could see Sori Island. The Sori found this amusing but their skepticism was clouded by doubts, for they "know" that there *are* bush devils on the mainland!

At market time the Lebei bring sago, betel nut, leaves, pineapple, opossum and pig. The Sori bring fish, clams, and clamshells, tortoise, shark, and all the fish of the sea. Sori and Lebei presentations of "self" are also contrastive: the Lebei are dramaturgical, myth-making artists, and the Sori present themselves as "logical," and no-nonsensical. The former are sensitive and peace-loving, the latter are warlike and quick to take offense.

We spot Lohai in #2 Sori sitting under a huge tree, for he is easy to see with his bright red shirt and white *laplap*. His wife Salai is at the house of Polai's mother, telling her about the Mesian-Polai "court," we have no doubt, for the mother saw Mesian coming and ducked into the door of her house.

Salai changes the subject, so to speak, by greeting me and telling me that Lohai is holding another "court." This is a case of an old woman who had no land on which to build a house. A certain man in the village told her she could build a house on his land. All went well for years, but she had planted a coconut which in time became a tree and now the woman claims that the coconuts are hers, but the man who owns the ground says they are his, he owns the ground, and if she and her children want litigation they will get it. He will have her thrown out of the house which, after all, is on his land.

I ask Lohai how he will decide this case. He says he will have to think about it and ask the *Kateket* (P.E. catechist, native trained to perform religious services in the absence of a Catholic priest on these outpost islands). Salai asks how such a case would be resolved in my country, and I say I think that planting a tree on land that belongs to another is making him a present of the tree. Any rights you think you might have gained in time have to be substantiated as contractually agreed upon in some way or another, written or verbal, but you have to prove it. Assuming of course, that the land rights are as presented, the man is probably right. Salai quickly interrupts and rolls her eyes in dismay heavenward, to her husband and to me, "We have exactly the same laws. Why does he have to wait for the catechist?" As usual, *kaunsil* Lohai is demolished by his wife.

He quickly changes the subject back to Mesian. How sorry he is about the "court" that had to take place in my house! If she had had a chance with Polai to "go married" it is certainly all ruined now, thanks to Lokes, who "buggered it up *quicktime*." (Lokes of course is not through with Mesian and is dictating letters in Pidgin to Ted in New Guinea, telling him that he must fire Mesian since I do not seem to see the importance of this gesture).

As we speak of Lokes, he is just arriving in Lebei with Steven who is here to attend to a woman who had a miscarriage. She had been working hard and long, bearing heavy loads and working the *saksak* in the bush. Steven tells me later that he counselled the husband about this and the husband replied, "That has nothing to do with it, she lost the baby and the other two babies because I did not pay her grandfather the dogs' teeth when we got married." (It would be futile to ask him why the other three children lived.) Steven, as usual, asks relatives of patients how they can hold such beliefs and still say they believe in God. The husband replies that he believes not only in God, but also in Christ and Mary, but he also *knows* that the *tamberan* man was asked to work this bad event on his wife.

*February 10.* At a meeting held by Lohai in Sori: Paliau has sent a letter to Lebei village, with a copy to me, explaining that he is a candidate for the post of elected official from Manus to Port Moresby. They are to read it, and then pass it on to #2 Sori and then Sori #1. Some men from Lebei ask me how they should vote. Another thing that these villages learn today is that the "tax" is to begin. The head tax will be three pounds for each man and 5 shillings for each woman. The South Coast tax already in effect is four pounds for each man and 10 shillings for each woman. There will now also  be a tax levied on dogs, which will hardly affect Sori, but the Lebei will be hard hit.  Mesian laughs at this, and whispers to me that she predicts the Lebei people will do what is done in Bunai village.  When the time for tax collection for dogs is near, many put a stone around the dog and drown it.  Some however, not sanguine enough to do this, will take their dog into the mangrove swamp and leave it there.  It is said that such become "wild dogs."

Steven then addresses those assembled.  He talks mostly to the women about hygiene, "Wash your hands, wash your dishes, wash your breasts before feeding the baby." (Later, every woman there confesses to me that she finds this suggestion absolutely ludicrous.) He asks them to please stop coming to his "hospital" and ask for "that medicine over there," or "those green pills" or an injection. He then gratuitously terrified them by telling of a woman in Rabaul who insisted to the Doctor Boy that her baby be given an injection. The baby didn't need it, but the Doctor Boy gave it one of water to stop her nagging, and the baby died.  When she went to court she lost the case, however, since it was decided the fault lay with the mother.  I doubt that Steven serves the best interests of Public Health with this story, but I have noted repeatedly that homilies here have to be macabre, it seems, and examples spine-tingling.  Lohai's idea of a joke is to come to the house and say (today's example) "Misis, why do you clean your house, haven't you heard that a plane crashed and your husband was on it?  He is dead."

I spend hours today working with the young Isi'ini, great grandson of the famous warrior and marksman, on the lineage of the Luhai patriclan.

*February 11.* Today Takaray insists on re-telling me the history of the eels, this version in Pidgin. He adds nothing new except this manner of telling it; instead of saying, "He chose the eel that was the largest," he has each eel step up, with the host asking the hero if he liked it and the hero saying he did not like that one.  Although Takaray dramatizes the story beautifully, the only way I keep awake is to try to guess which number would win.  I place bets on 3, 7, 10, but do not guess 12. The twelfth eel. Takaray replies overtly to my questions such as, "Why was it wrong for two women to be pregnant at the same time?"

"Because one has to be able to work while the other is pregnant."

"Why did he sit on the floor instead of the bed and why was it not a good thing for a guest to do so?"

"He sat on the floor to shame his host.  Then he would ask the host for something and the host would have to give it. The man of Pwa'apwep knew it. He said to himself, 'Look, he is sitting on the floor, and now he is even sitting on the ashes. He is going to ask me for something big'.''

The eel in Nranah's story propelled the canoe, and Lebei man did not have to paddle. In fact, the eel was "just like a motor" so when the man wanted him to slow down he did so. The eel was eaten by everyone, including children, pigs and dogs, and all died, for revenge in Lebei's stories is very inclusive. Ndranah wanted me to understand the subtlety of the transition between sleep and death, "You must understand Misis, that all night long they were asleep, but when the dawn broke, when they would have begun to think about getting out of bed, that is the moment they were dead." He also thought it important that I understand that when the eel and the man sang in perfect harmony everyone thought it was two people, but when they saw it was one person they marveled (this took about 25 minutes of story telling time).

My story teller of this morning is even more enchanted than the average Lebei with the idea of multiplicity in unity. He is even more astounded that the man "made so much noise with the slit gong that all thought it was many people and were so surprised to learn it was just one person."

I ask Takaray why I now have two origin stories for the Lebei: the first one of the Ponam women and flying fox, and now this. It seems that the Ponam women and the old man were the first to give rise to the Lebei people, and that they almost perished through hard times, and the man and two wives is the second origin. Why don't the Sori have an origin story, I ask. "Because they just don't," said Takaray, with an intonation implying that they were a culturally impoverished lot.

# Collectibles for Contrast Sets

Pwepwe hears all of this, of course, and asks me, when Takaray leaves, what I think of the Lebei language. I wearily say that it had its difficult aspects. "Actually," she replied, "It is simply a stupid language. They say *tjong* for basket, *tjong* for canoe, *tjong* for *garamut*." I demonstrate for her that the vowels are not the same at all, ranging from open to closed to an elision (oh, aw, and uo). She seems completely surprised and says, "Well, you must be right, but I never thought of it like that."

Pwepwe has an extraordinary intelligence, looks down on just about everyone and her acknowledgement of my small linguistic triumph makes me feel very very good. In addition, Lohai brings me six shillings which I earned, as did everyone else who worked loading sago on the Sunam that was to go off to Lorengau. I show my respect for their work by accepting my pay as everyone else does.

*February 12.* I play baseball with the young boys and I am amazed at the ingenuity displayed in the use of a coconut tree. It is a source of food and a source of the technical means of preparing it, as described earlier. Now Mesian immediately makes a baseball by tightly weaving coconut leaves, which serve admirably. The baby is amused by a coconut leaf toy flier, also of sudden manufacture, that whirls in the breeze.

Parts of trees are used as scoops, as shovels, and as canoe coverings. Shells of coconuts are used for making ladles. As even Lévy-Bruhl knew in his Paris apartment, they know well how to utilize their environment to procure everything they need. I have already found much to admire here, in their moral judgments, in the poetry of their myths and cries, and have yet to record in detail what I find admirable in the uses of winds and stars for voyaging or programming economic exchanges and other activities such as fishing. Still I think the "science of the concrete" (Lévi-Strauss 1962b:Chapter I; Lévy-Bruhl 1951:159—174) involves contradictions, though such contradictions are not a problem for the primitive.

I finish Lukas' account of the Sori—Ponam "War" of the cooking pots, and the fecal gift left for the Ponam. Lukas is quite intelligent, but not the ideal "informant." He, like, Lohai, gets involved in the paradigmatics of explanation, which is to say that there is no such thing as asking for a literal translation in explanation of a phrase and getting it. What one gets in reply is not only what is implied by the verb of action but a performance that would delight Ray Birdwhistell, formalizer of kinesics. For example, *lim nimey* means "he claps his hands." Lukas quickly arises from the tree stump, gives a cheerleader performance while shouting, "Fooray, fooray" and tells me that natives here are like Americans in this respect, for he had seen American soldiers making these "fooray," had I never seen them? He wonders, now, do Australians do that too? For these are *not*, he ventures, like Americans in many respects and in fact seem very reserved. Lukas' paradigms seem to include all his past experience, but favor the years of World War II.

It is not that this is uninteresting, but as Lukas is performing I watch old Tata going out to sea; I have grown very fond of her and

I pray for her safe return. She and Ebei are my best informants. There are six other old persons here, but they do not *remember* anything, or they are considered deranged by the village. NyaSabaso looks like walking death (see photo). I have tried talking to her but all she says is "*sa'apo dyam bwey*" (talk of the whiteman not got). Everyone forgives her for urinating on the beach in full daylight and it is said of her, "poor old one she is past her time." People of the village, however, do not share my concern for "the best informants." Their concern for me is that, in their opinion, I am too kind and generous with the Manus girls, who, they *just know*, are frivolous and foolish and will leave me when I need them most.

*February 13.* A fascinating session with Tata on the kinship "lines" of her totem. She once more tells me of tragedies in the village resulting from the broken *tambu* of the *manuay*. We talk of her age and she says she is very old indeed because she remembers the Germans, and she was even then married and grown up. She could be eighty since the Germans were here from 1908 to 1910. As she tells me that NyaSabaso is her age, I remark that Tata is in excellent shape. NyaSabaso, I am assured, is old, tired and broken in mind and body because long ago she broke a *tambu* of the *manuay*; and for that reason, too, she had no children. Tata owes her youthful vigor to the fact that she has never broken such a *tambu* in her entire life.

Then Tata and Pwepwe begin to speak in low tones about my closest neighbor, Sa'abwen. I now understand enough *Sa'apoy* to know that they are talking about multiple births and beg Pwepwe to explain the several words I do not understand yet. She tells me it is a terrible thing, but I really must know about this. Sa'abwen had twelve children and eight died. It was like this: the first one died, the second lived, the third were *twins*, and one died, number four were *twins*, and both died, number five were *triplets* and two died, number six died, and number seven died too. Both women were saddened by the fear that this did not bode well for the Sori, these multiple births. Just look at all the women who have had twins in addition to this one. There is the wife of Uweh, whose twins died from falling into the blood of a stingray in the canoe of their grandfather, Ebei, who had violated his totem. Well, they did live for several years after that, and I might not believe it, but I would have thought them completely normal children in the interim! Samahong had twins, and Siwa, and, oh yes, NaSapadye. They wanted my opinion and I refrained from commenting that that was a large number, for their interpretation of my reply would have increased the dread. I had really upset Pwepwe not long ago by telling her that indeed a woman can become pregnant with only two sexual events, in fact, it only occurs in one event. She looked at me in stunned disbelief, and I was very sorry I had misjudged the seriousness of my accurate remark.

*February 14.* I have been waiting three months for a tree from Harenggan from which a *saman* (P.E outrigger) for our canoe is to be made. Two brothers own the tree and they cannot decide which of them is to be paid for the tree. "*Em i bullshit,*" Lohai tells me in Pidgin. My luck is not improved by a miserable four hours working with a young man from Lebei who wanted to replace Takaray, who is off at school in Rabaul. He writes, but cannot read his writing. I have no success trying to explain that if one hasn't built up perception, meaning will not "come up" from hours of trying to read. It is not different, however, from having watched Mesian and Lomot continue to "pump" a kerosene lamp for over an hour *after* I had told them that it would not function until fixed. Nor pleading with Steven to stop re-arranging the batteries in the lantern because they had to be replaced with new ones. After a long time of observing this I finally handed him three good batteries, took away the leaky batteries, and he did get the lantern to work and took all the credit, "You see Misis, I told you I could fix this lantern for you." Just doing something with dogged persistence is what will bring results, it is believed.

One can see the Sori—Lebei contrast in their meetings. The Sori are orators. The Lebei seldom have anything to say but will complain to me privately that the Sori are willfull and inconsiderate. A Lebei is animated when he recounts a myth or history, his entire body is involved, his face assumes the expression of the person or the animal speaking. Direct quotations are acted out. A Lebei will rise from his chair and look startled, frightened, angry, etc. A Sori sits placidly like a detached historian as he tells his tale. The Sori consult the *tamberan* men, but it is with pride that they say they do not have one. The Lebei lack humor even more than the Sori, who do not distinguish themselves as purveyors of wit and humor. It is only from their own shyness and feeling ill at ease that they collapse into laughter, which becomes contagious in a group. For the Sori, an incident or remark that has brought laughter once will be endlessly repeated, and even more remarkably, will never fail to evoke the same spontaneous laughter among the same persons who have heard it many times. The song about Adan and the *pukpuk* (P.E. crocodile) is one such.

But there are incidents here that do remind one of the Western World. Everyone is amazed that I take photographs with a camera and that these materialize as well as those the *Mastah* (Ted) took! Imagine: a woman, a camera, and the result, a picture. Just like a man. How can this be?

Some observations on the audience as I work with an informant: The young have a habit of hastening to tell me the Pidgin equivalent of a phrase or word before the informant has a chance to look carefully into his repertoire for the exact translation. This is met by a crude rebuff to the youngster by the middle-aged members in the group, as the elders sit back and look pleased in *lapun* (elderly) dignity. A young upstart has been put in his place. But this discouragement is only temporary, as they are accustomed to crude rebuffs and a verbal lashing whenever they step out of line, which is almost always. An older person never helps a younger person save face but rather appears delighted to have been the instrument by which the younger person lost it.

The Sori resent the informants who come to work with me on Lebei linguistics and have now begun a new strategem. As the new replacement for Takaray stammers in confusion, a Sori woman will sit down before me with a *laplap* full of shells and will tell me their Sori names and for what culinary or decorative purposes they are used. Another woman will begin to make a *purpur* (P.E. "grass skirt") with my discarded kleenex and papers thrown into a wastebasket. Another will begin to name all the fish in the Sori waters so that I can write them in my notebook. Pwepwe, wanting to have center stage again, has begun walking into the work room with matchboxes in her perforated earlobes.

But I learn once more that there is no such thing as a casual remark. I say to a young bride in our audience, "Why do you not cut your hair?" Everyone is very disturbed. I try to avoid whatever disaster this comment might have engendered by adding, "Well I wonder why you didn't shave your hair off like Suwa here."

Everyone sighs with relief and explains that although, in the not too distant past, all married women shaved off their hair, *now* one will shave off her hair only as a sign of mourning for the death of a close relative. Suwa has done it for the death of her sister and not simply because she is recently married, as I must have inferred. The next morning, however, I am awakened by sounds that gave this tiny island the appearance of a vast barber shop. Every woman is getting a haircut. My question has implied my disapproval of long bushy frizzy hair, of which they are very self-conscious anyway. I had used the word, *"tihitihi"* which means "cut" and not *iyeou* which means "take away completely" or "shave." My question to the young bride had been interpreted as, "Why don't you married women get your hair cut?"

***February 19.*** In the morning Baripeo and So'ong, who was lost in the bush but found his way back, are crooning in their soft almost inaudible high-pitched tremulo style. "Go listen to them," a number of women urge me, with amused smiles. They are singing a *cry* that Baripeo had written about her son "America" when he left on a boat to go off to school somewhere. The women sit about weaving their *saksak* baskets, all their small children crawling about in the sand, buttocks and bottoms all covered with "whitesand." A little girl has fallen asleep between Sa'abwen's full and pendulous breasts as mama keeps weaving dried coconut leaves. The women steal glances at me from time to time to indicate that I should know that they consider this strictly third rate. These are not like Salai's literary and musical inventions. For the *cry* for the death of Luwi has to the Sori ear a classic grace and style. The perfume of the winds, the feather of the totem bird, the characterization and repudiation of the white man's culture and his bottles of vaseline give the Luwi ballad a place of prominence in the Sori literary arts, since it is recognized as elegant. Some of the women snicker at Baripeo's poetic attempts while others confine their disapproval to letting me know that this is not considered quality among them.

Today I learn how to make lime to be savored with betel nut and pepper leaf. First collect white coral. Place it on a fire from six o'clock at night to six o'clock in the morning. Put it in a basket and shake it until the ashes of the fire are removed. Then just put it away. It will crumble into a fine powder; then you put it into your *kampang* (P.E. lime gourd). I have been advised not to try it, since the person who does not know how to use it will suffer bad burning.

Getting rid of Lomot has purified in spirit the rest of the helpers in the house, who now vie to see who can be the cleanest and the quickest to please. The villagers are delighted to see the moral record set straight at last. So'ong has come with a declaration that he wants to marry her, so that, it is said here, he can get his job back at the co-op store, after having offended the Sori with his *hambak* (P.E. playful affair) with Lomot in their village.

# Diagnosis as a Group Activity

*February 23.* Last night, So'obwey, wife of Pranis was ill. Mesian suggests that we have a look, for she is about seven months pregnant, had worked much too hard that day making *saksak* with others and was now going to have her baby before its time. Apparently I am being called to help because everyone had acknowledged that whereas they could "help" with full term babies they are terrified at the thought of having anything to do with a baby "who comes before it is time." When I arrive I ask if she has had a show of blood. I know nothing about midwifery, but that is what my doctors had asked me when ascertaining whether a baby was actually on its way into the external world.

Several voices state at once, and Salai repeats in an after-echo rather pedantically, "She has no blood. She has had eight babies and all her blood is finished." The Rev. Hans left the village a short time ago, after having visited me, and he has sanguine self-assurance and success with such events. But at least Lohai has dispatched a canoe to Sapandruan where Hans was staying overnight in order to deliver the sermon to the Lutherans there tomorrow. The men have been told to talk to Hans, then to go on to Lorengau for a work-boat to come get the sick, parturent So'obwey. I ask Salai, "Do you think the baby is dead?" The reply is, "No, because the belly is hot. If the baby were dead the belly would be cold."

Then I ask Salai a question she considers really simple-minded, "Is the baby in the correct position to be born?"

"How would I know, Misis, how could I know? Can you know?"

I said I could. She wants to learn, so I show her and Salai is delighted with her new knowledge.

"Here is a leg, here are the feet, here is the head!" she announces in lecture fashion to the group of about 35 people in the crowded hut. As Salai keeps repeating to smaller enclaves that she and the Misis have ascertained that the baby is alive and in position, Mesian and I suggest that we might brew So'obwey some tea. Lohai steps into the middle of the house and announces that the Misis and Mesian are going to brew some tea, as though it is a special dispensation on his part. There is no matter so minute or delicate that his *nihil obstat* is not required.

Upon our return, the hut has been transformed into an amphitheatre with a light blazing at the feet of the ailing woman. Women, adolescents and men, both married and unmarried, crowd the doorway and the interior of the house. Steven does not know what to do; he has come to fan her, telling me she is "short of wind." I ask So'obwey where it pains her. There are at least a dozen voices that shout the reply, "in the belly," but So'obwey does not even have the strength to reply. All are staring at her, as if she will yield up the mystery of life and death. To me she looks very ill, and not at all in labor, but I assure Pranis that Hans *will* come back and will know exactly what to do. Pranis wants me to know that it is not *his* fault that she works too hard, for she thinks only of her family and her work. Her daughters are unconcerned and go about their small occupations. But for her husband, no one seems upset, but rather just curious about the outcome. Some of the older people make a joke occasionally of the usual, not particularly witty, kind.

I decide to leave now, and note that my leaving is a sign for everyone to leave. Salai tells me on the way home that she has a bad cough and what should she do about it. Lohai says, "Misis, I will tell you what to tell Salai. Tell her to go to the outhouse and *bekbek* there (p.e. defecate) and then eat her own *bekbek*."

It is not common for husbands to have such felicitous advice for their wives here, but then I have not always been as privy to intimate moments as I have been tonight, at past midnight, walking home with the chief of the village and his wife. Salai ignores him totally, wants me to notice the mint leaves planted in front of their house, and tells me they are very good in soup. She recounts, as though it had happened miraculously, "Look, I saw this on #2 Sori on a trip, put some in my hair for decoration, put it in the ground here just for a joke and all this comes up all the time."

I have never seen her so full of delight.

At 3:30 a.m. Mesian awakens me to tell me that Mastah Hans is here and could he sleep in the *haus kiap*. Hans is annoyed at Steven because So'obwey was *not* having a baby. She had pleurisy and Hans gave her procaine penicillin and put her in the care of Steven, who, he says, should have known what to do. I ask Hans about his experience and the knowledge of the people in having babies.

"Pranis summed it up perfectly for you," said Hans. "They know when it is full term and everything is normal, in which case the woman really has the baby by herself."

*The oldest woman on Sori Island*
*"Poor <u>lapun,</u> she is past her time."*

_Kaunsil_ Lohai of Sori Island, dressed for the occasion of changing the marriage rules.

# SEVEN

# Modernizing the Politics of Love, Sex and Power (with Mythic Nostalgia)

*February 24, Monday.* Lohai tells Lokes to tell me that I simply must attend the *tihineu* (meeting) at #2 Sori this morning because he is going to do something that has never been done before, and I should bring my notebook and pencil. I meet Lohai at the canoe, and he now confides that he is going to invent a new way for people to get married here because there are too many unmarried people about these parts. There are too many women who are alone without help with too many children without fathers and no one to support them except the mother who has to be gone all day either fishing or in the bush so that they can be fed. (Odd statement from Lohai in view of the extended family situation here!)

Those around me begin to joke about this. Is *SaLuhai* going to put her name up and will she hope that Mastah Ted puts his name under hers? (*SaLuhai* is the name given me by Simbuom, the eldest male of the Luhai clan. It means "woman of the Luhai clan," and now I am a *meri belong ples tru*; (P.E. a woman who really belongs here and is of the place). Everyone today is addressing me in *talk place* and I reply when I can in *talk place*, not in Pidgin. Mesian and I paddle the canoe while Lohai and Salai sit on the bottom. It always takes persuasion before I am permitted to have my way about this; they don't understand when I say I need the exercise.

Upon arrival, we are met with much joking about what was presumably a secret agenda. Some men express the hope that their

117

wives will take another husband, though this meeting is not to be for married people. Those particular wives make sure that I receive the message in the meaningful looks they give me which say, "Ha, he should know how I really feel about him." All this amidst much laughter.

Lohai begins the meeting by reciting the need for the program he is about to propose, expostulating the same rationale he had given me on the canoe. He goes further to say that the Australian government cares about fatherless children while several shout to me, "Not really, such a lie!" Lohai continues, "In the past there were and still are strict rules about how marriages are arranged, but now it seems that no one wants to go to all this trouble except a few families. And so, people just aren't getting married. Is it because our customs involve too much cost and trouble in affinal exchanges between families? This might be so, so let us change it now. Even the married couples who may make their homes available to a couple who like each other, hesitate or refrain from doing this because they know not what manner of relationship they are fostering nor whom it will offend. This is understandable. Now, there are many who will say, this is not a concern of mine, I take care of my wife and my children, what has this to do with me? Well, we must think of how the place came up. Young men who think only of themselves and how to sneak off for their pleasure and get away from responsibility are not thinking of Sori, nor of the whole of Manus, nor of society. Left to them, Sori would perish, and even they would not want this if they thought about it. It is not good for a child to have no father and never see a mother. What happens to a child who must think, 'I have come up nothing'?"

It was a good speech, and now he wants to hear what they have to say, "Please," he continues, "Do not talk about coconuts, or the Baripeo Society, nor the torts and wrongs you have received. Please talk only on the subject at hand for the moment, for that is all I want to hear."

There is a long, long wait. It is punctuated by coughs, by those who rise and walk away from the assembly, by the blowing of noses with hands, by the expectoration of bronchial mucous. I am the chosen recipient of meaningful grimaces by the young women and polite shy smiles from the men. I have now moved away from the mass bronchial congestion and am seated under a coconut tree so that I view the entire group. They surround *Kaunsil* Lohai in a circle, but are separated by sex into two groups. Lohai is wearing an American shirt and tie and an American khaki *laplap* which was made in Rabaul, New Britain, (so he told me). Elegant and with graceful movements, he is unquestionably the best speaker in these parts and the person most at ease before a group. He repeats, "Would someone please talk, but only on the subject, not on the nasty Lebei tricks in the bush to the Sori. The subject is, what is the way of the good of man, and how can we avoid what is not straight and not good on this subject of marriage."

As with any other group in the world, there is one here who needs to fill the void of silence with words, any words. Such a one among the Sori is Sapandariu. He merely repeats all that Lohai has said and he does it badly. Siwa throws me a look of exasperation at such simple-mindedness. A young man from Lebei walks over to me and says, "Don't feel that you have to cover up all of your legs and be uncomfortable and hot. This *tambu* on legs around here is very stupid. Americans have the right idea — a *tambu* on breasts. Now, it really makes sense that breasts would have a *bikpela tambu* (P.E. a major taboo) placed on them. But legs, it is ridiculous. I wish I were an American Negro. All this no good fashion of the *kanaka* here makes me tired."

Tuam has brought his photograph of himself with General MacArthur. It is yellow and tattered and I smile to think of the old soldier literally fading away on a small Pacific Island. Tuam tells me he will never, never part with this. Never.

But no one wants to talk, though Lohai keeps urging with a dogged determination. Bipi has done it, and Loniu and Jowan. With good results. Don't the Sori and Lebei think of anything but money? What good does it do to have 3—5 shillings or even a pound, for all it can do is go to the store and you never see it anymore.

Lohai is really saying many interesting things about culture change. He is upbraiding them for their not knowing that they are between two cultures. That they are only slightly enmeshed in a money economy but are not yet a money economy; that they are beginning a process of loss of identity, both personal and cultural; that they must develop an awareness of what is happening to them.

Someone remarks that the *kaunsil's* own sister Pwepwe is not present, so he sends for her forthwith. The idea of putting names to be matched in bottles is discarded as there are not enough bottles, so a board is put in place and several men write their names and the names of their friends on the board. Underneath each name is a space for two or three names of girls who might be interested in that

man. As the names are read off, the women in the crowd shriek
with laughter after each candidate for husbandhood. No one was
omitted. Boys of 15, Polai of earlier Mesian fame, who is leaving for
Kavieng for a two-month course on how to be a storeman, and
Teteh, the oldest widower imaginable. Even Teteh, of the long, yellow, filthy beard, who is considered ludicrous and repulsive by all.
The list provides the greatest merriment the women have known for
a long, long time. Though Lohai exhorts and pleads, no woman will
write her name on the board.

"Alright," Lohai concludes with this dismal failure, "The
women have spoken. You do not wish to be married. The responsibility of what happens to you in the future is no longer mine. But
there will be two more *tihineu* for you to write your names under
those of men you like."

When we arrive home Pwepwe remarks that this affair is very
stupid. What woman would write her name under a man's so that it
might publicly be scratched off by him? As we disembarked on Sori
Island, John Sapalona, the storeman, asks if his wife had put her
name in a bottle and if he was at last rid of her. But the trouble with
all the girls, he has to add, was that they all wanted to get married.

Lohai later admits to me the failure of the enterprise, but vows
he will continue his efforts to make people marry and to make the
men responsible. This is a curious attitude, for in Manus generally,
and here in Sori as well, the bond most cathectically charged is not
the husband-wife tie, but the "brother-sister pair." It is from this
pair that the descendants reckon rights, duties, obligations, affinal
exchanges, and so forth. The only true love story is not between
real people, but between a person and a spirit or bird or snake. It
will be remembered that Lapa-Lokoyan, a snake, was overcome with
passion for a woman and that engendered the Lindrow people, and I
am soon to learn that it was a deep hostility between the sexes that
began the heterosexuality of the Sori people. It is not the custom
here to be concerned with paternal responsibility. Children are a joy
and resource, and anyone will gladly take them. Therefore I begin to
worry, of course, that my attitudes have something to do with it,
though I could not find evidence for this in a perusal of my past
words and actions regarding marriage. Of course, my very presence
may have had an influence.

A few days later an Australian District Officer puts in a call at
various North Coast Points, since he was preparing the villages for
their first election, and he happens to have with him the village
books begun in 1957. Although the information is scant, it lists the

approximate year of birth for those in the village for whom this could be ascertained with reasonable certainty, and it lists the total population of Sori in 1963 as 166, as follows:

| | |
|---|---|
| adult males | 32 |
| adult females | 38 |
| children (male) | 40 |
| children (female) | 25 |
| average size of family | 2.6 children |
| number of women of child-bearing age | 30 |
| number of women pregnant | 2 |

These figures coincide closely with my own. Tata's birth date is estimated as 1904, although from the events she remembers she must be at least ten years older, in my opinion. I did not accept Pwepwe's declaration that Tata was over 100 years of age. Still, their estimate of A'Amau and Ebei as having been born in 1905 is probably correct by my criteria of memory of events and participation in them. The weathering of the skin of face and body adds years to age appearance, as it does here. In the official's notes there are brief accounts of visits by anti-yaws campaigns; these investigators had found the Sori "in good health." (As the accounts of many other visits, this was a one-sentence account.) There is a date on the levying of taxes for the Council area. (The head tax had recently been announced, as will be recalled.) There are six cases in ten years of divorce granted by the administration, with very specific instructions left for the maintenance of the children and the ex-wife by the divorced husband. Follow-up visits brought fines imposed on those who had not complied with this (*none had*); particularly upbraided were those who had failed to build a house for the ex-wife as well as for the present wife. The terms "child support" and "custody" were used and expressed in Pidgin.

Now what must have given these judgments added moral force in the eyes of "the councillor," as Lohai is referred to in the book, is that in several cases where the Sori, the Nrehet, and the Tulu brought cases to the administration over land use, the Sori usually won out in the District Officer's judgment. Example: "1) 26-9-1958 Busuotinang (Sakumetia) Island. Heard the case for both sides, Tulu vs. Sori, regarding use of this island: a) The Tulu admit that they are an inland people and that this island was a traditional camping ground of the Sori at "market time;" b) The Sori are an island people and controlled the seas, reefs, and probably the beaches in the old days; c) The Tulu have adequate land; d) The Sori have not."

"The Sori are to have the unrestricted use of the island after they pay the Tulu 3 pounds, being the value of coconuts planted recently by the Tulu. The Tulu are to complete the harvesting of the garden on the island by 31-12-1958. W. G. Murdock ADO."

*"27th.* Today the Sori handed over 3 pounds for payment to the Tulu, meeting in village unanimous."

In 1960, a case that the District Officer was not able to settle ended up in the Court for Native Affairs, Civil Jurisdiction, and was heard as a complaint under Regulation 59 (1) NAR. It was a claim of entitlement to the use of a number of sago palms in an area of about two acres said to be owned by a man of Nrehet. The decision was that "the natives Salai-Bwalohay, Pope-B, Sisamen-B and Sapalona-B all of Sori, Manus District, are entitled to work in common the sago-palms on the ground in question, being part of the land known as Paus, provided that Pai-Mani of Nrehet is entitled to reproduce of such food crops as he himself planted between the time of the death of the woman Ipiko-Tendewo of Nrehet and the date of this order, and provided also that neither party shall make any further plantings of food crops on the ground in question."

For both of these cases, Tata, mother of three of the above-mentioned "natives of Sori," had given me "stories" of the genealogy of the ownership of that beach property on the mainland; it belonged to Bwalohay, but she did not refer to this case. No wonder she was very eager to get it on the tape recorder! And small wonder too that incidents in her histories dwelt on the past generosities of the Sori toward the Tulu in sending them corpses to eat when the Sori killed in battle.

It is generally the case in the Admiralties too, that rewards go hand in hand with moral compliance. Lohai must have inferred that the least he could do for the Australians was to urge the village to act as Australians do about family morality. For all the other residual cases dealt with Lohai's attempts to bring to Australian justice the scoundrels who got a girl, or several girls pregnant but did not marry them. One example from the "village book":

> *"3-7-1963.* Complaint by Councillor Lohai that a single man of Sori #1, Si'iwin'ape made two single women pregnant. The two women are Senale-Drasui and Sagahun-Baboia both of Sori #1.

Senale will bear the first child.  S. was warned he will have to pay maintenance to the women and states today that he intends to marry Sagahun.  For action by PO on arrival of the first child.

"*3-8-1963*.  At Lorengau Councillor Lohai has come in to report that Senale has had a child, female.  As yet Siwing has not married either Senale or Sagahun."

Once again I am made aware of the need to understand the paradigmatics of informants reponding to one's questions.  One does not know *why* they choose to *instance* what they do in their replies, unless their ongoing preoccupations have been made manifest.  There is always a person behind any cultural mask, a person who is not unprepared for the intruder and who has his own repertoire of past events to recall so that he might influence future strategems (Romanucci-Ross 1983).

*February 27.*  This is the day of the election for the person to represent Manus District in Port Moresby.  There are two house guests here, young Australians, Graham and Terry from Ambunti, to supervise the election.  The voting is to begin at 8:00 a.m. and all from the three villages are now here; the usual joking is absent.  The voting begins late at 8:45.  Each person gives Graham his name, and the name of his village, then goes to Terry to give his number one choice.  Pictures of the four candidates are on the back wall of the booth.  I want very much to keep out of the election, but Lohai wants to know from me who is good.  He is going to vote for Malai because he has heard from "plenty *Mastah*" (P.E. many white men) that Malai is number one.  (They *say* they have not heard of the South Coast cargo cult of which the candidate Paliau was the leader.)

*March 3.*  It is well over a week that both men and women here have been working their entire days building a new school house.  The building is, like the previous one, made of sago palm leaves called '*a*.'  The new school to follow this interim one will have a base of blocks of ground coral.  The men have now been putting up the frames and going into the bush for leaves, which the women are sewing up for walls.  The leaf is folded over a stick either of bamboo or *marita* (of the family *pandaceae*).  This is then sewed together with a vine that grows around trees. Each woman from each of the three villages is expected to make ten of these leaves-on-stick sidings.  Although the two Sori villages and the Lebei consider themselves culturally distinct, this cooperation is politically imposed on them from the Administration.  There is only one *Kaunsil* for all of them and that is Lohai of Sori.  The Lebei consider themselves subsumed and long for their own Councillor.

All the men are absent from the village today, but all the women are sitting about working on their quota of sidings. Teresia has some small children around her and her son Cristop Ahen, who is looking at a book. "Book" is the only word I have heard Ahen utter, and his parents worked very hard to teach him that. Teresia asked me in modest seriousness whether she might ask me a question about my country based on what she had seen in the book: *Do we really dress up cats and dogs in clothing in the United States?* I suppressed laughter, since she would have been offended, and after my explanation that we do it only in books to trap children into learning to read, I feel guilty for explaining it with such authority. Teresia does accept as our fantasy the pictures of mice rocking on chairs and knitting, but she reserves the right to think that we really might dress up our pets. All the more a reflection of American affluence, since the natives here have no "real" clothes!

Father Fischer arrives, new to Manus, but not to Melanesia, having spent several years on the Island of Tanga. He is a big, pleasant American of German-Hungarian descent, from Winfield Illinois. He wants to talk of the election, avers that "300 of Father Freeh's people in Papitalai voted for Paliau." He now feels that Paliau will win and hopes for a rapprochement between Paliau and the Catholic Church. He speaks of "peaceful coexistence." Father Fischer tells me that he feels the church makes a mistake in intervening too much in native affairs and customs, citing an instance in which the pig "feast" after a funeral was discontinued by a priest. "The pig *kaikai* was their form of wealth distribution," says Father Fischer.

The group of women are listening intently to a story. I ask Salai to help me get it all down in my notes, since I understand much of Sa'apoy but not all of it. Salai fills in my lacunae with Pidgin, and here is the story that entranced the women working on the school sidings:

"A woman has cooked and eaten one leg of her baby with taro. Her husband comes home from fishing and sees the rest of the baby, cooked and uneaten in a saucepan with taro. She had hidden it on a rack above the bed. When asked about the baby, she says, "My mother has the child."

"How she lies," he thinks, "Just how far will she go?"

He tells her to go get the child. She returns, saying that her mother wants to keep the child for awhile. "Oh," he thinks, "There is no end to her lies." He tells her to cook the fish he has caught, and to fry some sago. She says she has already eaten, but he makes her eat. "Enough," she says, "No, it is not enough," he replies and makes her eat a plate of soup. She is stuffed, but he insists that she eat more fish and more sago. She eats and eats, thus being commanded by him, until her belly bursts. Then he takes the baby and buries it in the cemetery."

This is considered a fascinating story, and of the type the villagers tell each other. Lukas tells me that this story is a very good one and has been cherished from the times of the the important men of yore.

I borrow Ebei's canoe to go to Lebei to make tapes of the songs they sing. There are five participant singers using very close harmony. Although the taping is long, here are some of the characteristic songs:

*Sawa kemeteh oh* (let me have a bit of water). This song was composed by the Lebei celebrating the advent of the killing of a Bipi man. The Bipi was visiting someone in Sori and went to the Lebei bush to get some leaf for his betel nuts and while he was picking the leaf, he was beheaded by the Lebei, who felt that he was trespassing. It seems that the windpipe was not severed, because as he died he begged for water. His dying *cry* was, "I know you will eat me later, and when you do, eat me gently, but now, before I am your dinner, please give me a drink."

*Maniey niandro, maniey ndrokai.* This is a song of the white shell penis dance, a song exhorting warriors to fight well.

*Kaik.* A man asks a large bird to take him and his wife up high in the air but then to take them down again.

*Liyeu osakiani talu.* Tells of a man and a woman who like each other and are about to do "something no good." She tells him that there are bush devils where they are and he agrees that this is true and bad, but they go ahead and do "something no good" anyway.

Taum wants to reassure me that the Lebei songs are *never* songs about nothing. They are about sorrow, about brothers who have died in a fight, about small children who lose a parent, usually a father. In the past, he said, people would sit around in the evening listening to these songs and just cry and cry and cry.

When the *singsing* is finished, everyone wants to hear the entire tape. One doesn't mind repaying their kindness in this way, but the sandflies have been biting ferociously. I notice that the two girls I

have with me from Sori as well as my two Manus friends are hop-
ping from one leg to another in agony. Only the Lebei are not
responding to the bites. After this tape is finished, some people in
the village express amazement that I and my Sori companions are
going home — we have to go through the bush, "full of *marsalai*
bush devils," and then there is the cemetery. We manage to survive
this trek through the bush and arrive at the canoe. I paddle while
the young girl Samanaggay steers and poles us across the passage.

Sa'abwen has joined us and sits on the bed of the canoe with her
two children. We meet Lohai, who is coming across to get me, concerned that I am still out at night. As we arrive, Baripeo shudders as
she recounts that a *marsalai* took the leg of a pig she had left in the
house of the teacher from Tulu (her "friend"). It seems that
several men had gone to look at it and it was Sapandriu who came
upon two *marsalai* eating it. He saw them engaged in this activity
very clearly in the water under one of the several logs one has to
cross near the mangrove swamp. Later some men found the bones
and brought them back to her.

*March 11.* Over five months on Sori now, and like the others in
the village, I also wait for the boats on the horizon, watch their trajectories with hope and with disillusion. The mail has been sitting
here for three weeks, with no way for it to get out. The *Kaunsil* of
the Bipi is running a high fever, has a swollen, purulent knee, and
comes in for medication. I work on top of the canoe today, waiting
for my informant to come, and there I chat with John Sapalona,
who wants to know all about the American electoral system. He
wants the defeat of Paliau here, and appears to believe the assertions
of the Catholic information pamphlets that Paliau is "of the past"
and that he "talks rubbish" (See Our Lady of the Sacred Heart, Jan.
and Feb. 1963).

In the evening, John Kilepak, our canoe captain, confides to me
that he thinks the Sori and the Lebei do not know how to work with
anthropologists, as the Pere used to do: "We used to sit with Markrit
(Margaret Mead) and *Mastah* Potune (Reo Fortune) or *Mastah* Ted
(Ted Schwartz) and we never got tired. We knew and we still know
our marriage rules, we knew the fashions of our ancestors, and we
knew how to talk about it. These people, some know, and some
don't, but for sure, not a one of them knows how to talk about it."

Later in the evening, Lohai comes in to talk more about how
people in Sori got married, and still do, in the manner that is traditional. He has been coached by our Manus cook, Lokes, who smiles

broadly in the background. Lohai now seems to know what I have been seeking in the structure of the rules, and he wants to assure me that that is *still* how they prefer to get married now. This evening was interesting since I was able to talk to Lohai in a completely different manner. For example, together he and I noted some parallels and some differences with Manus rules of seeking marriage partners for children:

|  | Manus Tru | Sori |
|---|---|---|
| "Side of the Man" | *lom kamal* | *naru mwang* |
| "Side of the Woman" | *lom pein* | *naru bi'ibing* |
| Cross-cousins | *pwalapwal* | *bwaha* |

In Sori, a *bwaha* may ask his *bwaha* for a woman for his brother, or for a man for his sister. In contrast to the Manus Tru, either *bwaha* may ask the other, it does not depend on whether you are descendant from the male or female of the brother-sister pair. The Manus Tru ask only for "a woman to be returned," that is, your "side" has to have given a woman in the past before you can request one. I don't bother to tell Lohai that he has concretized a Lévi-Straussian "point" for me.

Steven and John, sitting by and listening to this, ask me why we don't pay for women in our culture. I try to explain our payment systems such as dowries, alimonies, etc. They find it very interesting, as I explain that such payments are circumstantial and optional. "That is the way it should be," they say, "It is the men who should be bought — or no one!"

***March 12.*** Lukas comes to my house to tell me a story of how the Sori people began. He and Pwepwe have decided that it is time that the Sori not be outdone by the Lapalokoyan story of the Lindrow, nor the origin stories of the Lebei. The accounts are worth recording here, since they give me a very different view of the Sori who, until now, have seemed very pleased to have me know that they find all such tales nonsensical "rubbish." Here is how Lukas explains the origin of the Sori people:

> "A group of women lived on the island of Noru; they had no husbands and they had no lovers. The sea gave them sexual pleasure and it also gave them children. When a male child was born, it was killed. They used to beat their hands in the ocean,

an activity called *tubweng*. As they did this they would sing,
"Number one male and number two male and the spear called
Nyowena, where are they, where are they?'

Actually they existed and they were somewhere off in the
bush on the mainland where they used to hunt and kill things.
They were expert at spearing. One day they got very annoyed at
this *tubweng* with the accompanying song and decided that they
would kill all these women of Noru. They went and they threw
spears at them; the spear points were not of stone, nor obsidian
flake, nor of glass, but only of the skin of the *kasta* nut. All of
the women were killed but one, who was pregnant. She escaped
to Old Sori Island and there she bore her son. Later, she with
her son conceived four sons, the founders of the patrilines that
are now the four largest units of patrilineal division: *Luhai,
Hi'inang, So'opay,* and *Babi.*"

Then he wants me to write down this other very, very old true
account about the Sori:

"There is a man, his wife, and their little son. The woman is
cooking pandanus and sago. As she does so, a drop of blood
drops from her finger into the meal. The little boy runs to tell
his father about the incident, to warn him. The father also
thinks that this woman is up to no good sorcery, with him as
victim. He suggests that they all go out to pick fruit, but after
he posts his wife under a tree, he tells the boy to go off in the
distance. He tells her to stand in a certain way so that she will
be certain to catch fruit. Instead of fruit he throws down a
coiled snake that fastens itself securely about her neck. Then he
makes her walk home carrying the basket on her back anyway,
as well as carrying the boy. She could not rid herself of the
snake and was unable to eat. The snake nibbled on her neck
from time to time. She was wasting away.

"With her problem and her sorrows, she goes to visit her
brothers. First, they help her get rid of the snake by taking her
to the sea and asking her to place her neck near the mouth of a
large clam. The clam eats the snake. Now there is the business of revenge to be attended to. The brothers find another
woman, for their sister is still too sick, to go pick white yams,
some of them edible and some of them not good to eat. The
bad yam is relegated to the dish that will be taken to their
sister's husband. After eating the third yam, the husband
notices that his belly is much enlarged. He is pregnant. He
feels that he is pregnant and is quite concerned that, as a male,
he is not up to giving birth to a child. When it is time to give

birth he goes to the bush, takes a knife and cuts himself open. He gives birth to twin girls. He wipes them clean with seaweed and then he dies. The girls drink sea water; that is all they need for nourishment and growth. One is *Arup* (number one girl) and one is *Asap* (number two girl). They are grown girls now and they are singing. A young man from the mountains hears them, comes down, looks them over, accepts their reassurances that they are not *marsalai*, and marries them.''

Lukas apologizes that he does not know, nor does anyone else, the names of the lines of the descendants of the twins. Those who knew them are long dead. This is a Lindrow-Sori story, for Lukas believes that these two peoples were once "one company."

**March 13.** That was all I could get of Sori origin myths, and Lukas did his reputation not much good in the village by telling me. Still, no one denied the truth of these beginnings, but when I asked why they thought Lukas should be chastised, they said it was not in good taste for him to tell me intimate things such as Sori beginnings. Lukas, they said, had become much too outspoken since his experience with American soldiers in World War II.

Interesting aspects of the Sori origin accounts include the unabashed hostility between male and female. Also the innocent woman is always suspect for treachery, and the tell-tale son who protects the father has come up in other stories. Pregnancy by ingestion of food is not uncommon in mythologies in other parts of the world, but the male who becomes pregnant and concerned about his inability to give birth, and who then cuts open his own abdomen and dies, could only have been plotted by some Sori ladies of yore. The resulting twins give rise to both the Sori and the Lindrow people. The similarity of languages is used to support the truth of this origin account.

These origin stories bring forth a host of comparisons of languages concerning the Sori and other groups nearby, for the Sori are obsessed with thinking about origins of language. In the ethnolinguistics of Lukas, he wants me to note that the Sori say *monong, lo'ona, maney* whereas the Harenggan say *modong, lo'oda, maddey*. Some words are the same, such as *gariay* which means *lie*. Lukas notes that it must be because telling lies is what many do well. The Lindrow, he notes, have a habit of dropping off the "ng" at the end of words. For "good" the Sori say *mwa'asing*, the Lindrow say *mwa'asin*. Therefore the Sori spoke the original language, which the Lindrow ruined. Luf, near the Western Island, has a language similar to Sori, as does Harenggan. Lukas compares them (from what he

has learned from singing in *lotu* perhaps): "Sori is soprano, Harenggan is alto, Luf is base." He refers to the purity of his pristine
tongue.

*March 15.* The rains occasionally do stop. Today it stops late in
the afternoon. The children of the village rush to the beach with
their toy canoes to race them in the wind. They are made of bamboo with pieces of citrus fruit for ballast and newspapers or a bit of
old, old *laplap* for sails. My work is interrupted because a young
man, Ndranah, with whom I had been working in Lebei, comes to
tell me that he cannot come anymore because the Sori are gossiping
that, although it appears he comes to work here, he really comes to
see a woman in Sori. But Ndranah is not alone tonight; he is accompanied by Takaray's parents and Takaray's sister, for they had all
been part of the court session with Lohai. The four of them decide
that they also want me to record what Ndranah has to say.

Like all Lebei males, he tells a story by acting it out: It seems
he was almost asleep when he heard a stone against his house. He
was surprised, and looks very puzzled as he tells it. Is the house
about to fall apart? No. Another stone. And another, and another.
Then he gets an idea: suppose he who is throwing the stones thinks
it is someone else and not he, Ndranah, who is in the house. He
lights his night lamp, makes it flicker and die. Another stone. Hah!
That must mean that the signaller-by-stone is expecting another sig-
nal. Ndranah gives a slight knock on our door to show how he did
it. Aha, the door opens. A man comes in and removes his *laplap*.
"Now," thinks Ndranah, "I know what I must do, I understand,"
he thinks . . . . . " I will get the spear for wild pigs. No. That will
kill him. The spear for fish? No, that too will kill him. The *tamiok*
(P.E. ax). Death. But I don't want to kill him. How can I kill a
man? I cannot. So I put out my hand and say, 'just whom were you
expecting?'"

The young man, Mana, had a ready answer. Takaray's sister
had been wanting to meet him at night, but he had not been
interested. Of course, Mana had been Ndranah's wife's lover in the
past, but he managed to convince Ndranah that this was all about
Takaray's sister. Well, if anyone was really asleep, then Mana did
not want to awaken them. He even found two girls to testify that his
version was true. Now Mana had a problem. He was being brought
to court to declare his intentions to marry Takaray's sister. She was
asked if she wanted to marry him, and she said that she did. The
parents were asked for permission and did not refuse it. Mana said
he would consider marrying her, but sometime in the distant future.
(A Sicilian tale, but not a Sicilian resolution.)

*Mesian, Pwepwe, and Adan.*

# EIGHT

# Last Days on Wild Island

## Winds and Stars of Sori

*March 17.* Samanaggay, a young girl, tells me that her grandfather told her stories about the stars. But an attempt to get him to tell me those stories fails, for "they are not true stories, only stories told to children." I will be able to learn "true" facts about the stars and wind and land, however, and the older people become my willing colleagues.

There are sets of stars that bring auguries of fishing: one such set comes up from the direction we call West, one from the East. Stars that come up on the South side are not good for fishing, "you will catch no fish when you see them." One set comes up near the moon, and at this time, too, "the sea is no good because it is the time of the *dyapay* (Northwest monsoons). Also, "if the face of the moon looks at the island, the island people will catch fish but the people on the mainland will have nothing to do. When the moon faces the mainland, the situations for these people will be reversed."

The following constellations are recognized and referred to with frequency:

| *Pusiha'o* | | |
|---|---|---|
| *Pung* | (seven stars) | (the Pleiades) |
| *Sausau* | (three stars) | |
| *Sotulumo* | (three stars) | |
| *Manuay* | | (includes North Star) |
| *Atohep* | | (Southern Cross) |
| *Oromanang* | | (Morning Star) |
| *Dau Apayap* | | (Evening Star) |

As indicated above, only *Pung* and *Atohep* correspond to constellations that we have chosen to recognize as such. How are the constellations perceived? One group of three stars represents two men going fishing with a basket between them. *Manuay*, consists of three stars around which they "construct" the fish hawk. The "seven stars" are arrows that were aimed at the famous cloud over Sori that had caused the famine. Two groups of three stars are interpreted as the mouth of a shark about to swallow the tail of a sting ray. "When the tail of the sting ray goes into the mouth of the shark, the bad weather will come up soon."

The trajectory of the sun, as it goes from solstice to equinox to solstice to equinox has been and still has the points of reversal of its course marked by large trees. Two of these tree markers are on the East side, and the other is on the West side of the island. What is observed is where, between these points marked by trees, the sun rises and where, in relation to the other trees, it sets. The movements that represent shifts in the setting of the sun are called "from *Hay* to *To'orau*" and "from *Hay* to *Um*" (see diagram below).

If the sun "goes to Um" then the Northwest monsoons will be on their way to the island. If the sun takes the *To'orau* route, the weather will be good.

The word for wind is *langa*, and the following are recognized as major winds: *Dyapay, Um, Hay*, and *To'orawu*. But these are further classified. I include what I was able to elicit as directions, range, and boundary by using a compass while working with my informants.

*Dyapay* ("comes from Bipi"): West-North-West    280°

| | | |
|---|---|---|
| *baray dyapay* | — | a little Northwest wind |
| *dyapay tinang* | — | a formidable Northwest wind |
| *dyapay awung* | — | comes from Sori Island (WNW 290°) |

*dyapay*
   *mbuhung*    —    comes from the Island of Noru
                          (West 270°)
*dyapay lang*    —    seems to come from the mainland at Lebei.

*Um*: SSE 135° (2nd reading 155° to 130° to 115° to 100° ESE)

*um lumbuhu'oh*   —   comes from *Sapoloay* (Southeast 135°)
*um lobohay*    —    comes from Nrehet
*um lobodyapay*   —   comes from inside Lebei
*uboho*    —    comes up in the night, very gently
*barang ubuhay*   —   a gentle south wind
*ubuhay*    —    a big forceful wind

*Siyeh*: a wind that comes up from the bush (from mainland)
      East 90°

*Hay*: ENE 70°

*bara ubwehay*   —   gently from the East 60°
*Ubwehay*    —    a big wind that comes from "inside
                          Ponam"
*Talawohay*    —    a strong wind that breaks trees

*To'orawu*: "it comes up strong and that's it" (NNE 350°)

*Awu*: a South wind that comes up To'orawu (North 360°)

*Lang*: a Southwest wind (SW 220°)

*Boundaries*

*Lang*    —    170° SSE to 225° WSW
*Dyapay*    —    245° WSW to 300° WNW "true direction"
                          270°
*To'orawu*    —    320° NNW to 30° NNE "true direction"
                          350°
*Um*    —    100° ESE to 155°

*Da'ahong* is East but not mentioned as a wind direction

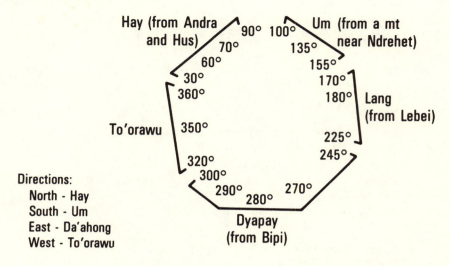

Note that both direction and force determine how a wind
shall be called; also, it usually comes from a place.

*Wind Directions on Sori Island*

# New Ways for Old?

The Lindrow people are considered poor and backward by the Sori,
who in turn are so considered by the Manus Tru. And it is around
this theme that many wish to talk to me today about woman-stealing
(elopement?) among the Lindrow and sometimes among the Sori.
Ordinarily, affinal exchanges are so heavy, that a young man must
work most of his life to repay the family for the girl he marries.
Woman-stealing is simply a good way to avoid the exchanges route, I
am explicitly told. The feelings are generally that it is wrong and
"cheap," but there is some sympathy with the young man who
wants to begin accumulating capital of dogs' teeth or shell money or
now, more importantly, strings of shillings for himself. Many also
want to speak of Lomot, who, finally "having won So'ong as husband through pregnancy," is miserable in Jowan; the tale in the
North Coast villages is that she threatened to jump into the ocean

and swim back to her native Pere village while So'ong restrained her begging her to consider her condition. Bets here are that she will have the baby, leave the heir with So'ong's family and go back to her beloved South Coast.

The rain is endless. Some women come to ask me to play the tapes of the Usiai slit gong drums and we do, and we dance in my large house to break the monotony of the rain.

*March 18.* Tonight the votes are being counted. Radio commentators make these points: many European candidates are leading over New Guineans or Papuans. Many places have refused to participate in the voting, for fear of giving power to those in charge of voting by consenting to vote. The missions have not formally intervened but have made their preferences for candidates very clear in sermons, etc. They have openly excoriated Paliau and have asked the North Coast, at least, to vote against him. To people here, to be cut off from the mission means to be cut off from with the rest of the world and specifically from "civilization," which to them means affluence and complexity in all things. The commentator from radio Port Moresby is impressed by the fact that almost everyone throughout the territory welcomed the opportunity to listen to a candidate, even if he were not their choice. Some groups in New Guinea wanted to vote for the President of the United States, Lyndon Johnson.

There is only one radio here in the village; it belongs to Tolau. Many listen to the radio late into the night even though none understand English, and the Pidgin commentaries are few and far between. There is no discussion about the election, nor is it possible to elicit one. Not even from Pwepwe, who, after her brother Lohai and his wife Salai, is undoubtedly the most opinionated person in the village. (They didn't like the outcome, and had predicted the election "wouldn't work.")

*March 19.* The election returns for Manus: the winner is Paliau. Paliau 2,788 votes, Malai over 1,000 (but not one of us heard the exact figure), Peter 100, Mohe 473, Cholai 187, Maiha 105.

# Notes on Cognition and Affect.

This morning I want to work translating tapes taken in *talk place* Sa'apoy, in particular on the *cries* that Salai sang for me. I play the tapes and get Pwepwe to help me when I have difficulty hearing the text clearly, so that she can repeat a phrase more slowly. She becomes saddened and her eyes fill with tears. Lokes comes to lean against the window and tells me that these song poems of Salai's fill him with sorrow. This is interesting because he does not understand the Sori language. Pwepwe goes to call Salai to help me, and as Salai approaches, her eyes too, fill with tears. She says, "I weep so much now I can hardly see the sago there. How can I tell you about them, they tear my heart, my voice will not be able to reach you."

I beg Salai to relax and hand her a cigarette, and beg her to try. First we work on the one about her totemic origins, then on the death of her mother's brother, and then on the funerary rites.
**March 20.** Salai comes back today to help me with the phrases that are difficult to hear on other tapes. But she doesn't like to work on the information I obtained on the constellations. She (as well as others present, who all happen to be related to her) wants me to know that these stories about the stars *are not true*. They are all lies. Salai wants to give me an example: "Now you take those three stars that some told you are about a couple of men fishing. Now I suppose that one time there were a couple of men here fishing a long time ago, and they looked up at the three stars and said to each other, 'Oh, look, these are three fishermen who have a basket of fish between the canoes.' Just because three crazy, stupid fishermen cannot see anything more than that in the whole world, well, this is not what I call a story." Salai practically spit out her contempt for such simple-minded analogies based on silly reflections of self that men were prone to contrive. A "story" is a very serious matter here.

In the evening I work with Makah, from Lebei. Although most here are very modest about what they "know," Makah at first says, "Yes, I will talk to you, and I know many things, anything you want to know." He is the *tamberan* man for the three villages here. So he divines, he diagnoses and he cures. For this professional status he paid three pounds; he bought it from someone who had bought it from an old man who had received the knowledge from a bush devil. Makah specializes in curing those illnesses called *sick belong ground* or, as it is understood here, sorcery. His fee is about 12 to 15 shillings for a cure. He claims that he cured the son of John Sapalona after his parents had taken him to Lorengau to no avail. And his work went well beyond the purification ritual that the Sori perform on anyone who has left the island for any reason (breaking a coconut with a weapon over a pandanus mat over someone's head and saying words with a victory leaf to ward off all illness and evil picked up away from home). But he will not tell me more.

*March 24.* Lohai has borrowed our shotgun and is delighting the village first with shooting a tiny crocodile, then a hawk. One of the exciting children's games in this village is the Sunday afternoon concerted efforts to kill a hawk with sticks and stones, since hawks attack chickens. Today the children walk about triumphantly with Lohai's bounty, then hang the dead fowl by his feet on a tree and pelt it with stones in tune with much jubilation. Yesterday Lohai and Sapalona shot two wild ducks with our shotgun and gave one to us and one to Steven. I could not understand why they did not keep one for themselves, since it is much prized as gourmet food, and rare at that. Then I learned that it is the totem of Sapalona's wife, and if she prepared it or was near its preparation she would suffer a paralysis of limb or lose her power of speech. Steven enjoyed his duck and laughed as he said, "Oh, Misis, these people, for them the wild duck is the *tamberan* man. They won't eat it. That is good luck for you and me. It is very good. Still, I am honest and I do tell them, 'God intended you to eat wild duck."

*March 27.* Sangong tapes the story of the sea turtles for me. For Ebei had given the story, but he had simply left out, in Sangong's view, something of essential interest. The women, in grief over the fact that some turtles had gotten out of the fence, into the sea, and had gone out to sea, had removed their grass skirts in grief, and performed a *cry*. It was the waving of their grass skirts and the singing that lured the turtles back to their pens. Ebei had also skipped the part about the great happiness of the men in learning of the efficacy of the fashions of their women. Even in lore, the Sori are in awe of their women, and in this respect they differ markedly from the Manus Tru.

The women gaze with delight at some photographs I took of them, and state in amazement (again!) that they came out as well as if a man had taken them. Sa'abwen persists in repeating that Sa'apoy (Sori Island) is truly beautiful as she looks at the photographs. People here never concentrate on the central figure or figures in a photograph, but rather they are forever concerned with identifying the tiny figures in the background or those standing far out in the ocean. They all hope that I did not show these pictures to Father Kopunek, who does not like their habit of wearing crucifixes sitting on top of a mass of hair that has abundant natural tease and feathering.

Usually very little or nothing is described about the emotional tone of the ambience of one's field research site; what happens to me here daily in this vein is puzzling to me. Today Mesian laughs merrily at a photograph on the cover of a music book — simply a slender man leaning over to play a guitar. She shows the picture to Pwepwe who begins to laugh heartily. Enter Samanaggay who is shown the picture and laughs hysterically. The baby Adan bursts into tears in fear of all this demonstration. Now, truly, nothing is more humorous here than a terrified child. Pwepwe for example, has taught Adan fear of a clump of seaweed which she calls *No-Nom*, which is the equivalent of "fearsome object." She can keep him within a cleared-off area on the beach by making a "fence" around him of this kind of seaweed and, as the baby approaches it, shouting "No-Nom." He backs away in terror from the strange greenish-brown jellied foliage. Having recalled this, I note incredulously that Samanaggay laughs until she weeps. Everyone who enters the house that day is shown that picture and laughs, bringing Mesian and Pwepwe into their previous laughing spells. I finally ask Samanaggay why everyone laughed and she says, "Well, don't you see, he looks like he is about to die."

*March 30. Easter Sunday.* A curious Easter parade for Mass. Everyone is dressed up either in their native best, or for those who can afford it, in their Western best. No in-between styles. Many wear grass skirts, dogs' teeth and flowers in their hair, and ankle and arm bracelets. It is the men who wear leather shoes, trousers, striped ties, etc. I want to discuss the sermon which was in *talk place*, but everyone says it was too long and boring. The catechist always talks too much, in their opinion.

*March 31.* I take motion pictures of the women actually making "shell money." A'amau comes to sell me a "shell money" belt, for soon it will be tax time and he needs the money. He claims the rights to this were his family's, but that a *Hi'inang* person had cracked his father's skull open by dropping a rock from a tree and that the *Hi'inang* folk have only their bragging big mouths, but no land and no prestige. They were never, he asserts again, the Big *Lapan*. They now pretend to have been in the old days, whereas his family was number one. (There is general village agreement on this.) Having no land, he continues, the best that wretched *Hi'inang* family could do was take to the sea and establish rights to the sea turtles. The cloud of the cloud story, he adds, hovered *only* over the place of the *Hi-inang* on the island.

Tonight Lohai and Salai come in to sing again for the tape recorder. Salai does not call Pidgin English *talk boy* (P.E. talk of the native) as everyone does. She calls it *"talk mastah"* (P.E., the talk of the white man). She then tells me that it is a foolish tongue, invented because white people seem to be incapable of learning native languages and so everyone had to help white men communicate!

"White people, most all of them, can use only this pitiful language and so they can only ask us silly questions like, 'is it raining?' or 'is the canoe coming.' We reply and then white people think that we think like *that*."

Lohai agrees that Ted (who just returned) and I may do some collecting of measurements for somatotyping in the village, so tomorrow we will do some photographing and measuring of skin folds. A'amau stops in before we go to sleep to tell us of the "court" that had been convened concerning ownership of coconuts and says that the mission takes coconuts without paying for them, saying that it goes for the school, "We have to give most of our copra to the mission, the mission really knows how to eat the native."

It seems that the catechist has begun to urge the men to resist the photographing of their nude bodies, even for "Science." Mesian and Lokes are disgusted saying that the Manus Tru have always cooperated with "Science" through Margaret Mead and Ted Schwartz before, but these people here are "*kanaka tru*, and *very* ignorant." What we learn later, however, is that the women did not mind at all being photographed in the nude for "Science," and Salai used this occasion to heap invective and curses upon Pahung, the catechist. Her language, I was told, was so bad, that the women did not want to repeat it to me. Salai excoriated groups of men publicly, wished they would get deathly sick and then have no medicines to cure them, medicines that the white men *might* discover if these *kanaka* pusillanimous males would cooperate. Some of the men were so shocked that they were demanding a "court" for Salai, who will, I am sure, more than hold her own in it.

We scrap this project and decide to leave, as planned, for the next adventure on the tip of Manus Island between the North and South Coast known as Mokerang.

*A Matankor Bride, Mokerang Village.*

## NINE

# Interlude on a Matankor Variation

*April 6, Monday.* All come to bid us farewell; Salai is sad and promises to come visit me in Mokerang. She tells me to use her name there if it will help in my work because the *Luluai* (P.E. chief) of Mokerang, whom she calls Potihin, has an ancestor who is a classificatory sibling of the same sex as Tata, her mother. Tata calls Potihin *nara* (son) if one reckons kinship by the Sori path, but she would call him *nagiriye* (child of the woman on the father's side) if she called him by the Mokerang path.

We sail to Mokerang in the *Peu* (shark), a ship owned by the South Coast Council. Behind is the stifling, debilitating heat of the island, and I rejoice in an ever-freshening breeze, the sparkling foam of the deep blue in our wake, the silver tuna flashing in the sunlight.

This is the *duupwiy* (good weather). Waters are calm, the breeze balmy. Lokes catches three tuna one after the other, and the Captain smiles at *me* (?). *My* presence, I am told, has caused a *mana* or a "lucky line."

We arrive in Mokerang after five hours. I had asked the Captain how long the trip would take and he had answered, "one and one half hours;" but then *if* you ask a question in the Admiralties, you will get a "precise" though at times inaccurate, reply. No one ever says, "I don't know," particularly concerning things that have no meaning to them. They do not reckon time in hours, but will not disappoint you by failing to give you an "hourly" reply, especially one that they believe will please you.

143

Potihin, chief, as he would have been under the old system of devolution of authority, and *luluai* as he is under the Australians, wants to let me know immediately, that here, although *"Matankor all the same"* i.e. Matankor, same as the Sori, every family has a garden.

Because of its location on Seeadler Harbor, the village of Mokerang, although "Matankor all the same," has had contact with "Europeans" as administrators, as employers of men who could leave the village, as visiting nurses, and, of course, as members of the armed forces. From the time of the Germans, this contact has been constant if not intensive. Yet in the months I have been here I have noted with some amazement that what are considered personal or village problems are always solved using protocols that reaffirm the ideologies and values of the traditional culture of the ancestors.[1]

For our purposes here, forms of social structure and exchange are sufficiently undifferentiated from the Sori that we can forego documentation of difference. In other contexts these differences are not without interest and so will be described elsewhere. A major difference between the two villages could be described by the term "ethos," the notion of emotional tone. Sori was silent and formal; Mokerang is a shouting, litigious and boisterous village where frequent quarrels are punctuated by the barking of dogs. (The Mokerang find this a fitting accompaniment and howl with laughter as it occurs.)

I will add only one bit of information to a general Matankor ethno-ethnography here, one that it was not possible to elicit on Sori island. Because the Catholic church, from a distance, counted heavily on the North Coast villages to ignore the call by Paliau for a council of native leadership and a native reform church, Sori villagers would not admit to me that they had known about the "cargo cult" of the South Coast. (Later, in Pere village, I am to learn that they did indeed know of this.)

In this village of Mokerang, after months of working with informants, Potihin tells me one day that he knows something very interesting about dreaming but wants me to assure him that I will not get my papers mixed up and get this dream to "bugger up" his land-tenure histories and genealogies. After cigarettes, chocolate mints and my assurances, I am rewarded with the story that to me has features of striking resemblance to the cargo theme of the myth of Lapalokoyan alluded to earlier when I was among the Lindrow of the North Coast.

# Dreams and "the Cargo"

"This is a true story. This man was not born. Oh, he began in his mother's belly alright, but then he was a man without being born. His father was Popu. You could not see him, no one could. Some people could hear him. Some people with special gifts, that is, such as my father, who could talk with him and who, in fact, was once so taken into this man's confidence that he held his hand. The man's name was Kiele."

"I thought you didn't give names to those who died before they were born alive."

"But I already *told* you! No, Kiele never died, he was born, but you couldn't see him. Well, this Kiele, he went to that place where all the dead are, who can know where that place is? But there is a place where all the dead are, for Kiele used to go there and bring back all things to eat and big bowls and all other things you might need. The dead worked these things, you see, and sent them back to the living through Kiele. It was unbelievable. There you sat, wondering what to eat, or even what to eat it out of, and Kiele would see that you got it. Kiele knew how to make the fish go into the nets. Kiele was around for a long time, even after my father died, but people able to communicate with him were not just being born anymore."

It was interesting to me that this tale of Kiele was evoked by a discussion on dreaming, and even more interesting that it is a story about cargo-cult idealogy. Such cults have been found and are still found in many parts of New Guinea. The central focus on the varied versions is that of the dead, who, pleased with the fact that the living are following their wishes (either to preserve the old culture or to take on the new one of the white man, depending on the particular place and cult) send them *cargo* i.e., the material things they very much need and want. One of these that occurred in the 1950's on the South Coast of Manus was known as the Paliau Movement. (See Schwartz 1962 for the most complete description and analysis. See Mead 1975 for a popularized version. Lanternari (1963), Guiart (1956), and Worsley (1957) have also written on the more general aspects of cargo cults in Melanesia and elsewhere.) Cargo cults celebrated either native achievement of white status through the acquisition of material goods received from the dead, or sometimes the eviction of the white man and a return to traditional native culture. Such celebrations cause great concern among the administrators.

Trance and possession are an important part of ritual communication with the dead. The returning dead would bring metal tools, textiles, clothing, canned meat, bags of rice, guns, tractors, etc. They would arrive by ship. (For had this not been seen, pale people unloading these things from a ship from who knows where? Besides, for the Manus, the dead eventually disappear off into the ocean.)

In Manus, the cargo cult was begun by Paliau. He had been a sergeant during the war in New Britain, and he had been given authority over the leaders there, and had probably heard of the cult started by Mambu before 1937 (Salisbury 1958). His cult version was that all native property had to be destroyed and the fashion of the native had to be gotten rid of, then the dead would bring all things. He became more pragmatic with the passage of time and then had as his goals the unification of Manus and working with the Australian Administration on objectives of education and health for the Manus People.

# Interface Informant on Human Sexuality

On many occasions I am considered "the authority" on what each culture here wants to know about the other's most intimate customs. Contact between natives and "Europeans" here has been constant in some places, but it has been formal for the most part, and from some of the queries I receive, one might ask whether "European" or native has ever vaguely considered giving the other the full status of being "human." I submit the following example:

*May 23 - June 4.* At the Navy Hospital at Lombrum, since baby Adan has amoebic dysentery, he is given Entero-Vioform, with no one knowing what was learned later (that it does, in some instances, cause severe neurological disorders, including blindness). Pwepwe and Mesian are devoted, helpful and loving, working with the nurse to take care of him. I catch up on grammatical points of Sori language with Pwepwe and have Ward Room Conversations.

The Naval Officers want to know mostly about homosexuality in Manus men. Does it exist? They are struck with all the holding of hands and other displays of affection among some young men. I can only say that I am not aware of homosexual behavior, and if it exists at all it is not noted, not talked about. I explain too that having lived in cultures where expressed tenderness of this sort is permitted, I do not think of it as homosexual. I have indeed, in both Sori and Mokerang, looked for the proper time and context to broach the subject. Any suggestion that a male could play a female role, either biologically or culturally, always met with stunned incredulity. Is it possible? But who ever heard of such a thing? Those who do such things must be crazy. Several men of Mokerang had told me that it was hard for them to believe their eyes when they saw American soldiers indulging in certain acts. Perhaps I could explain to them, are white people different inside? Punou said, "Yes, you white men have many important discoveries, some good, some bad. Ships, medicine, traveling fast and far, all that is good. But you people have also found some things that are truly, truly no good."

Some Mokerang want to know if these men have breasts or other appurtenances that women have and men do not. My denial causes them to resume their stunned and smiling expressions. Pwepwe joins the group and reiterates her usual line, that white people are too numerous and that will cause any group of people to generate a lot of crazies.

I stay with Naval Commander Anderson and his wife Marge. She washes her own underthings, and when asked, explains to me that Navy wives are instructed in a circular to do their own washing of unmentionables. Why? Because native males might get sexually excited as they wash the unmentionables of white women, with unfortunate consequences for everyone. But it is not only the Australians who have strange reveries about Caucasian-Melanesian sexual relationships. Natives always speak of native-white sexual affairs with glee, relish, and sometimes a bit of malice.[2] Contraceptives are not available here because they cannot go through the post. It is feared that natives and whites would then have no impediment to sexual intercourse. Still, the "Europeans" are dedicated to believing that "integration" is what they want.

## NOTES

1. For a village "court" case involving land tenure, see Romanucci-Ross 1966. For a definition of madness and a discussion on the "ejection" of the mad from the village social structure, see Romanucci-Ross 1983c. For illness and curing, see Romanucci-Ross 1969, 1978. For emergent patterns of drunken comportment and the "assimilation" of drinking into the cultural exchange system see Schwartz and Romanucci-Ross 1974.

*Margaret Mead at work in Pere Village.*

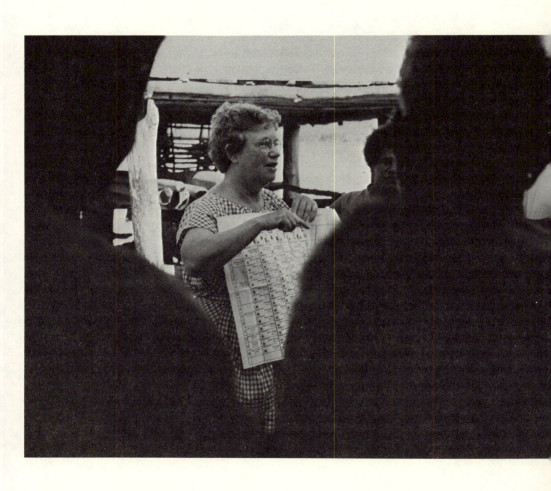

*Margaret Mead in Pere Village explaining the American Ballot.*

TEN

# Of Pere Village and Margaret Mead

*August 7.* Rabaul, New Britain. At the Cosmo Hotel I meet Ann Chowning and Jane Goodale on their way to the United States after field work in New Britain. We spend several days talking about problems of language and of access in the field. I must look dreadful, for Jane, generous and caring, gives me a dress of hers and a large bottle of multi-vitamins. I also meet Dr. Vincent Zigas who first came upon *kuru*, the neurological disease among the Fore speakers that intrigued virologists and provided a context for Nobel-Prize-seeking research.

*August 9.* Leave Rabaul for Manus. Results of medical checkup: a gratuitous chest x-ray showed a primary lesion — tuberculosis. The little island of Sori was full of it, but neither they nor I knew it at the time. There I had felt exhausted most of the time; overworking and breastfeeding, I was a perfect target for Koch's bacillus. My main informants had coughed continuously. I hadn't included TB among the calculated risks of fieldwork; did I feel magically protected by the purchase of Christmas seals every Christmas? Apparently I am not contagious at this point, as an inquisitorial catheter from mouth to stomach confirms.

*August 10.* Leave for Pere village on the South Coast. I can continue working, since I have been put on drug combinations to contain TB. Sailing three hours from Lombrum we arrive at Pere village, where work is progressing on our house. I am wondering what my work here will be. I suspect that I will be doing mainly my own analyses on Sori and Mokerang material, because Margaret Mead has laid a sort of "claim" to Pere village since she first stepped foot here with Reo Fortune in the late twenties, and since *Growing Up In New Guinea*. (She will be staying in our house in Pere.) And Ted Schwartz studied the Paliau cult and movement here in 1953—54. Anthropologists are very territorial; Margaret had always spoken of "her" Manus, sometimes meaning Pere people, sometimes meaning all the Admiralty Islanders, although she described the others using the Manus Tru descriptive categories for the other groups.

*August 14.* There are several aspects of Pere village which are very striking to me in comparison to "my" (!) two Matankor villages (Margaret's "other" Manus). First, there are the frequent meetings. People here sit around a "place clear," a rectangular space with logs that are meant to define the boundary of the "place clear." In Mokerang there was a formless and indifferent attitude toward attendance, and at the meeting itself everyone strove to be as peripheral as possible. In Sori people focused on the speaker but tended to sit apart in small clusters. Pere gets the prize for the longest meetings and the belaboring of "points," a word that Paliau introduced into the Manus Tru language. Sori runs a close second. Mokerang can be appreciated for the brevity of its meetings. The Manus ask us whether we want them to speak in their language or in Pidgin, and we prefer the former. The other two villages never manifested awareness or consideration of an audience in this regard.

Secondly, the play of the children here is spontaneous and constant. They play fearlessly in the water and the village rings with their laughter. One has the feeling that they are encouraged to enjoy their childhood. Children in the other two Matankor villages of Sori and Mokerang are not very much inclined toward play and appear constrained to the observer. If small children play in the water, parents and others scream with alarm and someone is sent to drag them out of the water.

Then, too, Pere is in disarray and sadly neglected with its bogs and fens. Paths are not swept. One is enveloped with flies, "marshiness," malodors and decaying houses fetid in the tropical sun, as fungus blossoms fill the air. Minds here are on the *new* village that is to be built at nearby Tchalolo. Inspection reveals that only two or three people have driven the posts into the ground for their dwellings, although "places" have been marked off for individual constructions. People here are busy fishing, gathering fruits of the sea and of the mangrove swamps. This is quite a contrast to the lethargy about food gathering encountered in Sori and Mokerang.

One very good thing about being here is that Mesian comes to work again. She seems to have survived the end of her sad love affair with "New Guinea Joe" and is resigned to the failure of her escapade and the triumph of her parents. I take her with me to nearby Tchalolo to visit an Australian schoolteacher, Gus Buckham, so that I may observe the teaching-learning situation.

I talk with the Doctor Boy in Pere. Nine people are being treated for TB in Pere at this time. They are being given streptomycin, P.A.S., and Isoniazid. There are about 19 more who will probably be added to this list since recent chest x-rays show that they have active TB.

*August 15.* It is only after many, many months of close association and after sharing a few hair-raising experiences that Pwepwe, who has accompanied me, has begun to speak of her feelings to me. I had been named Saluhai, or woman of the Luhai clan, and Pwepwe was told by her family that she was to listen to me, for my words would have the same weight as the words of Salai, Lohai's wife. Nevertheless, Pwepwe remains a closed, reserved, rather "cold" girl of about 27. It is unusual for a girl this age to be unmarried in Manus, but not as unusual in Sori as in other places. She longs to be warm and friendly, and I watch her try, but she cannot quite succeed. She is good at suppressing her fears, such as when the plane took off for Rabaul, or when we sat down in a restaurant to eat.

She tells me of a recent dream in which she found herself on the island of Baripeo, and under a huge stone on this tiny coral island near Sa'apoy (Sori). From this huge rock hung a chain, just like the chain in the bathroom at Bill Pokumbu's house (he is the "houseboy" for Commander Anderson). In her dream she began to pull this chain but felt forces pulling her back. Spirits seemed to be restraining her and she could not move her arms or legs. Terribly upset, she began to perspire and became short of breath. In her dream she told of this occurrence to her brother, a brother she saw in Rabaul. He told her that the very same thing happens to him and that she must not worry about it. This dream worried her a great deal and in the morning she told Lokes about it. She accepted Lokes' explanation fully, and this only added to her fears. Lokes had said, "Do you think that this place where we are now in Pere is a place true? It is not, indeed. This is the old burial grounds and there are many dead here. It is they who annoy you in your sleep."

Now the occasion for her telling me about this dream was as follows: she and I had been walking baby Adan to sleep. As we approached the burial grounds for the village, he suddenly came out of his slumber, cocked his head and pointed to our house as he whined, signaling to us that he wanted to go back. Pwepwe quickly explained that the dead were annoying him and that we had best get back quickly.

I try to give Pwepwe a more analytical explanation of her dream. I remind her that we had passed under a huge rock on our way to Tchalolo and she had even noted its resemblance to a huge rock at Baripeo. That when we stayed at Anderson's she had showered at Pokumbu's house. That she saw her older brother at Rabaul for the first time in four years (he works as a carpenter at Vunapope). But she counters that she does not *understand* Pere village. There is something really wrong with it. *Of course*, the dead would torment her with things she has recently *seen*, why not? And with what else?

"Well, I guess you're right about that," I said hopelessly, "You are right."

*August 16.* Much more is made of *lotu* here than in other Admiralty Islands villages in which I have lived. The Pere people are melodious with their spoken prayers. The front of the church features two carved posts that are about forty years old. This evening there is a long meeting about church affairs. Unfortunately, it is all *talk place* and I don't know any Manus Tru yet, but Lokes (our cook) gives me what he considers the important "points" in Pidgin.

I spend the afternoon taking notes on children and their play. A young boy called Posin catches a seagull with a small fish and a string for bait. Another young boy has fashioned a toy of a large beetle stuck on the end of a slender stick. The beetle makes a whirring sound (in agony?) as the child shakes the stick. And I look sadly upon our cat Pihlawa, permanently crippled because an anonymous artist-with-events tied its leg with a rope so that it would not run away.

*Bombom* fishing begins with ten men going out in five or six canoes. With branches of coconut leaves they make a huge circle. The ends are either attached to several of the canoes or held by men. Then the men come together, making the circle continuously smaller. The fish, not daring to venture beyond the circumference of the coconut leaf circle (once they are encircled by it) are finally driven into the large fish nets opposite each other at two points of the circle. They are then gathered out of the nets and put into canoes. John Kilepak wants to help me record this for my countrymen back home and wants me to see the operation up close from within a canoe. Some of the men are busily spearing fish between the four *bombom* operations. The Manus Tru make it appear so easy to do. Six, eight, then ten fish suddenly appear on a spear. The catch: 240 brightly colored fish. Time: 75 minutes. Equipment: spears, canoes, coconut fronds and ten Manus Tru men from Pere village.

Pwepwe tells me excitedly that this is what they have been try-ing to describe to me on Sori in the history of the Luf-Harenggan encounter, but they didn't know how to say it. She is glad that I saw it, and participated, and that there are now films to "show people in America how it is done."

*August 19.* Karol Matawai wants to tell me about what is here called the *kaniya kasonai,* or "the food regarding a marriage." First I am taken to what looks like a wedding feast. For awhile, during the Paliau movement, they had stopped having these exchanges, as they tried to do away with much that had been traditional. It was part of the cult effort to bring in the "*cargo,*" all the good things of the Europeans which their dead ancestors would give them if they cut off their past. Now the old traditions (certainly the old exchanges between the side of the groom and the side of the bride) are creeping back into the culture in Pere, sometimes in covert form. Paliau had pronounced such exchanges of durables (dogs' teeth and shell money) for consumables (food, etc.) as wasteful and nonpro-ductive. Nevertheless, the "recursiveness" of tradition is relentless here.

As Kilepak explains to me, the Manus Tru seem to have been relegated to a role of exporting trained young people to go and be productive for other places. They go as teachers, as Doctor Boys, as students and workers to places more backward than their own! Just what is a feasible economic venture for the Manus Trus besides copra? And the world market prices are depressed. So, with nothing on the horizon for the investor, they see going back to the old exchanges as an investment across affinal lines for some sort of security. I agree with Kilepak that Margaret's emphases were quite misplaced when she wrote of their joining the twentieth century (Mead 1956).

Ancient Pokenau, now among the venerated old in Pere, was an informant for Reo Fortune and Margaret Mead in 1928. He looks glumly at me through the open door, not at all pleased that I am working with Kilepak. Like Potihin, he wants to be treated as the fountainhead of all knowledge. However, he is not offensive about it, as was Potihin, and joins Kilepak and me one afternoon. He whispers into Kilepak's ear, as I ask for a sentence matrix or a phrase. I think he does accept my explanation that because he is old with loss of teeth and other respiratory ailments, he provides difficulties for one who does not know the language. That is, he understands that his defects are only articulatory, not intellectual.

The next morning, having broken the ice, he comes to my door and says, holding up his spear, "I went fishing last night, but no success yet. It is not time."

"Oh, time for what kind of fish?"

But he is coy, "You don't know, do you? Mastah (Reo) Fortune, he knew. But you, you don't know. Mastah Fortune even went with me."

This is my punishment for not asking Pokenau about things in general. But now it is meted out to John Kilepak also. Once Kilepak used to go fishing with him all the time, and he was good, but now he is a "man of the beach," that is all. One just cannot rely on Kilepak as an informant for fishing, no sir. I want to assure him that my respect for his knowledge is boundless, but he does not give me that chance:

"Look, Misis, the way to do your work is this: first you come up to me and you point to your eye and you say, 'uh-uh,' and then you point to my eye and I say '*mara*,' and I tell you whether it is right the way you say it. If it is not right I make you say it again and again. Then you point to your mouth and now I understand so you don't have to say 'uh-uh,'" I just say '*pwan*.' And then you point to your ear and I say '*nrelingeh*' and it is the same, you say the word and I make you say it right." Pokenau did this for every part of the body that he felt was fit for this discourse.

"Now that is what Markreet (Margaret Mead) did long ago, and if you want to become like Markreet that is what you have to do." I do not have the heart to tell him that I have all these things recorded, and that I have to go beyond this. I know by now how much it means in Pere to make an irrefutable point eloquently, so I say, "You know that I am not well and that I cannot do too much work that tires me all at once." I point to my medicines and he agrees that I must not work so hard with him. He nods his head in sympathy. Yes, I must not tire myself too much and yes, he has learned that I wasted all my good soul, yes, *wasted* it all on the Sori and Mokerang people who were and are not worthy of my efforts.

But how could I know until I got here that here there was true knowledge? All is forgiven.

*August 21.* Paliau, now recognized by the Australians as a native leader who cannot be ignored, receives invitations to almost all official functions of the Navy and Australian local government. As an honorary member of the Naval Officers Club, I too get invited to the Officers' Mess dinner. Paliau is assigned to be my dinner partner and "escort" for the evening. He behaves quite better than I do but nevertheless when in doubt he watches me closely. This is not the thing to do, for I certainly do not know my part for the port and sherry ritual — the Australian miniature version of the kula exchange, though the similarity would surprise them. I send something in the wrong direction while several guests across the table squeal in mock agony at my clumsiness. Paliau is hurt for me. I tell one of my tormentors that I am only an American, and one of them replies, "Well we all have to be Something." It is all in the jocular, but Paliau pales. Am I going to have to suffer this man disgracing me, what should he do? So for Paliau, I reply,

"Not at all, some of us succeed admirably in being Nothing." Smiles directed at me from the offender's superiors tell Paliau that our side has won. He rejoices with relief as the offender says, "Touché Madame."

It is a desperate creed with Paliau to never lose an encounter.

Margaret had written that children in Pere are free in their play and I find that they are certainly much freer in their play and more generous in their laughter than those in Sori or in Mokerang. Pwepwe agrees and feels that the parents here should be chastised for allowing them to arise at two or three o'clock in the morning to sing endlessly their repertoire of Manus songs at the top of their voices. "In Sori they would be spanked immediately," she notes with distaste, and she would be among the beaters. And we both know that in Sori they would have to clean up all the public "grounds" on the island for having transgressed on the privacy of others. But here it is their unquestioned right.

Once again I note the "sense of humor" characteristic of these islands. Pwepwe's strategy for making friends (which might be a feminine universal) is to give some tidbits of gossip to the wife of the teacher here, a nice quiet girl from Baluan. Pwepwe's gossip is, of course, of Mokerang and not her native Sori. The most hilarious thing she can think of is the raft of incidents about a poor "crazy" young woman of Mokerang, and what brought the loudest laughs are the lines about her ejection, as they construe it, from her village to the Catholic sisters' place at Patu. Our maimed cat has Mesian telling the baby with much hilarity, "your pussy is going to die." All find it funny to see the little cat limping with paralysis. Our decision to finally allow them to drown him caused much merriment, all day.

*September 2.* A "court" case was called by Matawai who is "the committee" of the village and custodian of our canoe. Mesian accused Niandros and her sister of stealing her brassiere. She had hung her wash last week and when she went to take it in in the evening, the brassiere was missing. On Sunday Mesian saw Niandros' sister wearing *her* brassiere (nothing over it, as is the style) at the basketball game. They designate a young girl Piwen as private investigator. Piwen goes to the girl and tells her that she is wearing a brassiere that belongs to Mesian. Niandros said her sister had received it from a male friend and gave it to Niandros.

At the court hearing, Matawai testified as to the laundering and the hanging of it. Niandros and her sister pleaded innocent, claiming that they purchased it in Lorengau. But Mesian triumphantly disproved this by saying it was made in the USA, as clearly marked on the label, and that the Misis had given it to her, as indeed I had. The court put the blame on Niandros and publicly upbraided her by saying that everyone knows that she makes money by being loose with men in Lorengau, but that she need not add lying and stealing in the village of Pere. Mesian was pleased that many, many people had come to this court case, as the crier had gone through the village before the meeting.

Cases in Pere are often over brother-sister relations that triumph over espousal support, adultery, and other situations (e.g., involving the value of children) in which traditional attitudes prevail. Anything having to do with the government will not be adjudicated in the village. Accountability for money and the ease with which it is lost is becoming popular in cases tried in the village "court" (see appendix III for sample cases).

*November 21.* Lokes asked me for 10 shillings needed for his sick daughter, but I learned later that he went to see his young paramour Niandros instead. She later emerged with a blouse and skirt bought for her by Lokes in Lorengau. Pwepwe refers to Lokes now with contempt as "this very young man." He is 50 and Niandros is 16.

*November 25.* The "court case" of Lokes and Pipiana (Lokes and Pipiana have been married for 17 years, and they have two children). Matawai performs the judicial function. I do not feel I should stay for the case, since Lokes is our cook and "butler" so to speak, and general factotum. So I go to Tchalolo to view the progress of the village being transported. New huts are being built and then carried there, but the "map" of the village carefully follows traditional placements. The medical orderly and his wife have already moved there, although their house does not have the walls up yet. Cardboard and tin keep the water out of half the house, that is all, but they couldn't stand Pere anymore because it "stank finish."

Arriving home, Pwepwe and Mesian tell me excitedly that they tried to listen to the court case, but Lokes kept ordering them out by saying they had to get lunch ready for the Misis. But they did hear Pipiana tell the court that her ears had so tired of listening to his lies. So, with a lack of exciting news about the case, I work on the "Manus Tru" grammatical sample.

Margaret Mead has given Matawai a record player, and he has borrowed records from Gus Buckham. He doesn't like any of Gus' records, except for the "liklik pikaninini" (P.E. little kids). I learn later from Mesian that this is actually the speeded up voice of the performer, which to us produces a comic effect. Since he is so happy, will he please take the battery of tests: Weigl, Bender, Stewart, Raven, Holtzman? As Ted "does" Matawai, I "do" Benedikta, an older woman. Matawai has a great deal of confidence in his ability to take psychological tests, because once during World War II some American soldiers made him and others guess which pack of cigarettes was the chosen pack. Matawai guessed correctly and got the cigarettes.

He also summarizes the "court case." It seems that Pipiana did admit she was pregnant while Lokes was in Mokerang with us, but that she lost the baby. Most think it was probably an abortion and that is what Lokes believes; hence he wants a separation. The leaders of Pere want Lokes to move to Tchalolo, but Pipiana does not want to move there. Matawai wants to tell us about his judgment of the case and the lecture he gave Lokes publicly that went like this: "I used to have adventures with many young girls but for the past year and one half I have been virtuous. Why? Because I have been elected as 'committee' and I take this seriously and feel I should set an example for the young boys. How much more so should Lokes act, for he is older and very respected. What sort of example does he set for the young boys?"

The villain of the piece turns out to be Mesian, who, the court established, *told* Pipiana about Lokes and Niandros with the result that Pipiana went up to Niandros and beat her. There is a Pere law that informers must be fined. Mesian will be fined three pounds, for it is thought that anyone who spreads stories, true or false, can only cause trouble and danger.

Matawai and the other "judge" came to the decision that nothing had been proven about Lokes and Niandros. They found kinship reasons for her being in houses which Lokes frequents. (As in other villages, an established couple acts as cover for a couple that wants to have a light affair.) In the meantime, Mesian has gone to the village elders to say that she has done no wrong. Her version is that Pipiana said to her that Lokes wanted to put off the reconciliation so that he could play with the young girl of this village who does this sort of thing. Mesian said, "Oh, you know about it? We have known it all along but did not want to tell you."

It was decided that nothing is settled and that things can remain as they are, with Lokes and Pipiana leading separate lives until some future date. Mesian, however, had her moments of satisfaction. She had every motive for revenge against Lokes for the grief and humiliation that he had caused her in the "court" in Sori. And she had a score to settle with Niandros for having stolen her brassiere.

*November 27.* Old Pokenau comes to the house in tears for fear that his son, Johannis has been lost at sea, for he went to Pak island two weeks ago and the weather has been very rough. Now for three days the weather has been calm and sunny, but no Johannis. He goes back to his house for divination, spitting out betel on a leaf. The side of the leaf on which the spittle ran told him that either his son would return, or that if he did not, pieces of his canoe would be found. No sooner has he finished telling me this than Johannis arrives in his canoe and Pokenau is gloriously happy.

*November 29.* No *lotu* this morning, as it is raining. A controversy about taboo. Mesian yesterday ate a *mwing*. Pwepwe and Lokes were shocked and would not join her in eating it. Why? Because the old men of before never ate it. It is a bird that shows you where the land is when you are lost at sea. How can you eat it? Do you think that after such foolishness you will not perish? Or that something truly no good will not fall upon you? Some old men here are very cross at the young boys who killed this *mwing*. I run to ask Pokenau about this, as I run to him with a question now anytime that I have an occasion. He said that once, long ago, some of them broke the taboo and ate this bird. They all defecated water and blood after that. It convinced all of them that you must not eat the bird that shows you the way to the land.

I receive a report on the progress of the "new" village. In three months, 56 houses were finished, while 24 are not yet finished. Four families have already moved there. Tchalolo is considered a good place because the people of that clan are all dead, so no one could come later with claims.

Today I also get Pere wind directions (according to Tchokal):

| Wind | Compass Reading | Tchokal's Comments |
|---|---|---|
| *Kup* | 100° ESE | (repeats degree reading after I say it) |
| *Malenkan* | 160° SSE | It is southeast from *Malenkan* direction. |
| *Malenkan Tru* | 180° | "South." |
| *Lan* | | North. *Lan* and *Malenkan* are the same wind. |
| *Ay* | 170° SSE | West. |
| *Tchar* | 325° NNW | Northwest. |
| *Tolau* | 10° NNE | It is true North. |

Joana (the midwife) has just returned from Pak where she spent two weeks. She and her brother Johannis Matawai (of the joyful return) had gone to mourn the death a of sister of Pokenau. For this, she and her brother were paid a pig, a sea turtle, one bag of rice and more for six housebuilding feasts.

I ask her if any babies are due to arrive here and she says indeed there are and she was worried about them while in Pak, but if she could not be here some other women would have done the best they knew how without her. Joana is not pleased with the way the men of this place follow her instructions. She tells them to buy sheets, *laplap*, soap and powder, and to make a new mat for the baby, but they do not do so. They are just too *kanaka* (P.E. too bush native), too hardheaded for words. And, when she is gone, the women who become midwives do it all *kanaka* fashion.  They get rid of the afterbirth the old way.  They push down with their hands while the woman stands up.  She thinks this makes it more difficult, for in the hospital they are taught to get rid of the placenta while the woman is lying down.

*November 30.*  Johannis Matawai gives his house-building feast.  These feasts turn out to be a distribution of food.  He distributes the pig that was given to him on Pak island and killed and smoked there, as well as a sea turtle caught on the way back.  Pokenau asks us for eight sticks of tobacco for this feast.  Bapau, too, is having a feast that features the distribution of pig.

Tchokal comes to talk to Lokes about another court case concerning him and Pipiana.  This one deals with the division of property.  Lokes had sent a letter to Bunai village saying he wanted to terminate his marriage to Pipiana and to divide the property.  Those who would be in charge of the "court" say they want no part in breaking up a marriage of such long standing and that if Lokes wants to do this, he can go to Lorengau to do it in the courts of the white man.  Lokes tells us he does not want to do that because in such a case he would accuse her of having had an abortion and she will go to jail.  He turns to me to say that this is what he can never forgive her for, that abortion.  Even though it was not his child, no matter, he would have liked another child.  He is not angry with her for having had a "friend," they have both had such and both been "befrienders" over the 19 years, but it was humiliating to him to have only two children in all that time.

How does a woman abort here?  She hangs from a height, she beats her belly against something, she falls down, or throws herself on her stomach.  There is something she can drink that is taken from a tree, but no one, and that is *no one*, knows what that tree or substance happens to be.

Pwepwe interjects here to report that about seven years ago in Sori one woman aborted several women on that island.  The men were extremely angry and the chief tried in every way to learn who the abortionist was and what she had given the women.  All they could learn was that it was something from a tree.  It is "well known" on Sori that many women do not have many children because they drink this.  (It is also probable that the unhygienic conditions of childbirth very often induce infections that cause sterility and thus limit family size.)

# Problems in an Incipient Money Economy

*December 2.* Pranis Paliau was to have brought a sum of money to the Edgel and Whitely store to pay off a village debt, but instead he became very generous with it and used it to get his brother out of jail. In addition, he had ousted his wife and was courting the wife of another. This recalled to Mesian how difficult it is to trust people with money. Now here is Lokes who has not repaid her loan to him. Being very generous with her salary, he has spent it on others. Her uncle in Bunai has been after both Mesian and Pwepwe to give him their salaries so he can buy a sewing machine for his canteen. Then they could sew on it and make things to sell and earn enough money to buy themselves a sewing machine. Pwepwe is so leary that she had 25 pounds saved with me and 15 pounds saved with Sapalona at the cooperative store in Lorengau. She wants to get all her money to Sapalona but doesn't trust anyone to take it there.

It is a real problem for anyone who earns money here not to be severed from it. It would be difficult for things to work out any other way. To ask, to "*sing out*" for what one needs has always been legitimate and expected. To refuse to lend (give) money when one knows that employment is short term and that eventually one will again be in a state of interdependence with others (whom one had refused) must be a hard decision. Those who ask for money simply appropriate it once it is in their possession and they always have a good excuse: someone is sick, someone is in jail, someone needs something desperately and one has the opportunity to have someone indebted to you.

The idea has now emerged that one can make money from a *piley* or *perey* (i.e., the "traditional" exchanges I have described). The *perey* that Kilepak is involved in now is the *kanyoliai yayem* ("mother's teeth"). One asks to be repaid for the teeth of the women of the clan that masticated the food for the child or children who are now members of another clan. There are several people who live on Buke and towards whom Kilepak stands in this obligatory relationship. To various persons he has sent: 4 pairs of long trousers, 3 pairs of short trousers, 4 singlets, 6 bed sheets, 1 axe, 14 shirts, 7 dresses, 1 chisel, 3 forks, and 50 *saksak*. They have also requested, but he has yet to send: 1 pair of shoes, 1 Coleman lamp, 1 watch. He will invite them here and give them some bags of rice. At that time they will announce when they will pay him. He expects to receive one hundred pounds from them.

# Reflections on a Midterm Visitor

Margaret Mead has been here for two months now. I deliberately omitted from my notes the daily interactions with her and her *modus operandi* in the field, for Margaret always wanted to be in complete control of any interpretation of her actions and her life. I wrote about Margaret as a fieldworker later (Romanucci-Ross 1976, 1980), and include here some of my notes of a personal nature, (bare sketches for a future collection of bark paintings):

As colleague, as friend, and particularly as "family," as Margaret likes to put it, she is ever thoughtful, caring and aware of all possible dangers. We are urged by her to be well prepared in advance for every possible contingency, and on the many occasions her advice is taken it serves us well. She has a wondrous appetite for foods, beverages and anything that can be considered cultural data in any guise. Ted and I do our own work and she does hers: we three do not collaborate on minor details of research although we are, of course, collaborators in the major research design of the areal integration of the cultures of the Admiralty Islands (Schwartz 1963). Because of this, every few days we have sessions called "theoretical," and for these she appears to have a great fondness. She impresses me with the fact that it is necessary to have labels for ideas, or no one will recognize them, and also that it isn't enough to *do* something, you have to be telling your audience what you are going to do, what you are doing, and what you have done. To me it smacks of a world of appearances, and yet I know that she is describing the real world "out there" and that I had best pay attention.

Ever interested in the behavior of children and in the process of formal education, she wants to go to the elementary school at Bunai quite frequently, and for that we accompany her on the canoe and take photographs for her on those occasions, as Ted does for all her other occasions. In preparing for the first of such trips, her excessive concern for all the technical details of equipment, etc., so frustrates us that we both think the other has the film. Margaret has an enormous distaste for "incompetence" and so rather than admitting that we "forgot" the film we just photograph as though the camera is loaded, to avoid a tantrum. (I always marvel at her unflagging interest in *children's* tantrums. Although Ted sometimes appears to welcome her onslaughts of anger, I will do anything to avoid them.) We return to Bunai on some pretext or other the next day, to take the shots we faked the day before.

As Margaret describes her visit to Pere in *Letters from the Field* (1977:268), she "was living neck deep in the past" from the moment the old women of Pere wept copiously in greeting her until their tearful adieus when she left. (When I ask her why they cry she said, "because they and I both got old since the first time I was here.") She reads and re-reads (much to my astonishment) her monograph on Manus Tru kinship (Mead 1934). For one thing, she is rather peeved by Ted's discovery of some minor errors in that work and keeps trying to find plausible explanations for their differences, although Ted is correct, and he *has* spent a great deal of time learning the Manus language and kinship system, as well as the rest of the culture. She does not like it at all when Ted decides to "cover" a keening session for a deceased person (that she feels is her territory) or "a quarrel," for she does not want the Pere Manus to be thought of as "quarrelsome." Since Pere is not my "field," it is my assigned duty to intervene and get Ted to cease and desist from "covering" an event, which puts me in the position of the ill-fated messenger. My solace is to think of myself as SaLuhai, the Makankor girl, and I put myself to working with Pwepwe on disentangling some texts collected in Sori or Mokerang which are "recognized" by Margaret as "mine."

She is pleasant to live with and it is with some embarrassment that I sometimes find it somewhat intellectually stifling to be engaged in constant talk about "culture": culture as an abstraction, and a mosaic of "ideas" expressed or plucked from innumerable small conferences in likely and unlikely places on the planet. It must seem a strange admission for an anthropologist, but I nurture a niggling conviction that if we could stop constantly thinking and talking about culture we might learn something interesting about the *people* here. I never express this opinion, needless to say, and I *am* ashamed of it and don't quite know what I mean. Ted is a more congenial colleague, always ready, at sensible intervals, to play chess as we listen to classics on tape, or to turn to a work of science fiction. Whyever not? Ideas, new ideas, have to come from "noise," as Bateson said. Of course, it might occur to us to think of our "informants" as informants about new meta-logical ways of dealing with cultural materials, but no one accepts this now, and very few will later (Romanucci-Ross 1980b).

Mead loves being around people of all sorts, but she *misses* people of her own kind. Therefore, she is pleased to suggest that she accompany me to Rabaul for a followup of the TB non-treatment regimen that a "European" physician there has assigned to me. At our hotel in Rabaul she is really irked by an affable drunk who comes to sit at our table to ask what we are doing later, and whether we "girls" have ever been to Thailand. "No," she thunders, and I cannot suppress my laughter thinking that it is probably the only place in the world Margaret has not been. I later receive a sermonette because I "do not know how to act around Australian men" and because my behavior this evening does not reflect my training to be "objective" as an anthropologist. In one of the few times I am able to express my true feelings, I say that being trained in the ways of science does not mean you are no longer the person you were brought up to be, and that not knowing that makes you a poorer scientist, not a better one. And I find that many things in the world are to me comic, and I see no reason to treat that harmless bloke "in his cups" as anything less than a person, who is perhaps a bit fallen from grace at this time, but who *did* leave in the grace of God and without rancor. I learn a rather remarkable thing about Margaret tonight — she *likes* to be "told off." Bored to distraction in the hotel room, she is delighted when I manage to pick up a dinner invitation for "me and my girlfriend." The administrator and his wife are dumbfounded to learn the identity of their mystery guest: soon the phones buzz and Margaret has about 35 whites in the area for a post-prandial talk. She cheerfully talks into the night on everything from the future of the territory to the Buka "baby farms" to the chances of nuclear war. The magic is there, for 35 territory "Europeans" (as it was earlier and later for 3,000 people in San Diego, or on a national television network). Margaret gives everyone her enchantment and her best, always and anywhere.

There is a second highlight of this trip to Rabaul. Dr. Vin Zigas had asked me to see that he got to meet Margaret, and I thought that she would be delighted to know him, as I was. As a medical worker in the Territory, Vin had "discovered" *kuru* among the Fore people of Okapa in the Eastern Highlands of Papua New Guinea. In 1956 he had been the first to clinically document the sickness and to initiate research that attracted others, including Carleton Gajdusek. Vin has an infectious charm and enthusiasm and can never stop telling me how he and "Carlety" together are really going to puzzle out the etiology of *kuru*.

Now there is an occasional person to whom Margaret can take an immediate (and to my mind) irrational dislike; poor Vin is one of these. Entertaining, amusing, charming, interesting, highly intelligent and all that, he *is*, but she remains untouched, with a hidden scowl which I can recognize anywhere, anytime. When I later ask her how she can be so negative about one of my favorite people in the Territory she comes up with the excuse that he had the temerity to visit her bringing a lady friend. Knowing that this is the last thing that Margaret cares about, since she relates to *people* and not to sexually-motivated behavior, I look for quite some time for a possible explanation. What finally emerges is that Carleton is one of "her" scientists and this Dr. Zigas, physician, neurologist, virologist, is not welcome in the race for prizes. She has a fierce (and again to my mind) irrational loyalty to her circles: "family," colleagues, or fellow scientists with characteristics that please her. Knowing Vin as I do, I assure her she has no cause to worry about the outcome of claims in the *kuru* domain (whatever their eventual worth), for he does not lust after glory.

It is often intimated, especially by novelists, that anthropologists live out their fantasies in the field. For Margaret, this fantasy is to have tea in the afternoon in the manner of an English lady. She is a dynamo of energy from daybreak to 10-11 at night, except for the afternoon nap and then tea. We have to wash up (with a bucket shower), dress up (in my only *other* washed cotton dress) and act English. Now English tea parties are incomprehensible to Italians, who, like the French psychiatrists of the 19th century, view this form of English behavior as an exercise in controlling a deep-seated ethnic madness. The "point," it seems to me, is to give as little information about yourself as possible to people who appear to care even less than you might imagine about having it. And conversational trajectories must appear as though all are about to gently grasp a Sentiment which forever eludes everyone. Needless to say, none of us plays "English tea party" very well. Margaret and Ted are soon engaged in arguments ranging from Manus kinship to the nature of the community of scholars. There is an air of aggressive intimacy in their battles, from which I am emotionally excluded. Anything I ever say to tip the balance of power of argument will later lead to my being reproached by one or the other for having done that. I therefore listen with all my conscious attention and the "third ear," but I also daydream of snows and saints, and of Vivaldi and *vino bianco* — something to feel merry about in the steam heat and tropical torpor of an equatorial afternoon. Ah yes, and as one of our Melanesian culture-bearers wanders by in the shade of the pandanus roof down below, I wonder how to get the culture-bearer to *really* yield his cultural secrets.

Margaret has time for anyone going through our village. Patrol officers, American servicemen overseeing a missile tracking station in the interior of Manus, and Australian women from Port Moresby looking in on the women's club, they will all leave Pere with buoyant spirits for having talked with her. She even tries to distract me from my illness by taking me for evening walks and singing me songs of her youth, vaudevillian lyrics shorn of the original melody.

Rapid culture change (as noted in the introduction,) is one of the ideas, possibly the major one, to which Margaret Mead is deeply committed. Although she insists that "the primitive peoples of the South Pacific" are her "laboratories," she does not admit to having brought her cultural heritage with her, those perennial middle class American values. The linchpin of these values is precisely that in one generation, in 25 years, differences that "took mankind many centuries to overcome," *can* be quickly overcome. This is, of course, the dominant theme in *New Lives for Old* (1956). The people of Pere provided this model for the world. I do not find among the Pere this "understanding of the American political system," nor do I hear the Shakespearian cadences and sonnet-like style of discourse that I have read in *New Lives for Old*. Ted had told me (and later referred in an article) to her 1953 resistance to the idea that the Manus of Pere were full participants in the cargo cult. According to her earlier writings they were too "rational" to participate in cargo cult behavior, and that they did participate did not emerge until six months after her departure (Schwartz 1983). These, too, were Mead's "other" Manus!

Margaret and I are visited one day by a man who had belonged to the cargo cult. Among other conversational items of interest he tells us that one of his cousins left a pound note on a table and that night a dead ancestor brought him a record player (i.e. "cargo"). Margaret glares at him, and like a teacher correcting an erring pupil says in Pidgin, "Now record players don't come up on a table from the ancestors, they come up along hard work. Everything you see that we have in this house here has come up along hard work."

I feel sorry for our confused Manus guest, who certainly must be thinking that he sees a great deal of hard work going on all around him in Manus by the Manus, but nothing "comes up" out of it. But I understand her irritation, since she had described these people to the world as a model in moral and political evolution, so what *is* this chap doing here talking like an old myth-making cultist of times of before *New Lives for Old*? Just a few weeks before this she had called a meeting to try to get people to change their personal naming system, to use name and surname (as we do) for each individual so that they could keep bank accounts and so that administrators could identify health charts, work records, etc. Several persons refused to consider this, and so it was tabled, to my understanding, forever. They made this decision on two points: one, the ancestors knew as much about naming as anybody; and two, the tyranny of the majority should not prevail unless *everyone* wants something changed. She finds these foils to her attempts to make their lives "easier" quite frustrating.

I do not mean to say that Mead is wrong when she says they want desperately to join the modern world. "They" are a faction and have very little idea what the modern world is about. Another small group wants to retain the traditional ways of the ancestors, and yet another group wants to remain "in the middle" taking elements of whatever comes up, not really caring what happens as long as things go well for them in their immediate family goals. Those who push for change eventually change the course of events, but not necessarily in the manner they intend. I do not think that Hegel would be at all surprised by the religious cargo cult positing a thesis, engendering an antithesis and causing the society to end up with a synthesis of the dialectic (Macran 1929).

(As I have mentioned, John Kilepak was brought to California by Barbara Heath in 1970, and I recall his being mostly speechless as he encountered the twentieth century, so to speak. He kept asking me how he could possibly describe all this to the Pere and the other peoples of Manus, especially "my" Sori if he encountered one in Lorengau. He was particularly fascinated by my electronically-controlled garage door and by the "baskets" that can be ridden above the treetops at the San Diego Zoo. Since the myths of the Manus (Margaret seemed to think they had neither "history" nor "myths" — see Mead 1934: 1975) are full of allusions to *marsalai* baskets and *marsalai* doors to caves that open and close mysteriously, one can only guess what meaning they must have had for him and what beliefs they must have validated).

Although Pere is not, in the research sense, "my village," I feel I have heard enough, understood enough, and collected enough materials and commentaries by the Manus to convince me that culture change does not proceed even here in a manner that is linear and spectacular after a cataclysmic historical moment of truth, anyone's truth. While conducting research in Sori and Mokerang, I collected data that could be described as linguistic, economic, religious and political, and that dealt with ritual, land use, trade and exchanges, courtship and notions of the self. These data, when compared with other "areal" data, reveal a basic structure shared by Admiralty Island cultures that does not make for revelations of culture change; i.e., the culture does not go into "reverse" when one hits the Southcoast version of Admiralty Island cultural themes. Margaret simply does not wish to "consider" the traditional behavior I have illustrated here.

Mead does garner enormous amounts of information with some insights that hold up well under later scrutiny, despite the fact that she works through Pidgin and not the native language. She is gifted in being able to observe much in a very short time span, but also in sifting out what does not please her. Learning to use a language foreign to English is not her *forte* nor is she among the most fluent of Pidgin speakers I have known. (Mead had argued in the past that knowing a language was not really necessary for knowing a culture, but deemphasized this view in her later years). Careful scrutiny of her fieldnotes reveals what I consider a very limited range of "informant" types in her village. This, in my opinion, might help explain why her generalizations have at times been found questionable by other researchers. After reading all her fieldnotes, I thought that by talking with everybody and trying to learn all points of view in my Matankor villages, my notes would please her "as more of a good thing" in note-taking. Not so. Her exasperated verdict after reading two volumes of my notes on Sori was that "like Gregory" (Bateson) I wrote down "just *everything*" and "like Gregory," I would never be able to find anything in my notes when I needed to look for it. Margaret always "takes things down" with the thematic in mind, to be sure, but she is always indexical and topical as she works, so that later what she needs will be easy to find. I tend to be excessively (?) phenomenological (even before the discovery that one could "be" that in the modern social sciences) and keep collecting with some constant concerns: how can I know now what the questions will be later? How can I avoid divesting a people of their creativity in presentation of the self, while also burdening them with the need to "explain" themselves to the rest of the world, and to future generations?

*December 3, 1964.* A Modern Manus Song (expressing chagrin, for the "new work" does not profit family nor group and does not lead to fulfillment of the still highly valued traditional goals.)
(Words not in italics are in Pidgin; others are Manus Tru of Pere Village).

*O pein a pati Manus*
   (you, girl of Manus)

*O le* skul sukul nesing
   (you go to school, nursing school)

*Yo nopwa ku* winim wok *eoi*
   (I think you will win your work)

*Pati tchapona kol e yotalu*
   (it's for raising the place that belongs to us two)

*Pe yetape kone* lusim wok *eoi*
   (now why did you lose this work of yours?)

*Kone nyamali kamal pati tau*
   (you looked at a man who is from far away)

*Kone tawi mamatchi le kol etalu*
   (you bring shame it goes to the place belonging to us
   two)

*Nrowiyan, konan, kwaso*
   (alright, never mind, you are married)

*Kone waso le kor e tau*
   (you are married in a far away place)

*Kone* lusim *papum pe yayem*
   (you lost your father and your mother)

*Alu nopwa pwa ku* winim wok *eoi*
   (you two think that in the future you will win your work)

*Atu* wok *eoi notu* lus *kapwen*
   (hard work of yours has been lost for nothing)

*Tcha kae si tatan tipalan e awa*
   (what kind of custom has been lost for you folks?)

*Awa matu katutilani kae titan a wiyan ne muan*
   (you folks stop and think of it, is this 'way' good or no
   good)

*Katutilani mamachi ti wei*
   (think good. Shame is here now)


(Note the words that are in Pidgin: gain, win, work, lose, school.)

December 3 also brings more information on illness and war. Kilepak says that there is a certain animosity between the medical orderly and Petrus Pomat, the *Kaunsil*, over the cause of illness and that it is of long standing. Petrus is the son of Isole, described and photographed by Reo Fortune in *Manus Religion* (1935). To know this is to have a grasp on his traditional perspective. He believes that medicines *may* help a child recover from illness, but medicines are to no avail if the parents have been fighting or if one of them has wronged the other. During a recent dysentery epidemic, the babies of three couples died. It is generally believed that these babies died because of the wrong-doings of the parents. Kilepak believes this too, "Tonia and Tomas are very jealous of each other. This is their wrong. Their baby got sick and did not get well even though they went to Lorengau and had the attention of doctors and medicines. Tcholai and his wife must have quarreled." I do know that Pomat, reporting to the village after that trip to Lorengau, interpreted a statement by the doctor about needing their cooperation to mean "I, the doctor, am enough to cure your children, but I cannot do so unless the parents help me in my work, that is, to keep things straight between them." (See Romanucci-Ross 1969 for an analysis of this hierarchy of resort in curative practices.)

# The Birth of a Baby Girl in Pere Village

*December 4.* When Joanna referred to a woman who was due to have a baby during her visit to Baluan, she meant Maria Ipwau, who had been thrown out by two husbands and was now about to have an illegitimate child. Today, I am called at 6:45 AM and run to Ipwau's house. I decide she is not about to deliver yet so I come back to the house to have breakfast and get dressed properly. Back with Ipwau at 7:00 to find Joanna seated legs akimbo, behind Ipwau who is lying on her side. The two other women with her are her "sisters," although the "real" (in our terms) relationship is that these "sisters" are both daughters of Ipwau's mother's brother. Ipwau's other two children died as babies. The two women present both have their babies with them.

This is taking place in the part of Ipwau's house where the cooking is done, and it is over the sea. On half hour later, she is moaning softly and Joanna rubs her back and places a pad of lint between her legs. She is working from behind and apparently intends to remain there. Now Ipwau sits up and holds on to the post. The "sisters" show no interest in this, but rather play with their babies. Joanna asks me to talk to her saying that she cannot talk to me because her work is taking all of her energy. Ipwau is lying on her side with one leg on the floor and the other resting, or rather pushing against a post of the house. She is rubbing her own abdomen, and now Joanna joins her in this. Her younger "sister" decides to leave as the pains are about three minutes apart. Ipwau says "sorry" in response to the pain. Younger sister's baby screams and defecates, and as she is wiping him with a dry coconut fiber ripped from an old coconut lying about she threatens him sweetly with *moyap* (white man) meaning me. I jokingly correct the word to *piyap* (white woman) and she laughs. Joanna also joins the laughter as her attendance to her working the abdomen has her saying, "Sorry, Jesus."

Now at 8:11 the breathing is heavy; there are contractions and Ipwau pulls her legs together with pain. Now she sits up and Joanna presses against her back with both hands. As she lies down, sits up, lies down and sits up again, and again, she is very concerned about her pubic area becoming uncovered. Eight minutes later a piercing yell — and I begin to notice the Mbuke pottery on the racks and the fishing traps. What a solace to give them all my attention! Yes, I must copy the designs of all fishing traps, for sure, tomorrow. Younger sister now pokes me so that I turn my head to observe what is happening now. The baby's head is emerging and Joanna takes it with her hands. With no pushing, not bearing down, the baby is born, to have its face washed and its mouth cleansed of mucous by Joanna.

The baby cries a bit, then is wrapped in a towel and placed next to its mother. The placenta is removed by a push, gentle but firm, on the abdomen, then put into an enamel basin and covered. It is later buried in a hole on the beach.

Two old women enter after the birth, and one tells those assembled that they must open the window. Water is being heated to wash the baby, and Joanna teaches them to wash as she was taught at the hospital. But the position they all agreed upon for the delivery was that of the woman lying on her side with legs apart and one pushing on the post. Now, this is not what Joanna was taught at the hospital, it is the "native" position. What she was taught at the hospital is considered ludicrous and much too painful for the woman. The women here absorb what they want from the Australian notion of midwifery, but keep what they think is better from their own traditions.

Ipwau will lie on her mat for five days. If it had been her first child, she would have had to lie for ten days. Joanna will stay at her house to look after the baby. In the old days, intercourse was not allowed for one month or two, but now "it's up to the two persons involved." All the clan relations of the mother look after the food needs at this time.

***December 6, Sunday.*** This morning at Lotu, Tapas does, it appears, have a sermon that is not concerned with Adam and Eve. He tells the congregation today that it is the sixth of December. This is the constant reckoning of time to Christmas, which has been going on for six months. Now, if you know a white man (*Mastah*) is coming to see the place you clean it up and get rid of the garbage, right? Alright, Jesus is coming on Christmas so let us clean up our thoughts and throw the garbage out of our minds. Let us not talk foolishness, or to no purpose.

Not bad! And I use this occasion to solicit Niandros, Tapa, Sori and Piwen to come and take the psychological tests. Also keep my promise to myself and take photos of a fish trap for crabs, and a trap for ordinary fish. Both are made by men but used by women. The one trap is made of bamboo; it is to catch all fish. The large nets are made to float on the reef to catch the bigger fish. (The "rights" to net-making can be brought by women who marry into a patriline.)

And on this day, also, another baby, a boy, for Nyalawen. This time, Joanna begins by telling me that white women do not know how to have babies. How could they? They listen to the doctors who are men! What do men know about having babies? The *kanaka* way is the only way to do it, and they have been having babies as long as anyone, and they have not forgotten, though it is nice to be clean about it. Two loquacious women are keeping Nylawen (sullen and silent in a sheet) company. The older woman has had 11 children, and only two have died of illness, "only two." The other had seven, but four died of illness as infants. All proceeds much as the previous birth, except that the husband of the parturent hovers outside, fixing the posts of the house. The women are delousing each other and I am being devoured by mosquitos.

The women are laughing hilariously among themselves, and I understand enough *Manus Tru* by now to know that Joanna is telling them that I said that white women scream as though being slaughtered when they are in labor, and that I didn't have more than two children because that is all I wanted to have. They find this particularly funny, I must be truly deluded! The two women cannot tolerate the mosquitos and leave. I keep walking about to avoid them, but some other women enter to try to kill them while Joanna washes her hands. They think I don't sit because I cannot sit on the floor, so Kiteni goes to my house for a chair. As Nyalawen moans, her husband peeks in the door to scold her, and to tell her she must stop acting like a crazy woman. His tone is severe and unsympathetic. A few seconds later, the baby appears very quickly and, again, with no pushing or "bearing down," and the father leaves. All continues as with the other birth. After five or ten days, the child will be named by its mother's brother or its mother's mother.

Joanna thinks that many parents have intercourse, soon after birth, but that this is not good for the mother, or for the baby, who will become weak and sick if they do this too soon.

I leave the house to see a seven-year-old boy who has hit a younger brother of Nyakupwen. As she scolds him he says, "You cannot rebuke me, you carried two little sea turtles and they both died," meaning of course, she has lost infant twins, which means she is morally reprehensible on two counts. Mesian and Pwepwe are horrified, not that such a thing is said, but that it is said by such a young boy.

*December 9.* Another birth, handled by Joanna like the previous ones, but differing in some interesting ways. No one, of the large attendant company of both sexes, pays attention to the mother-to-be. Everyone is busily chewing betel, eating leaf, taking lime. Benedikta, the parturent's mother, comes to tell me that her dog had five puppies this morning, a stellar day for birthing. She and her daughter's husband laugh at her moans and tell her to shut up and lie on her side. There is little empathizing with her. It seems she had earlier had a miscarriage, which everyone blamed on her laziness.

Joanna rubs hibiscus on her abdomen to speed up the process, then Joanna begins to knead her abdomen. She does this so violently that it shakes the whole house. Now there is talk about straightening the *thinkthink* (mind, thought). The talk comes from her mother and husband to the young mother. They are telling her, in Manus Tru, that all is not well between her and someone else and that is why she will have trouble. When a young girl named Ana enters, Benedikta turns to me, "This baby that she has was given to her by her sister because Ana's baby died, but now this baby is hers, it is hers altogether, do you understand?" I supposed this meant she could keep it, although had Ana wanted it . . .

Benedikta first squirts milk on the face of her smallest child and as she feeds it she tells me that since her first baby her milk has never dried up, and she has had ten. A little boy who is related to her leaves and she calls after him affectionately, "You bloody shit," (in English!)

When the baby is born, its head is deformed but no one seems concerned about that. Smoked fish and *saksak* arrive. This is for the *lonken*, the first small feast and usually given indoors for all present and also for the midwife. The *kaniyen puaro* occurs later outdoors and it is the big feast which many attend. There is a payment from the side of the man to the side of the woman for the *kaniyen puaro*. Now it is usually paid in Australian pounds. Someone from the side of the man (the father's mother) has decided to name the baby Paliau. Long ago, the child used to be named by the mother's brother or whoever gave the *kaniyen puaro* on the side of the woman. Of course, the brother usually gave the feast, but it could have been someone else.

*December 10.* Try to follow up on attitudes toward the baby's misshapen head, but all I hear is, "Oh, it will be alright . . . the baby Paliau's head came out like that because his mother is lazy and does not like to work. She sat around too much." She was also blamed for losing her first one because she lifted a drum. She will be blamed if this one dies, but no one expects it to die.

Although there were no births during my stay on Sori island, Pwepwe tells me that they do nothing like they do here, nor have they ever heard of it. The delivery position is that the woman sits on a box, or something similarly elevated, and the woman helping her sits between her legs to receive the baby. The umbilical cord is placed on top of a sago or coconut palm. No one knows why, they just do it.

# On Changing Styles of Shame

Early this morning, a vicious storm threatened to make our house collapse. I heard a loud crash and something did collapse, the men's toilet, a small structure over the lagoon, now just a heap of tin and *saksak*. There has been no effort to reconstruct it, and the men are using the women's toilet. Pwepwe tells me that because of this, several girls have been attending to their needs on the "bridge" (a long plank) leading to the outhouse, and they do this from dusk on, "which is disgusting because they can be seen both at dusk and by moonlight.'' She rushes to Lokes to report this indignation. Lokes looks up from his cooking and sermonizes to her as follows:

"Before, we did not know what shame was. We lost this at the time the *Kaunsil* was established and as we waited for those warships to come that were going to bring us all the cargo from our Dead. Everything really went to pieces then as we gave up all the things of our ancestors and had nothing to put in its place. At this time, men and women began to bathe together and did not wear their *laplaps*. They used to just hang their *laplaps* on the trees and go to bathe in the same place and go in the water without clothes. It was terrible, really. We lost all shame, and at that time we thought it good, but it was *not* good. Some of us know that now, but some just keep doing those things and keep living without shame. Many of those things we did were no good.''

Pwepwe has a delicious occasion for a rejoinder with her usual Sori *hauteur*, ''that is why we of the North Coast did not want to join you in your *Kaunsil*. We heard about all those things you were doing and we thought they were no good. We know that the *kaunsil* put all these things into your *think-think*. Now you know the real reason for our not joining you. We don't like that sort of behavior and that's all there is to it.''

*December 13.* The usual ''vomiting and diarrhea'' is upon us again this season. Fourteen babies have died recently while being treated for this illness in Lorengau. There are many deaths in all the villages but the total is not known, since they are not reported. I know of eighteen in two villages nearby.

*December 18.* Another birth, and when I get home Lokes asks me proudly how I ''found'' the baby. A lovely boy I said. And he says, ''It is mine.'' (Well!) But not at all: he asked for the baby when Monica was pregnant and Monica and her husband and all those involved assented to this. They already have children after all, and Lokes' father and Tomas' father were brothers. When will he take it? After it is about six months old. Lokes is joyful over this. But later, his brother, Simon Matawai, who is here visiting from Lae, comes to see me because he wants me to know that the baby's name is Tchanan (his father's name), and that he, Simon, named it and that the baby will be his, not Lokes'. Even though Simon is not married, he gets it because he asked first. After he has the baby he will have a wife. In reply to my question, ''How can they give it away?'' Lokes looks at me as though I have learned nothing, ''because it is not giving it away, it is all in one family. Because Tomas is like our brother and we are all here, not far away.''

*December 19.* A man from Loniu meets us in Lorengau and asks once more that we procure for him a certain kind of lemon hair oil from the U.S. To get us to do this he has carved a crocodile (poorly), and a not-badly-done bowl. He asks us this time with some urgency. Why? Because it is magic and he had to have it to win at "lucky," a card game. Walking back to the canoe I am not pleased at the sight of two small girls taking care of a baby and trying to terrify it into silence by pointing at me and saying, "*Piyap, Piyap*" (white woman).

*December 20.* Paliau asks us to come to the *lotu* so that we might tape record his talk. He has become rather arrogant and self-centered. Perhaps this very trait helped him form a group around himself and to turn a religious movement into a political movement. I note that he spends most of his time in his talks scolding or reprimanding people (usually because they don't forge ahead with economic development). I wonder when or if they will ever tire of it. I have to tape the talk, as Ted had to go to Lorengau. Paliau apologizes to me because it was not long enough! He is saving his talk for Christmas.

On the way home, walking with Kilepak, and stargazing; he tells me that the Usiai people used to watch for *Tchasa* (the Pleiades) from a platform they had built in a high tree for this purpose.

A question of identity, or why Karol Matawai no longer has either of his washtubs. Napo of Mbuke looks so much like Kilepak that it used to be said they were one and the same person. For this reason he can *singout* (p.e. request) for things from Kilepak's relatives. Kilepak is older brother to Matawai and can *singout* to him. Therefore, Napo did *singout* for Matawai's tubs and got them.

*December 23.* No rain for twelve days and clothes must be washed in the river. Today I go along for the experience. Twenty-five feet of rowing from island to shore. Then we push the canoe through mud that is knee-deep with each stop. Then through the mosquito-ridden mangrove swamp, with canoe and outrigger often too wide for the stream. Deborah, my daughter, here for the holidays from Ascham School in Darling Point, Sydney, gets out and lifts the outrigger while Mesian poles and I walk. Much of the time we push the canoe over spots where the water is not sufficiently high. We had left Pere village at 8:00 A.M., and we arrive at the washing place in the bush at 11:00. The washing itself does not take much time. The water comes from a small crystalline waterfall, sparkling in the sun. We stand in the pool and scrub the clothes on rocks. Then we shower and shampoo in the waterfall unaware of selves and bodies; one with the world. The water has "risen" since we left, so it only takes us half the time to get home as it did to arrive.

*December 25.* It is Paliau's idea to have services from 3:00 A.M. to sunrise. I cannot imagine why, but it is probably a syncretic notion of midnight mass and Easter sunrise services. The bell begins to summon at 1:30 A.M., so that we can begin to think about getting up. Paliau sends several to call us, but we get there before most.

The altar is decorated with fruits and flowers. In front of the altar a crèche, the foundation of which is a box of sand such as one finds here in the cemetaries, but the frame around it is in the shape of an old-fashioned baby carriage, covered with green leaves. I am told that this is Bethlehem. The *House Lotu* is crowded. Almost all of the girls and women are dressed in white, and the men in shorts and shirts, ties and European shoes.

The young people sing "Silent Night." There is a pageant featuring Joseph and Mary (in flowing blue draped from her head to her feet). She walks up to the crèche and places a plastic doll in a small cot under the cover of the baby carriage. They are followed by angels in white sheets, with paper visors on their heads (halos?), but the effect is more that of nuns. "Angels" keep flapping their arms for a wing effect, through the entire performance. Mary and Joseph are also accompanied by a Girl Scout and a Boy Scout, both in uniforms. Three kings in table cloths and paper crowns come to a paper star illuminated with a flashlight in the center. They place three packages at the bottom of the crèche. The appropriate Biblical passages are read in Pidgin. Paliau first bows to the crèche and then begins his exhortations to the flock to work hard, and for the women to be like Mary and the men to be like Jesus. He interprets, "give to Caesar that which is Caesar's" to mean that they must pay their taxes. Paying taxes is a good thing and Jesus was all for that.

At 5:00 A.M. many are falling asleep. Samol comes up to slap a boy who has fallen asleep, nevertheless does not succeed in waking him. The young girls are all resting their heads on the girl in front (except for the unfortunates in the front row). But Paliau is not yet finished and has a long long talk yet to come.

All villages are devoid of activity on Christmas day in spite of many promises of dancing, feasting, etc. For one thing, I am sure, almost everyone is at home sleeping off the sermon.

*December 27.* Today there is a meeting on the "economic development" plans. In pristine democratic fashion, each speaks his piece. Arguments against Ted's idea that they buy a freezer for fish: it won't work unless *one clan alone* is responsible for the enterprise, for people here work only in clans. One could never be sure that all dealings are honest. It will work only if each clan has two men representing it. Some will be so displeased to see others making money that they will not sell them fish, in fact, will do all they can to sabotage the effort. Also, there are not enough fish caught to justify the activity. People here immediately trade fish they catch for sago and taro and would have nothing to eat if they did not do this. After all these valid arguments, they came up with a consensus that Ted's idea was a good one and they would try it. (As of this writing they have not done so.)

I think that all their objections are quite realistic, particularly the one about exchanging fish for other food. I guess they want to be courteous to Ted for his "original" idea. Ted gets back to "working the land." He has to repeat everything at least half a dozen times. It is the style of speaking here and the redundancy, (with no recorder) makes good sense. Arguments against working the land: they are salt water people, have never worked the land and never will. Pokenau adds that he once acquired land (through an Usiai relative); it was not worked. He knows therefore that salt water people do not work land. It is better to go back to Ted's freezer idea.

*December 30.* The Sunam does not arrive and we have no way of knowing why, so we leave for Lorengau by canoe.

*A Manus Tru is born.*

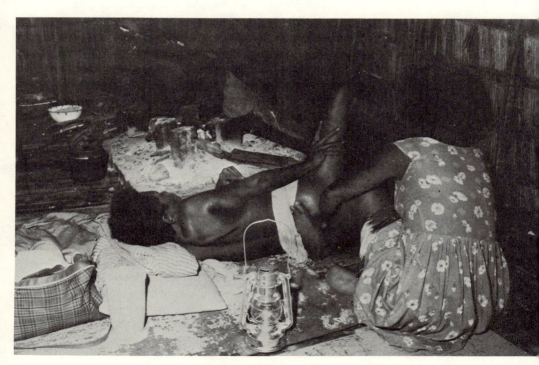

*The birth position.*

*Going home.*

# ELEVEN

# In the Outer Spaces of a Phenomenal Field

*January 1.* Lorengau is a good place to see old friends from the villages in which I have worked. The Sori Islanders have their Baripeo Society for trading copra, and it is here that I go to visit them. Sori people who come into Lorengau are usually marooned until another ship goes back that way. Often it is months before this happens. One Sori has managed to find some work loading trucks and unloading cargo from ships during this long wait.

*January 2.* I play tennis with Australian friends. Not an ego-enhancing experience, but I hold my own. Discussions among them are about the new sexual freedom, the pill, and how women have finally learned how to have orgasms. Not all are pleased with these developments. I also learn from a physician friend that a girl of Pere is being sent home after nurses training in Rabaul, having been discovered to be in an advanced state of pregnancy. This makes her the fourth from the Manus group to whom this has happened within just a few months. Pwepwe enjoys traveling with me and sermonizing about the degradation of South Coast Manus people.

Today she affords me an opportunity to observe once again what some have called, "the joking relationship with a cross-cousin." She meets him at the E and W store while she is carrying Adan. He says, "I see you have a baby."

Pwepwe: "Yes, and are you enough to have a white one? I have seen all of yours back at Lindrow and they are all black no good true."

183

Pwepwe is titillated by all this, which she finds hilariously funny. She is not delighted, however, by her brother Lohai's visit to us. He apparently wants to tell us about a *singsing* in February that he is sure we will not want to miss. But he really came to get ten pounds from Pwepwe (she is disgruntled about it because she is trying to save money to buy a sewing machine, but she will not deny his request).

*January 15.* Still at the Traveling Officer's Quarter, living out of suitcases, troubled with primus stoves that don't work and a refrigerator that has broken down. Lokes and his helper know that but they keep using it as if it were working. They put the butter and milk in it and serve rancid butter and sour milk next morning.

I work on language with a man of LaPahan. He is being punished for not paying his taxes by having to work on the roads in Lorengau. In the meantime, we share this domicile with travelers and have so far put up teachers in transit, a posts-and-telegraphs man, a German mechanic, a German senior draftsman and a man from the Treasury Department. And also one young Australian schoolteacher whose parents requested that he be examined by a Territory Administration psychiatrist since he married his native wife. (He now owns a certificate of sanity.) His inter-racial marriage included new notions about wealth in the marriage exchange. Initial layout from the teacher to her family had to be 1,425 pounds Australian; however, he gave them 250 pounds which they ogled and gladly took. They married both according to her village customs and also according to his. Eventually they had to leave the village, because his in-laws plagued him constantly for shorts or *laplaps*, or food or money and were taking all that he earned. When they learned that he was planning to leave with his wife, her relatives did all in their power to get *her* to leave *him*, and reported him to authorities as responsible for the death of their premature baby. Burden of proof was on him, and he had to disinter the corpse, etc. They now live in another place, where he teaches, and is concerned about the future of his small daughter as a "hapcas" (P.E. for half-caste). "Europeans" and natives alike thought this marriage was a stupid disaster, thoughtless of him as regards the future of his children, not only because he married a native but a *bush kanaka tru*, not even one who was educated.

# Paliau at the "Center"

It is well known that many of Paliau's followers believe that he has supernatural powers. Some who have opposed him are certain that some misfortunes that followed were due to Paliau's wrath having visited them and their families.  Apparently, some students from here attending the government schools in the Territory went to Lutheran services, since there was no Paliau church and feared that the spirit of Paliau would know and would punish them.  A Manus student in Lae who felt he had done something wrong was tormented by the spirit of Paliau over this wrong.

Paliau does take credit for everything good that has happened in Manus and even the Territory, saying that he started it all with his idea of the Council.  He even seems to want to take credit for the Gospels in the manner in which he cites no authority but Christ Himself and how he, Paliau, related Gospel teaching to the everyday economic and moral problems of the native.  Many of the improved attitudes that he takes credit for, though not all, were results of Australia's changing attitude towards the territories because of pressure from the United Nations, and perhaps Australia's own changing ideological emphases and balance-sheet analyses.  He does not take credit for things that are happening *now* that are reverberations of the Australian changing role, as for example, the discontinuation of an education course for European teachers, a reduced budget for education, and a lowering of salaries for native workers.  Some changes were due to the Paliau movement; e.g., meeting the demand for government schools instead of Mission schools, and having some voice in government through the South Coast Council.

# A Conversation in Sori Language

The conservation takes place (between Pwepwe and Sa'apa, indicating linguistic and cultural change.  Sa'apa relies on the Administration's boat, the Sunam, for transportation; he is concerned about the children's schooling and what his "name" should now officially become.  Such topics require loan words from the language of the contact culture.

P:  *Pwa'apwa ahu tineng tu ariey ari maneng*
    Pwa'apwa the two mother of him stay on top (or) they
    come down (Are Pwa'apwa and his mother at their
    place up there or have they come down here?)

S:  *Ari maneng*
    they come down

P:  *Ahu maneng ana apihe*
    the two come down (at what) time

S:  *A maneng ana mwiinyeng ana payap*
    Come down (at) yesterday (at) afternoon

P:  *Dyeu bwe ire aley ahu bweye.*
    I like to go to see the two (that's all).
    *Dyeu dihisip hey dyipeh alangow masaruwang*
    I one that's all I miss events a lot.
    *ma dyeu pa la bwey*
    so I (neg) go (neg) (Since I am the only one here I
    pass up a lot of things. I cannot go.)

S:  *Munow iro alebwey ho nao'oy matarop*
    we here maybe all children three
    *sang aho bari "selim" ho ara oh apising*
    road of all concerning sending (P.E.) all go place no
    good.
    *munow letu na tandro "Sunam," "Sunam"*
    we stay to wait the "Sunam," "Sunam"
    *na may, abo. ire bwey? hi narip*
    it goes, alright. It goes, no? It comes.
    *nanyaong "copra" dyeu na "selim" ho masip*
    to fetch copra (P.E.). I send all them together
    *narip bwe munow masip narip. dyeu na bo*
    (they) go not we altogether go. I work at
    *"tinktink" nasap a "pilay" na "kamap"*
    thinking (P.E.) a small "feast" (P.E.) comes up (P.E.)
    (We remain to await the Sunam. *When it* goes, alright
    we'll go then. It does go, doesn't it? It has to come
    here to fetch the copra. I could send them altogether
    but they wouldn't go unless we can all go together. I
    think a small feast is coming up.)

P:  *Mane "day" a "skul" Ba'abiep abo ho*
    suppose the day (P.E.) of school (P.E.) (is) near alright
    *matarop ara wa ara abo "skul", bwey "day" apihey
    mwa'asing*
    three go now (they) go along school, not "day" not yet
    (it's) good (If it's close to the day the three have to go
    to school they must go. But if it's not close to that
    day, it's good.)

S:  *eh he. dyeu ari (domonay) pater. hi aneu ala Kavieng*
    yes. I go (thought) the Priest (P.E.) he now go
    Kavieng
    *Bwey hi atu. hi na "wasim"*

not he stop.  me he Baptize (P.E.)
*hi na tapey ahang bari ahang Katolik*
he puts name of him belong him name of him Catholic
*ahang oh api la pi'isang*
name of "the place" it goes like what?  (Yes, I think
the Priest won't stay but will go to Kavieng.  He
baptizes one and gives a Catholic name.  And then
what does one do with the name of one's clan and/or
patriline?)

P:  *ahang oh mu atop ahang lobwa'oh*
name of place you put name of patriline
*Amu ire yi, aha bwatumbumu*
of you (people) it goes along the ancestors
*bade'e oh mane tapap naso'onga lobwa'oh*
the origin place suppose you and I call out the patriline
(You keep both the name of the clan and the patriline.
You are called and can call yourselves by both.)

S:  *Arua.  dyeu api bo "tinktink" api*
it stops.  I might work "thinkthink" (it) might
*láyi dyeu a'ap sip aha haama abo.*
go with it I find one name of man alright (It shall be.  I
might think of a name for a man that might go with
other names.)
*bwey ay bwey api la pi'isawa.  dyeu ari*
no oh it might go how?  I lose
*lamani na sap ho haama a munow*
"finish" a little.  All men belonging to us (are)
*Labaanai hi ari nyaong aha Laba'anai*
Laba'anai he took finish the name Laba'anai
*Lemo ari gisey Lemo abwey yem*
Lemo took finish Lemo it's finish now
*api la aha seng dyeu tana bwey wa*
he goes by what name I don't know now

Oh no, how might it go?  I'm a little lost.  All the men
of our group are Labanai.  Those were names that were
taken (and cannot be changed).  What name he goes by
now, I don't know.

# Romances Abroad Resolved

*January 25.*  We move into the house at the Council Center even
though it is not finished.

And, at last, continuity on the Romance of Mesian, (for she did eventually marry a man who was her family's choice.) She comes to visit us. She is here because her "husband's family" has come from Baluan to take him to catch a plane for Rabaul. She tells Pwepwe that she is sad on Baluan. Why? Because the place has too many stones and it is hard to walk. Because her husband treats her badly, does not care when she does not feel well, and even invited his girlfriend to a dinner that Mesian had to cook. He simply told Mesian that this was his girlfriend and that he expected her to act towards her in a civil manner. She is never out of sight of her in-laws. If they go to work in the garden she has to go work with them. If they stay home, she has to stay home with them. The food on Baluan is "terrible" and Mesian asks Pwepwe to give her some rice and a toothbrush for old times' sake. Tara of the Baripeo society told Pwepwe that he knows Mesian's husband well; it is no secret that he intends to keep the boy Tcholai and send Mesian back to Bunai to her family. All this, of course, is a source of satisfaction to many.

*January 27.* Visitors are the Australian teacher and his Papuan wife, as well as Lomot, who comes with her brother and her father, Kilepak. Lomot has left her husband on Jowan after many threats to do so. She tells of her unmitigated misery in that marriage and she has lost a good deal of weight. Lomot's laziness and devil-may-care attitude cannot sit well with his family, for husband So'ong will later join her in Pere village. It is not usual for the young husband to follow his wife to live in her village, which gains "a man" while his village loses one. I had noted that So'ong's family had not paid a bride price for Lomot, which must have indicated their displeasure and low expectation.

*February 2.* Ted and I (accompanied by Carleton Gajdusek who has been living with us for a week) film the Show and the *singsing* for the dedication of the new native society store. Some Australians tell me to take Carleton on as guest, as they have wearied of his unexpected arrivals and expectations. ("He is American, *you* take him on.") Our films of the *singsing* include the Pitilu women dancing on canoes, the bringing of food from the canoes for a feast, and the Lebei ritual dance drama of the *marsalai*, which they had performed for us in Lebei village.

*February 3.* Ted and Carleton Gajdusek go to Ndrossun and Sapon to collect 65 blood samples. CG's idea is to start with the small children, after which adults would be ashamed to refuse. Have everyone hold vials, since then no one would leave with your property.  Do it all quickly with no explanation and little talking.  Informed consent for the third world; I don't like it, but then my advice is not solicited.  Since I am not participating in this particular white man's burden of medical "scientific" discovery, I spend the day transcribing tapes on "cargo cult" material.

*February 18.*  A visit from Mr. Ian MacDonald of the copra-marketing board from Port Moresby.  Traveling on the Malaita, he stopped here to talk with Paliau, to tell him that Manus could and should be producing more copra.  He tells me that the Indonesians are not selling it now, and thinks they are eating all their coconuts.  There are various grades of copra, and it is a question of balancing production to meet the types of demand.  Buyers who want lower-grade smoked copra, as for example, for detergents, want only that.  Copra is still in demand for the production of margarine because of its high melting point.  With Mr. MacDonald came Sili of Bipi.  Nyawaseu, now working for me, asks him how much longer the Northwest wind will last.  Sili replies, "If it blows hard it won't last long, but if it goes easy it will last a long time."  (The wage-fund theory of weather, as the rent theorists in economics, as Freud with the amount of emotions one has to spend:  The psychic unity of mankind!)

*February 19.*  Paliau has often said that he will use any means to get villages to join the Council and today we have had a good example.  Paapi from Mokerang has come to visit while Paliau is here.  He comes to tell Paliau that *Luluai* Potihin has determined that most in the village do want to join and he wants to do something about it, let those opposed do as they wish.  (This is a most unusual attitude in Manus policy-making, in which unanimity *is* sought, courted and its lack assures failure of an enterprise.  A lack of consensus paralyzes any event).

Paapi reminds me, as I already know, that the *tultul*, Pokumbu, and his relatives are opposed for reasons that they do not clarify, though I think it is because of their Catholicism.  Paliau reminds Paapi that Mokerang has been remiss about joining the Council, but in Port Moresby, does he know what they say about Mokerang?  (No, what?)  "Well," Paliau says smugly, "they say that you people are like the Lapangai at New Hanover Island who want to buy the American President Johnson, you are all *that* ignorant."  "And," he adds looking at me, "like that business about Wapei at Rambutjo."

I find this oblique reference to cargo cult activity interesting.  He was referring to the cargo cult period when Wapei went into trance to visit the world of the Dead and reported to the constituency what had to be done so that the "cargo" might be sent by the dead ancestors (Schwartz 1962). I often wonder if the native Seventh Day Adventists are as naive as their missionaries assume when they refuse to do something or demur from a church activity by saying they will stay at home and wait for Christ. Some have told me that they wonder why the missionaries are busy going about the world converting others when they know Christ is coming. Missionaries should stay home and await the event.

*February 27.* Dinner with Peg and Cyril King. Discussion: "feelings among Australians about the upcoming independence for the territory of Papua New Guinea." The Kings do not like the idea that their children are thinking about a future in the territory. Richard, for example, wants to be a Patrol officer. They want their children to think of assimilating back into Australian society; but childhood and adolescence up here are not a preparation for that in any sense.

Some are asking us what kind of radio programs they should be beaming to the natives. Several tell us of the feeling of "defeatism" among Europeans in Port Moresby, where there are 28,000 people of whom 23,000 are indigenous. The latter feel, or the whites think they feel, an unmistakeable hostility towards all whites. They ask us if this is true in Manus and we feel impelled to say that *we* have not experienced any hostility, in fact we have the impression that the Manus would be distressed to be abandoned by the carriers of "Euro-American culture."

# Perils in Paradise and Their Remedies

*March 3.* Nyawaseu is now taking care of the baby, as I await the results of Pwepwe's biopsy, to learn if she indeed does have leprosy. Medical opinions here vary. It is interesting that a New Guinea physician trained in Fiji thinks she does, and an Australian physician thinks she does not. Both tell me they have sent eighteen leprotamous lepers from Manus to Analawa, just last week. The tuberculoid type are treated here. Most of the leprosy in Manus is confined to the villages of Lessau, Nihon, Salien, and Jowan. I note that these are all Lindrow speakers.

The days go on and I work on Dictionaries and tape transcriptions, and on linguistics and kinship with a wandering Trobriander. I also work with Sili on the Bipi language.

*March 14.* Church in the morning. I am horrified at the Catechist from Hus who harangues the congregation about Lent, and threatens their "gluttony" and pleasure-seeking with leprosy. He uses the example of a recent member who was sent to the leper colony at Analawa near Kavieng. This man, he reminds his listeners, once did a sort of silly dance step on the church lawn, and furthermore he was a bit too fond of beer. His final shot, "So you do not like to pray, my friends? Perhaps you will find plenty of time to pray later, with the fathers at Analawa." On the way out I meet Norman Dietsch, who tells me that Paliau has given him permission to teach non-sectarian Christianity at the church in Bunai. He will go there to give lessons every two weeks.

*March 18.* Dr. Kahu Sugoho brings me the report on Pwepwe: "Histologically, the skin biopsy shows occasional tubercle-like focal collections of inflammatory cells in the dermis together with a more diffuse infiltration of the upper dermis. Leprosy (dimorphous type)." Kahu tells me that this is the infectious type and that she must be taken to the hospital and then to Analawa "as soon as there are five or six others. We wait for a group so they do not feel too lonely on the boat."

Tears for Pwepwe, but also for my baby, who I am told, will have to be checked every three months for the next twenty years.

*March 19.* Michel Gaston Baelen is a medical assistant who is doing fine detective work on leprosy in the territory and has vast experience. He wants to see Pwepwe as soon as she returns from Sori. Michel had been on a medical mission to the Western Islands, then travelled to Bipi and covered almost every village down the North Coast to Bundralis and Liap. He found 180 suspect cases and did as many biopsies. The heaviest concentration of leprosy is among the Lindrow speakers, he confirmed to me. They were, until rather recently, inhabitants of the interior bush in Manus. Some of his leprosy cases (about 20) were children from the ages of three to ten. Buka is another area of concentration of leprosy. As yet, no "Europeans," but yes, last year there were 13 persons of "mixed race," as they say here.

I drive to Lugos to visit the Dietsches since I cannot think of anything except poor Pwepwe on the boat of sorrow. Norm tells me that recently 16 persons from Lugos were sent to Analawa. Particularly touching were the young boys who were just finishing school and were looking with great hopes to promised jobs. Several of them sobbed and wept bitterly. Adan cries for Pwepwe as he sees her getting off the Sunam; I pick her up with the car, but I am unable to tell her.

Michel examines her, and as we speak in French, to her great confusion and apprehension, he says she is the non-infectious type and I should keep her on as a nurse. I cannot, I protest, and Michel says that I have "a Biblical attitude toward leprosy," and that I do not "appreciate the leper as a social problem." I tell him my attitude may be irrational, but I will not apologize for it. He is stuck with it. I ask him to tell her that she is non-infectious but that it is better that she not take care of the baby at this time. He does and then says, "Do you know the name of your sickness?" She replies with much embarrassment "no."

"It is *sick tomato*."

That is what they call leprosy, but of course they do not recognize it in all its stages and forms. (After I returned to the States I learned that Pwepwe's "biopsy" was in error and that she did *not* have leprosy! Still, unfortunately, many others were not in error.) Twenty-seven more cases from Lugos of suspected leprosy are brought in for biopsies. Michel shows me several cases so that I will be able to recognize the stages.

I find some people who have come in from Sori and we discuss the death of a man from Lebei, one whom I drove to the hospital shortly before his death. I tell them that the doctor thought it was a brain tumor and I explain what that is. Yes, they agree, that was undoubtedly it. And perhaps I would be interested to know what caused it? By all means, I would. Well, begins Lukas, it was sorcery. The white man has three ways of finding sickness and what causes it: those x-rays, that way of finding "sick tomato" (leprosy), which is to look and to cut and then look again, and thirdly to find that one has a fever by putting that glass stick in the mouth. But, these things do not tell you what *kind* of sick it is, and then you have to know yourself that it is *sick belong ground*, or sorcery. Nrayah died of that, and with him it was like this: he fished too much. He, a bushman, of all people, going in for too much fishing. Well, when he went back to the bush, the bush spirits smelled the smell of fish on him and were very angry with him. Therefore, that thing in his head which I described so correctly made him faint, tremble, spit and die. They all shake their heads in agreement and hope that they have enlightened me. Do I understand? Yes, I nod, I do.

Michel shows me three cases of leprosy. One young boy of 14 has the leprotamous type, infectious, and will be shortly dispatched to Analawa. He has nodules on ears and arms. I later learn that he is from the Lowaya section of Bunai village. Another man has the non-infectious tuberculoid type. Also from Bunai, but from the section Yiru. The third is a sturdy healthy-looking young man from Malei Bay. He spent two years or so at Analawa and became non-infectious, but then came back to Manus and did not take his medications for three years. He is now infectious. The dimorphous type can become infectious, and without medication it often does.

*March 24.* A visit from Oto Sinda of Pujow. Now about 27, for a man of his age he has a great deal of traditional knowledge. He likes my interest in such knowings and wants to tell me of yet another divination technique, one which his father practiced. You roll a leaf (the kind chewed with betel) as though you were rolling a cigarette. You say "*lulu*" and then ask your question. You might ask this, "Is there an opossum up that tree?" Then you put the leaf in your mouth. If there is a small amount of red saliva from the leaf and the betel lime inside the leaf, that means that that the opossum is there. (If you chew betel, lime and leaf, you should have red saliva.) If the leaf buckles it means there is no opossum.

One consults the betel lime by sniffing the stick with lime on it. If your nose gets "buggered up" that means you had better not go to your appointment because a man or a bush devil will kill you. Sinda himself wants to tell me about a magic formula that was worked on him by his father. Since that time he has had unusual powers of knowing what will occur. This magic is called *kau*. Hung about an unmarried boy's neck is a *wakey*. It consists of a bundle of two bones (from the back of the neck) of the *melissa* (fish), and a little grass that has been picked and dried in the sun. Then you take some paint made from red earth, and add coconut oil. This is added to the grass and the bones of the *melissa*. All this is wrapped up in the grass with grass wound around it; then the rope is noosed about the neck. (Before that, the boy is beaten with it on both knees, both elbows, on breast and back.) Sinda still had this magic *wakey* until a mother's brother of his from Bipi asked for it and he was obliged to give it to him. He could not refuse his *keli*. But when he had the *wakey* he could tell whether an opossum was up a tree, whether he would shoot a wild pig, whether a member of his family who was far away had fallen ill. The magic is very weak now, he admits, but he still feels it. When he had the *wakey* in his possession he felt it quite strong. Through this *wakey* the father predicted that Sinda would not marry before he (the father) died. It happened thus.

His father had told him that the right side of the body is always good news and the left side is bad news ("it breaks true right down the middle"). He still feels messages on any part of his body. On his breasts he feels news about his children. Feelings on the left thigh or the left breast are signs of sickness to come upon his children. ("Feeling?"). It is as though he is pricked by a sharp object. If the fingers or palms of the hand are thus "pricked" it means "stick." Such a sensation on the right hand means oar of a canoe, i.e., some friends are coming to visit you. A similar sensation on the left hand means that such an object is digging a grave for a man who is dead.

If tears come to your eyes for no reason, that means that a man has died. Sinda asks me to recall the day I drove him to the hospital here in Lorengau. He had had a pricking sensation in his left foot. The pain shot up and that meant he would be sick; had it shot sideways, it would have meant that another man would have fallen ill.

Yes, the *wakey* had weakened, but he still has it in his blood. No, it cannot be used to work evil. It is only for knowledge, but now that it is weakened, he cannot tell anyone when death will take them. Any questions about death will not be replied to by the needle-like prick. There will be no answer.

It is fitting for Oto Sinda to come and remind me that the "center" is still the traditional belief systems, even in Lorengau.

*April 13.* I am asked to testify on the "Papitalai Mission Case." This concerned a claim by the Catholic Church that a native had sold them land. Reluctant to do so, I am assured that no one will be angry with me. All I will be asked is what I learned about what constituted "agreements" on the part of the native groups involved (as though that is not a powderkeg). The Counsel for the Catholic Mission approachs me to say that I shouldn't feel bad about the way it turns out, for he himself advised his clients, the Mission folk, against fighting this case and told them, "If you lose, you lose face. If you win, you lose the good will of the people." Also, he had spoken with the German fathers who knew something of the transactions and said that the Mission claim was not legitimate.

It proves to be a defeat for the Mission. The only land awarded them is the land on which they have buildings and on which coconut trees are planted. The Lands Commissioner rules that "there is no clear evidence that the Mission acquired anything" and therefore it is allowed title to non-contested land only.

On the land involving a section, the counsel for the Mission makes some men an offer to split the land in dispute, half for the

Mission, half for the claimants. This offer is refused outright. The Mission had no witnesses over this supposed land transaction. For the Papitalai case they had one witness who had been a very small child during the supposed transaction. He wore an enormous cross on his chest during the cross-examination. In these two cases, the Catholic Church "lost" 1000 hectares.

*April 14.* Paliau goes to Bunai to take credit for the two cases that spelled a sort of defeat for the Catholic Mission in Manus. He claims credit for the generosity that in the above case gives the Mission more land than they thought they would get. Although they lost 500 claimed hectares here, the Lands Commissioner gave the Mission a large sago swamp close to the Mission buildings. The Commissioner did this because he said the natives were terribly "bigheaded about it all." Paliau says that he wielded influence for generosity (?) so that the natives wouldn't be acting too "cultish" about the dispute. The litigating "natives" tell me that it always pays to make a not totally just claim of absurd proportions because it will lead to a compromise that gets you something in the end anyway. Both they and the Mission made absurd claims and they were both clever to do so. Since I attended all the court sessions, I know that the Commissioner awarded the swamp lands for reasons he made explicit, and actually it came as quite a shock to the native claimants, as it was explained to them in Pidgin. Yet Paliau and the claimants tell me how it happened through *their* generosity and interventions as though I had not been there.

*April 29.* A meeting featuring the UN Representatives from France, USA, Great Britain and Liberia. Paliau is not present, having been sent to Australia to study the procedures of parliament. However, he has sent a "paper" to the UN stating that Manus still has needs: docks, roads, schools, bridges, etc. He mentions that all these things have been promised, but never delivered.

The UN representatives tell them they are here to listen to their complaints and will they please come close to the platform. That leaves us (me and some Lutheran Missionaries and other "Europeans") out of acoustic range. I learn later, however, from some of the interpreters, that Sili of Bipi brought one general complaint that natives are not paid enough and that not enough money gets into the hands of natives. Joseph Malai talked of the necessity for secondary industries such as copra processing, but when pressed, he was not about to explain just how he thought this might be done. Peter Pomat of Nrossun was interested in practical education after school hours for the young.

Home again to write my final "letter from the field" to Margaret.

Lorengau, Manus

Dear Margaret,

Your letter arrived today and I will send it off to Ted who is in Bunai. I test people here from the groups we want to concentrate on everytime one turns up, and fortunately they space themselves charitably. You might like to know our *modus operandi* in Lorengau: Lokes and Pwepwe are well-trained (JK, too, and he is here most of the time waiting for Ted to ask something of him). They quickly tell us when they know of someone in town who belongs to a group we are interested in (of course we keep them briefed daily on our lacunae). I never fail to ask any native I meet where he is from, and try to learn whether he is worthwhile for linguistic work or knowledgeable for ethnographic inquiry or myths. The trip in the Holden seems to be enough compensation for the informant. Pwepwe keeps me informed of canoes that come in (conveniently "moored" at Council Center waters) and of likely-looking informants. Then there are the *Kaunsils* themselves who come to meetings here at the Center, and some happy opportunities, such as being able to check my Baluan Grammatical sample with Mwembup while in Peri, with Tuain the *Kaunsil* of Baluan, who is older and wiser (and with whom one would work *in* Baluan).

Another stroke of luck was to get about ten hours of Bogandi, the *luluai* of Lessau on tape. We would have considered going to Lessau to work with him. (He never comes here. . . . but he came in now to bring in his son, who has leprosy and must be sent to the colony at Analawa). He is North Coast Usiai. . . not really originally from the coast at all, of course, as their histories and myths will tell you. It was particularly interesting for me to get his version (probably original version) of some of the stories that I got from Sori informants. It proved what I had suspected, that the Sori are great demythologizers. And very adept at it too, sticking closely to all the events that are factual, omitting the transfigurations of snakes into men and that sort of thing. (Of great interest to Bultman and other intellectualizing Protestants). I've tested about 12 Sori here thus far, which would save Ted about four days in a testing program if he goes to Sori for the Feast of Pahung and to do some testing.

I have tested several Usiai in the past several days, and the results so strikingly differ from Manus and Matankor groups that if Ted is getting such results among the Bunai Usiai we will perhaps have found the "something" to formulate personality differences. Great preoccupation with design, not just sorting: on the Weigel. . . . dramatic hesitancy (almost hysterical hesitancy and fear of being wrong and untouched and unmoved by reassurances that there is not right and wrong in performance. This, the "Manus" we've tested seem to accept with no qualms) BUT very imaginative Holtzmans (relatively, of course). These are just a few indicators, and possibly my brief encounter on testing Usiai will not be substantiated by Ted's experience, but we'll see.

All this work has a kind of drudgery to it. . . would not have been congenial to my early temperament, (which time and disenchantments have tempered considerably). . . yet I have learned to live happily with it and even *like* it. (I consider this one of my valuable assets on assignments in collaborative work, though from a personal point of view it has been a dissipation of what were clearly my youthful talents. . . of course I can and do "blame" my parents and their (our) culture for discouraging virtuousity in women). If I do not write so frequently it is because Ted writes to you about the state of affairs and our work, and whatever I might have to say would be duplication. I did write you last week though, sending some clippings from the S. Pacific Post on Baby Farms and a story on you in the "*Nius belong yumi.*" I thought the enclosures might interest you and I hope they weren't lost.

Adan is just fine here, doesn't seem to pick up the viruses he always had in the villages. He speaks all the time now and you would find him at a much more interesting stage than when you saw him. JK insists on teaching him Manus (*ko to kay, okume, okala* and all that). He learns from JK especially because he is very fond of him. Debbi is very happy at Ascham School with her math and finds her new math teacher "competent and very interesting. We slave for her. We will be first-rate mathematicians."

I will stay with Caroline while in Sydney. She seems very sincere in wanting me to.

My dearest love to you,
Lola


*May 22.* From a group of visitors, I learn that most of the natives at the "UN meeting" were also out of acoustic range, as was I. Still they want to know from me what transpired and I tell them what their "complaints" presumably are, as told to UN representatives. They all express the view that nothing at all will come of it and thus echo Potihin, the *luluai* of Mokerang, who had said,

"What the white men say and do, they say and do for themselves alone."

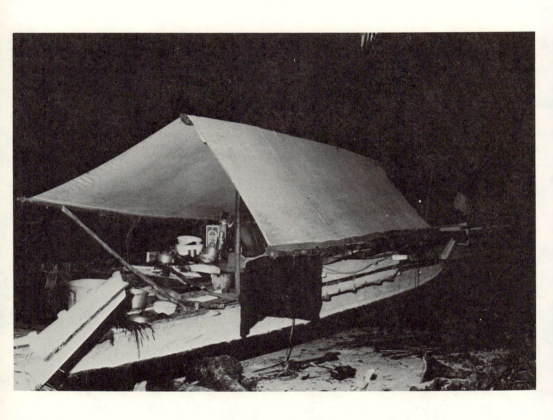

*A canoe transformed into living quarters.*

*The moving of Pere Village.*

# Epilogue

As I left the field, it was among the Manus Tru, mostly of Pere, that the directions of change were most evident, when present at all. One saw this beginning to occur in the marriages and exchanges between lineages. People moving about the islands and the territory with greater ease tended occasionally to marry others, of whom the families could not approve, causing many problems. The foregoing narrative alludes to several such liaisons, with their attendant cultural misunderstandings and often unhappy sequelae. Still, inter-racial as well as inter-group marriages had begun and continued to occur throughout the territory; only a few from the "European" or native groups found such unions an "outrage." Some natives voiced a sense of disillusion about the ignoring of educational levels by some white men who married native women; they felt that no one's rules were being adhered to, and this in itself was objectionable. Some "Europeans" appeared to object to "role reversal," as in the case of a white woman who married and supported her native husband on her salary from the Administration.

Money was beginning to enter the affinal exchanges in the "payback-through-time." Known as a *pilay* or *perey* (P.E.), a feast by cross-cousins for arranged marriages featured exchanges "responding to" a big feast with two hundred pounds Australian, rather than the native "hard currency" of dogs' teeth and shell money. When you give money, it is viewed as getting goods of some sort that you want. ("Suppose you would like to have a lamp. Well, you have only to express this wish out loud so that someone can hear you, then when you come with your money for the "exchange" at the feast, someone will have brought a lamp there for you.") Some individuals, such as Kilepak think of it as a way of realizing a profit. *But*, this incipient money economy is still linked to exchanges of goods between lineages as described earlier. There is an awareness that "Europeans" do not use their money in this way (i.e., that we depersonalize both marketplace and money), but there is not an eagerness to relinquish traditions of exchange and gifts. There are "court" cases over the accountability for money, but the accent is on accountability, not money. It might as well have been coconuts, as an ancient case in Sori demonstrated.

Young people have begun to go to work as teachers, nurses or clerks at other places in New Guinea, and it may be recalled here that Kilepak and others expressed to me that this is all the Manus are getting out of all this "progress": losing its best young people "to the *kanaka* world around them." They are losing resources for the exchanges, they are losing resources that might make Manus "come up" in the world.

Shortly before I left Manus, the Australian Administration had been trying various educational methods to combat cargo cults. Some natives had been taken to Australia to see how objects that they had requested from the ancestors to be left as "cargo" were actually manufactured. Showing these "cultural exchange" natives ore in the ground, steel from the mills, factories in various stages of turning out finished products was of no avail. The usual response was that some part of the secret was still being withheld by the Australians: "How did you people put the ore in the ground in the first place? What are the other little secrets you are keeping for yourselves?"

In viewing our films, Pere villagers found comedy in making comparisons between themselves and certain other groups in the world. Films made in Africa (the purpose was to show how a village built its own maternity clinic) did not have the desired effect. They were amused by masked figures, dancing, costumes, feasts, processions of women with pots on their heads, and anything *kanaka*-like, all of which provoked uncontrolled laughter. I had no better luck than the Australians trying to get some reflexive thoughts from them on cultural difference or similarity.

# On the Nature of Culture Change

In *New Lives for Old* Margaret Mead put forth generalizations about cultural transformation on the South Coast villages of Pere and

Bunai based on her observations from June to December 1953, and from her interpretations of Ted Schwartz' field research from January to June of 1954. What she had noted about the Manus during a burst of cargo cult activity and incipient changes in political behavior was meant to come under the rubric of contributions of the Manus experience that had "implications for the world" (Mead 1975:435). After expressing concern that (what was in her view) a precocious episode as exhibited by the Manus Tru might not be generalizable to the rest of the world (Mead 1975:435—436), she then decided that it was, and made the following "points":

- The Manus Tru had a desire for complete and total change
- Rapid culture change is not only possible but desirable
- Changes were made by entire units (kinship sets) and therefore no individual felt alienated, lonely or disoriented.

Within the narrative that precedes this epilogue I have described processes of choosing or rejecting cultural elements from both the native culture and Western civilization, as I observed them among the Manus Tru during the period of my fieldwork there. The expressed attitudes toward change differed for the Manus Tru, for they spoke of themselves as those who were spearheading change, but the *actual choices* for traditional behavior or culture change did not differ markedly from the two Matankor groups (the Sori and the Mokerang) with which I spent most of my research time. There were certainly factional differences of opinion among the Manus Tru concerning their cargo cult and political experiences and (as Lokes related to Pwepwe) many of them looked back with some shame and regret.

I have let both Matankor and Manus Tru speak for themselves, i.e., I did not "edit" or generalize and more often than not, they themselves defined the frames in which information was given to me. I have tried to be as conscious as possible of interpretations and have tried to bracket them as such, in full knowledge that one can only approximate such consciousness. These people wanted much from the outside world, and wanted to contribute, but they did not want to lose their traditions and what they considered of value in them. On this point my observations and interpretations differ widely from Mead's, even for the Manus Tru of Pere village. In concrete situations, many described in detail and expressed their awareness of the cost-benefits of taking on the ways of "Europeans," and appeared confident that "Europeans did not know *everything*." They were not, for example, eager to give up the notion that mind and nature (to paraphrase Gregory Bateson) constitute a "necessary unity" (Bateson 1979), nor to concede that Westerners know more about childbirth, for, to them, all groups have been proficient at that from the beginning.

The system perturbation caused by new religions or new European-style political movements inevitably had the effect, after a period of meta-stability, of driving some members of the group back to the stability and comfort and predictability of the native systems in such areas. The period immediately after Independence in 1975 drove many Manus Tru back to Paliau and drove both Paliau and his followers back to his comfortable and familiar cargo cult politics. Paliau is now 70 years of age and his adversaries are no longer the Australians but the new native government, established as a result of the Independence. Perhaps from this new antithesis there will be a new synthesis, but there will not be a new creative paradigm for the body politic.

The intellectual world was not bereft of historical interpretations of how cultures change before the advent of American anthropologists of the 1920's, or Mead's brief forays (see, for example, Mead 1975:455−457) into past events in world culture history. Still, small aggregates of little encounters on the edges of what is culturally familiar to us can certainly produce "patterns of culture" in the head of the investigator, especially one who feels obliged to solve problems of great import with solipsistic input from one's field experiences. (To the intellectual credit of our Manus Tru friends, even those most active in the cargo cult and political movement, they gave little credence to Mead's assertion to them that "the world wanted to learn from them.")

The mere act of doing fieldwork, being involved as an observer *and* an observer-observed, is in itself a de-contextualization of what one is to study, and therefore cannot later lead to analyses devoid of this recognition. Because fieldwork can complement but not replace reflective reasoning (enlightened as this "reasoning" may be by "training") the object of our studies must remain the disentangling of the "mappings of mind on mind" (Romanucci-Ross 1980a). Nor can we afford the Enlightenment view that affections and passions are "perturbations of the mind" (Cassirer 1966:105). I have followed Mannheim's admonition for the social sciences: that method has to "make explicit what is *de facto* going on in living research" (Mannheim 1959:37), and I strive to show how and why the groups and individuals in my field investigations "stand in different truths" to use Hiedigger's phrase (Heidigger 1967:14).

As I indicated in the Introduction, John Kilepak came to Monterey, California in the summer of 1979, sponsored by Barbara Roll. From her home there he came to La Jolla, and it was of great interest to me to observe Kilepak's encounter with the "twentieth century." In no way did what he had experienced in *New Lives for Old* prepare him for what he found here. For what does it mean to say of cultures in the South Pacific that they have come from the Stone Age to the Twentieth Century in one generation? Or that they have "evolved" within a fraction of a human lifetime that span of development that required centuries or millenia for the Western World, as Mead asserted? How long does it take for a costume change from a *laplap* to shorts or skirts? To handle a shilling rather than a stick of tobacco or a pram of shell money? To prefer tinned fish and tinned processed meats to native fare? To speak Pidgin in addition to their native tongue? (Or for that matter, for some to add English to the linguistic repertoire?)

Such "cultural transformations" have been witnessed by many throughout Melanesia, Micronesia and Polynesia, but such changes have hardly qualified for the adjective "startling;" nor would any have characterized these transformations as "crossing the widest distance between cultural levels that had ever been known in human history from a recent past in the stone age to the electronic age" (Mead 1975:x, xi). To be requested to vote and to comply does not mean that one understands the electoral process, as has been illustrated several times in this volume. To be enticed into consumer spending does not mean a "country" understands the concept "balance of trade." Tuvalu, for example, exports copra and depends on supplies flown in monthly, with a disastrous balance of trade (De Beer 1983:12). Nauru has one of the highest per capita incomes ($40,000 for every man, woman and child) in the world; such felicity is achieved through exporting its own soil which is pure phosphate and which should run out in less than twenty years. Food and water have become a problem but it is shipped in from Australia. (Trumbull 1977:224−226). We have witnessed some pathetic attempts, after nuclear testing, of American officials trying to explain to certain Micronesian groups why they could not return for many years to their native islands, and why, after they did return, they were not to eat the coconuts.

Many South Pacific cultures have preceded Manus into the twentieth century, just as rapidly as Manus, in Mead's sense, and a good deal earlier. We have ample documentation of the political, economic and medical sequelae for those erstwhile primitive cultures and island paradises that had the questionable fortune to be dragged into the twentieth century. More often than not, it was a responsible journalist rather than an anthropologist who took the trouble to record and analyze the tragic consequences in the history of exploitation and the emerging search for identity and pride by natives in their own traditions.

In some ways, the people of Manus, to my mind, skirted much of the moral idiocy that manifests itself in some interpretations of change in the twentieth century. I refer here to the notion espoused by many that to ignore history is to repeat it. Where this notion came from is hard to guess, for we know from the world of praxis that to repeat and to be reminded of an event is to reinforce the possibility of its happening again. (Child abusers were abused as children, a learned "art form," so to speak.) Potihin, *luluai* of Mokerang told me of warfare in the old days and added that children were hidden in the houses, as I might have guessed. (For safety?) No, so they did not learn that such cruelty could be perpetrated and endured.

In the 1980's, two trends in Manus are indicative of what I consider the "recursiveness" of the traditional culture in culture change. In curative practices, once again the ghosts of the dead are being asked for the cause and the cure of illness, and all of this within a socio-moral frame. Secondly, cargo cult activity is being activated once more, having been revived several years after Independence. Paliau is rewriting his theology, now including notions of hearing, seeing and speaking no evil and rearranging his ritual by surrounding himself with nubile young girls dressed in white (personal communication, Ted Schwartz, 1983).

This is not to suggest that the Manus want to retreat from our century, for the ancient parable appears to apply universally; one cannot return to innocence. But with "native" disenchantments across the South Pacific came the insight that there will have to be a return to traditional identity to understand what being part of the modern world means to them for their present identity and their future.

The works of anthropologists, both here and elsewhere, are not irrelevant to such an endeavor. For it is not easier to know the self than it is to know the other. Indeed it is questionable whether one can know the self at all without knowing the other. The ability to recognize "contrasts" with a certain disengagement is a prerequisite to knowing "self" and "other" and this applies to cultures as well as to persons. A culture, as George Devereux says, is a way of being human. Can one really understand what it means to be human without knowing *all* ways of being human ?

Anthropologists have engendered skepticism when they have tried to address what some were pleased to call "universals" among "the problematic," and choosing such sites as "South Seas Laboratories" to solve these problems for everyone. Social structures and webs of relationships in such groups should never have been tapped for answers to questions that those groups never asked, as they designed such structures and relationships. Authenticity in Knowing and Being will not be extracted from interpretations based on inaccuracies of perception and translation of a culture.[1] It is for this reason that I have opted in this volume, to try to illumine a process of discovery through the encounter known as anthropological field research.

It has been suggested that what has been significantly lacking in even the most recent and enlightened of cultural descriptions is "the interaction of informant and ethnographer as 'inspectable' and as 'part of the interpretation'." Without this, neither reader nor writer will have that "explication of the interpretative pathway linking concept with interaction, or the interpreter with the actual experiential encounter" (Foster 1981:6). Such lacunae will continue unless the investigator "takes field notes" in a manner that goes well beyond the disciplines involved in his "training" in anthropology. One might begin by feeling a revulsion towards "objectifying" the other in one's analytic (moral) philosophy.

Sensation, perception, imagination, insight, inquiry and its formulation, reflection and judgment all contribute to the description of "facts." The investigator is involved, committed, engaged, and because of this there is no disjunction between "rational" problem-recognition and problem-solving and the "irrational" investigator. Illuminating the *process* of discovery has to become the most integral "core" of the anthropological enterprise if we are to avoid future resolutions of conflicting reports as incontrovertible solipsisms[2].

## NOTES

1. Roy Wagner has written insightfully on the anthropologist's manipulation through interpretation of: nature, culture, self and other (Wagner 1981).

2. The most recent attempted "resolution" in the annals of anthropological inquiry is the Freeman/Mead controversy over the nature of Samoan culture and personality. (See Brady 1983; Freeman 1983, 1984; Romanucci-Ross 1983).

# Appendix I

This is an example of *difference in numeral modifiers* from a Mokerang Irio speaker, Iyamou. After giving me some examples below, she added that she found our "straight" modifiers very inadequate. In their system one had only to give the number and the listener knew what objects were being dicussed. A casual perusal would seem to suggest otherwise, however "Straight" counting (one to ten): stones, dogs' teeth, mountains, islands, days, "moons," pigs, fingers, snakes, betel nuts, dogs, shell money are all counted "straight":

| | |
|---|---|
| sih | mawano |
| mawo | maharucholo |
| macholo | maharuo |
| maha | maharusi |
| malime | masongol |

However, if you are counting using woman = *(pihin)* or man = *(aamat)*:

| | |
|---|---|
| hamo | mawonomo |
| maamo | maharieulumo |
| machelumo | maharuumo |
| mahamo | maarusomo |
| malemo | maseol |

*laplap* = *(chalau)* or shillings:

| | |
|---|---|
| séé | mawonoé |
| mawéé | marichuluwé |
| machuluwé | maruwéé |
| mahaaé | marusuwé |
| malimeé | masongol |

canoe = (*rul*) or tree = (*perekey*):

| | |
|---|---|
| seh | malimémawonowey |
| maawey | maarichuluwey |
| machuluwey | maaruruwey |
| mahaawey | maarusuwey |
| malimewey | masongol |

knife = *mooro*

| | |
|---|---|
| haapal | mawonopal |
| maapel | maarichulupel |
| machulupel | maaruupel |
| mahaapal | maarusapal |
| malimepal | masongol |

tobacco = (P.E. *tabac*)

| | |
|---|---|
| hamwat | mawonomwat |
| maawet | maarichulumwet |
| machulumwet | maaruumwet |
| mahaamwat | maarisamwat |
| maleemwat | masongol |

leaf = (*laukey*)

| | |
|---|---|
| haukap | mawenokap |
| maakep | maarichulukep |
| machulukep | maaruukep |
| mahaakap | maarisakap |
| malimekap | masongol |

# Appendix II

*Sori Kinship Terminology* (consanguineal unless indicated as affinal)

| | | |
|---|---|---|
| F = father | D = daughter | B = brother |
| M = mother | C = child | W = wife |
| S = sister | H = husband | |
| s = son | | |

| | *Male speaking* | *Female speaking* |
|---|---|---|
| Ari | MB | MB |
| Baruey | WBC (or male married to a woman of your father's side) | (husband affinal); FSH |
| Bwaha | MBs, FSs | MBD, FSD |
| Bwatumbu | F$^3$ (and vertical infinite same as female except HF) | MMB, MMBs, MMBD, FFSs, FFSD, HF (affinal) also vertical infinite |
| Dyi Pe | BW (affinal) | BW, HS, MSsW (affinal) |
| Giriye' | FM, FS, FSD | FM, FS, FSD |
| Masawa' | SH, MSDH, WB, (affinal) | — |
| Mburu' | W (affinal) | H (affinal) |
| Na'ari | SC, MSC | — |
| Nabuso' | S, FBD, MSD, FBSD | B, FBs, MSs, FSss |
| Nadasi | B, FBs, MSs, FBss | S, FBD, MSD, SC, FSsD, HSD (affinal) |

| | | |
|---|---|---|
| *Nadyahe* | | HSs (affinal) |
| *Naru* | C, MBD, FSsC, SC, BC, WS (affinal) | C, SC, MSDC, SC, BC, HB (affinal) SC, BC, HB (affinal) |
| *Nyabarip* | MM, FBW (affinal) | MM, FBW (affinal) |
| *Nya'ana* | WF, sW (affinal) | HM, sW, HBW, HSsW, wife of *nagiriye* (affinal) |
| *Nyabwau* | MF, FF, FFB, MSH (affinal) | MF, FF, FFB, MSH (affinal) |
| *Nya'ari* | MBW (affinal) | — |
| *Papu* | MMB, SsC (this term is really a Bipi term and the Sori equivalent is *Bwatumbu*; however, it is sometimes used). | SC, FFS |
| *Sarapu* | WM (affinal) | — |
| *Tamay* | F, FB | F, FB, FSs, MSDH, HB (affinal) FSHS (affinal) |
| *Tiney* | M, MS BW (affinal) | M, MS FBW, FBSW (affinal) |

Note the following:

*Bwaha*    refers to person same sex and same generation as speaker but whose parent is of the opposite sex of speaker's parent i.e., cross-cousin.

*Nabuso'*  opposite sex from speaker, but child or grandchild of sibling of the same sex of the parent i.e., parallel cousin of opposite sex.

*Nadasi*   same sex as speaker and child or grandchild of sibling of same sex as parent ie., parallel cousin of same sex

The term *tiney* can be used for all women of the mother's side.

*Tamay*    for all the men on the "side of the man" of the brother-sister pair, *munarumwang*.

*Giriye'*   for all women of the father's side

Some reciprocals:
*Tiney* or *Tamay* — *naru*
      *Ari* — *Si'ari* or *ari*
      *Giriye'* — *Nagiriye'*
      *Bwatumbu* — *Bwatumbu*
      *nyabarip* — *nadasi*
      *nyabwauara* — *nyabwauara*
      *Bwaha* — *Bwaha*
      *mburu* — *mburu*
      *nabuso'* — *nabuso'*
      *nya'ana* — *nya'ana*


SORI #1
Sa'apoy
Residential Groups—December 25, 1963
Census to village map:
          = indicates marital relationship
          ( ) indicates patriline membership
          __  (underlined) = female
          w  = widowed
          1  = *lapun* (old person)

Person from Sori unless otherwise indicated.

All are *Luhai* except Ebei and Uwey who are *Hi'inang*

1. Ebei   w   1 (NaSoare)

2. Uwey (NaSoare) = *Sabo'ohang* (Nandru'wy)
      *Nyuwobadep*

3. *Nyomang* = (deserted by Nupepa - see #22)
      *Longay*
      Bwasausau

4. Bebi (Nalohey) = *Arulunyarai* (from Harenggan)

5. Ani (NaLuwy) = *Pwepwe* (from Harenggan)
      Abiap
      Pwapwa

6. Kaseo (NaSisapo) = *Landay* (NaDyawo)
      Hapwey
      *Sabara'o*
      (given to Landay by her sister Sa'abwen)

7. Talau (Nasipoha) = *Piseh* (#2 Sori) (Babing)
   *Sa'amang*

8. *Nyasidyay (Nasipoha)* w 1

9. Lohai (NaLohey) = Salay (Nandruwy)
   *Saggey*

10. *Tata* or Nyaubalo'ohay (NaLuwy) w 1
    *Pwepwe*

11. Sapalona or John (Nandruwy) = *Si'ining* or Teresia (Harenggan)
    Ahen  (Cristop)

12. Sisamen (Nandruwy) = *Luminya* (from Lebey)
    Sisembung
    Balo'ohay
    *Aruplorungam*

13. Tara (NaLuwy) = *Sa'atamang* (#2 Sori) (So'opay)
    John
    *Sasarasang*

14. Iyapeng = *Sualomburo'*
    Bweyaiyai
    Smbu'uso

15. Simatilau (NaSimbuhon) w
    Ndripot
    *Samburong*
    Lemong

16. *not inhabited*
    belongs to Kubiliwau who was Doctor Boy from Ponam, but
    who has gone back to Ponam

17. *Nyasapaso'* w 1

18. Boboyang w (Nadyawo)
    *Saidyop*
    Siway
    Sapawin

19. *Beripeo* w (NaSisa'apo)
    America
    *Cristina*
    *Sa'ahe*
    Pwandrelang

20. *Sambuarey* (#2 Sori) (Babing) (deserted by Pamaleo, who is
      now living with Siwa)
      *Sangam*
      *Sapsap*
      Lalang
      Batorau
      *Nubweahmi*

21. *Nyaswelang* w 1 (Naluwy)

22. Nupepa (NaLohey) = Dzoppa (SuwaPak)
      So'olay
      Lohey
      Sapato
      Santiri

23. *Nyasasawung* w 1 (NaLohey)

24. Posoyay = *Sadyam* (from Harenggan)
      *Samanasung*
      *Sa'iye*
      *Sugumso* (Suwagumao)
      Sibounauw
      Sapaso
      Nupepa
      Uwem

25. Sapaloggay = So'a'aro (#2 Sori ) (Babing)
      Hi'inang
      *Apusing*
      Siggay
      Sapamanri

26. Barasoru w (#2 sori) (So'opay)
      *Sanga'aley*
      Aumau
      *Samanasang*

27. NyaSapaso w 1

28. Laubsing (Nadyawo) = *Sa'aro* (Lebey)
      Tale

29. Nasumanu w 1

30. Pwayyam (Nadyawo)

31. Logo = *Suwabe* (#2 Sori) (Hi'inang)
    Sialey
    *Sa'absing*
    Naowang
    Siarap
    Sabahapkas
    *Pimma*
    Mbuiyay
    So'onley

32. Karol = *Kapap* (#2 Sori) (So'opay)
    Pwa'ala
    *Sa'aba*
    *Rita*

33. *Nyabwa'ala* w 1 (#2 Sori) (So'opay)
    *Nyubwede'eng*

34. Lukas (NaPwasa'awa) = *Sodofina* (#2 Sori) (So'opay)
    Isi'ini
    *Saynyaunyau*
    Mamehenye

35. Naruawa (NaLohey) = *Arukapiang* (#2 Sori) (So'opay)
    *Samanaggay*
    *Suwahausip*
    Ausung
    *Dinowhambak*

36. Pamaleo (NaLuwy) = *Siwa* (Nadyawo)
    Nyohang

37. Unyohang = *Sa'abwen* (Nadyawo)
    Sa'aneng
    So'ong
    *Pwepwe*

38. Men's House
    Sirip
    Santiga
    Bepi

39. Men's House
    Simbuom (Nyasasawung) 1 (see #23)
    A'amau
    Si'iwing
    Lukas sleeps here occasionally but he has his own house

40. House for storing Copra (Baripeo Society)

41. "House Sick" (not in use)

42. Old dwelling, unoccupied

43. Copra House (for smoking copra)

44. Sapalodyang (NaSimbuhen) = *Arukisepong* (NaLohey)
     Nadanai
     *Kawa*
     *Siwa*

45. *Haus Kiap*
     (Lola Romanucci-Ross (then Schwartz) and Adán Anthony
     Schwartz)

46. The Co-op Store

47. Toilet for House Kiap

48. Men's toilet

49. Women's toilet

50. Men's toilet

51. "Police house" (Lokes)

# Appendix III

*"Court" Cases from Pere Village*, as recorded and explained to me by Prenis Paliau who had been chosen as "the committee" by the village.

*February 17.* Tomas Tchokal vs. his wife Maria Niandros. They were angry about Lucky (a card game). Tomas wanted the lamp to go play Lucky, she did not want him to play, so he left the lamp at home, but without telling her, he went to play Lucky anyway. Now it seems Tomas won sixteen pounds and ran off with it to his sister's house (Nyapin). Maria talked to her brother Pokiap and suggested they play Lucky with Tomas, with Tomas' 16 pounds, then keep it for themselves. But when Maria went, in anger, to find Tomas at his sister's place, he did not return her anger nor reply to her words, but went instead to "the Committee" to complain about her. Prenis told them that he "was not enough" to settle this kind of dispute; they should go home and work it out between themselves. He said he was not certain but it was possible that Tomas had originally won the money from his wife and her brother and refused to share it with them. In any case, who is he, he wonders, that he should get inolved with brothers and sisters doing things behind a spouse's back, for whichever way it started it came to the same thing, one member of a brother-sister pair had joined with a sibling against the spouse, and the other ran to a sibling for defense. Such things, thinks Prenis, should not be judged by "the committee," it is shameful of him to even think about it.

*January 28.* Lokes (our cook) has been brought to court by Niandros, his young mistress, who is also present. At this hearing she named Lokes as the father of her child. She says that a nurse in Lorengau told her she is three and one-half months pregnant. Lokes admitted that it was his child. Prenis gave judgment that Lokes must pay one pound per month for child support. Lokes agrees, but on the condition that he gets the child because he wants it. He also wants to marry the mother of the child. Prenis told him to ask his wife Pipiana if she would consent to Lokes "taking a second wife." Lokes says that at the time he was working for us in Sori Village on the North Coast, his wife became pregnant by another man. He did not mind, but told her to take care of herself because he wanted to have that child when it was born, no matter who the father was. But, apparently, she "buggered up" the child in her belly deliberately, that is why, when he came back, he began to have sexual relations with Niandros, so that he might have a child by her. Lokes also adds that he would take the child if only Pipiana would consent to look after it, but she will not, that is why he has to marry the mother of the child that is his. But Prenis told Lokes that he cannot get rid of Pipiana. For one thing, Pipiana would take his two grown children, both of whom are now educated, and he, Lokes, would get nothing out of this but having to pay child support. If Lokes chooses this route, Prenis will have nothing to do with the hearing, but will want a patrol officer to hear the case. However, Prenis has a suggestion, if Lokes can get Pipiana to divorce him, he, Prenis will give him the children. Niandros wants to give the child to Lokes but does not want to marry Lokes. Lokes and Prenis are both angry with Pipiana for not wanting to take care of this baby that is Lokes' and that Niandros is willing to give him. Pipiana was called in to "show cause" on this point. She reminded "the committee" that she had repeatedly brought Lokes to court over this sexual affair he was having with Niandros. Lokes repeatedly denied it and refuted her evidence. She says that since Lokes denied that he had anything to do with Niandros, now how could this be his baby? Yes, if Lokes had a child by any other woman Pipiana would adopt that child, but not by this one since Lokes denied that he was her "befriender." Prenis sent them both away, but he told Lokes that he must really play up to Pipiana and "grease her good" because that is his only hope, for Niandros has already promised, i.e., given him the child.

*February 13.* Niandros took Lokes to court to ask him for two pounds, thirteen shillings, six yards of material, two baby blankets, three small soaps and two more yards of material for baby clothes. Lokes complied, but he is then given advice from Prenis: give nothing further until you see the child born alive. Prenis added that these things would be assessed as so many months of child support paid in advance.

*January 28.* Aloisia Nyakakes took Karol Matawai her husband to court. Karol had struck her or beat her. Prenis asks Karol why he beat his wife. It seems they were discussing "stories of the big men (i.e., important men) of the past. Aloisia talked of Poli and Tchaponan, saying that Tchaponan was "big" and Poli was "small;" therefore they did no longer call each other brother. Poli then began to call Tchaponan "father" because Tchaponan was much older and therefore could take care of Poli, and Poli thus became his "son." Then he begat one called Poki, then Aloisia, then Alexander Kitemong, then Yakop, then Tchowka. Then Tchaponan begat Prenis Pikiap, Josep Potuan, Rene Kapwemolai then Maria Niandros. So, Aloisia claimed, she could call all of them brother and sister. Karol said this was not true, the story that Aloisia told of her father was a total lie. Aloisia replied that he did not like to hear stories about the big men of times of yore because he had become crazy with his "running around nothing." Karol became angry and beat her. Prenis ruled that Karol must pay her. Ten shillings would be enough. And Karol paid. Karol's argument had to be heard however; he maintained that they could not call each other by sibling terms just because their parents were "siblings." What was wrong with Aloisia is that she did not know how to comport herself properly and all she knew how to do was run about the village to all her so-called "brothers" and "sisters" being close to them. But actually, Prenis says (to me) that it is certain that Karol has been having affairs and he took her remark that he did not know how to listen to stories of big men belong before because all he knew how to do was to "run around crazy" (a reference to his philandering). Prenis said he did not want to hear who was right or wrong in these allegations, but Karol had to pay her ten shillings and then he was through with them.

*February 24.* Ana Tchimolen "got a court" against Yakopa Piwen. It was about a certain amount of sago. Ana's husband gave this sago to his sister. But Ana was not told of this. The sister worked this sago for her husband; it was part of the "work" he was to give as part of a marriage exchange to some people from Mouk who brought money to pay for the bride. None of the money was given to Ana's husband, therefore Ana got nothing for this sago. Ana said that her husband had given her that sago palm for some "work" of her own for her to give to her brothers, and then he just went ahead and gave it to his sister without telling Ana. Prenis asked her how much "exchange" the sago had brought. Kowai (called to court because he had received the money) said it was four pounds, but, the money was no longer in his possession, it had by now all been spent by him.

*February 27.* Pwating, and an old man of Pau "brought court" against three boys who are living with various sick Usiai who have come to the village to get daily medication from the Aid Post. They went into the bush with a dog one morning and there found an old man with a piglet. The dog attacked the piglet and ripped his stomach open. The old man brought the piglet to court so that Prenis could see the damage. The dog belonged to an adult male at the house for the sick, but Prenis blamed only the boys who took the dog with them. Prenis' solution: he asked the old man for the sale value of the piglet and then had each of the boys come up with ten shillings each. Then he asked the old man if he wanted the money he should give the boys the pig (which might or might not survive). Or did he want to keep the pig, with the money kept on deposit in case the pig died. The man took the pig, which recovered and Prenis gave him 15s in damages. The remaining 15s were returned to the parents of the boys.

Prenis also heard another case about a man (Pokenau) whose wife wanted to leave him but he did not enter it into this book he has lent me. He said he got very tired of recording, for he writes very slowly. There have been several cases since, heard by another "committee" who does not record anything at all about them.

# References and Selected Bibliography

Bateson, Gregory. 1979. *Mind and Nature; a Necessary Unity* New York: E.P. Dutton.

Brady, Ivan (ed.) 1983. Special Section, Speaking in the Name of the Real: Freeman and Mead on Samoa. *American Anthropologist* 85(4):908-947.

Carnap, Rudolf. 1937. *The Logical Syntax of Language.* Translated by Ameth Smeaton. London: Kegan Paul, Trench, Trubner and Co.

De Beer, Patrice. 1983. "Paradise Threatened by the 20th Century." *Manchester Guardian* Vol. 129, No. 12, week ending Sept. 18, 1983, pp. 12 and 14, col. 1-5 and col. 4-5.

Brandes, Stanley. 1980. *Metaphors of Masculinity; Sex and Status in Andalusian Folklore.* Philadelphia: University of Pennsylvania Press.

Cassirer, Ernest. 1966. *The Philosophy of the Enlightenment.* Boston: Beacon Press.

De Vos, George and Lola Romanucci-Ross. 1982. Ethnicity: Vessel of Meaning and Emblem of Contrast. In *Ethnic Identity; Cultural Continuities and Change.* George De Vos and Lola Romanucci-Ross, eds. Chicago: University of Chicago Press.

Dumont, Jean-Paul. 1977. *The Headman and I; Ambiguity and Ambivalence in Fieldwork.* Austin: University of Texas Press.

Eyde, David. In Press Recursive Dualism in the Admiralty Islands. *Societé des Oceanistes.*

Fortune, Reo, F. 1933. A Note on Some Forms of Kinship Structure. *Oceania.* Vol. 4, 1-9.
1935. *Manus Religion.* Philadelphia; American Philosophical Society.

Foster, Stephen William. 1981. Interpretation of Interpretations. *Anthropology and Humanism Quarterly.* Vol. 6, No. 4, 2-8.

Freeman, Derek, 1983. *Margaret Mead and Samoa; the Making and Unmaking of an Anthropological Myth*. Cambridge, Mass: Harvard University Press.

　　1984. Fact and Context in Ethnography; The Samoa Controversy. *Canberra: Anthropology* vol. 6, no. 2.

Freilich, M. (ed). 1970. *Marginal Natives; Anthropologists at Work*. New York: Harper and Row.

Guiart, Jean. 1956. Culture Contact and the "John Frum" Movement on Tanna. *Southwestern Journal of Anthropology* 12:105-116

Grossman, Marie Louise and John Hamlet. 1964. *Birds of Prey of the World*. New York: Bonanza Books.

Hall, Robert A. 1954. *Hands off Pidgin English*. Sydney: Pacific Publications.

Heiddegger, Martin. 1967. *What is a Thing?* Chicago: Henry Regnery.

Hélias, Pierre-Jakez. 1975. *The Horse of Pride; Life in a Breton Village*. New Haven: Yale University Press.

Inglis, Amirah. 1975. *The White Women's Protection Ordinance; Sexual Anxiety and Politics in Papua*. New York: St. Martins.

Lanternari, Vittorio. 1963. *The Religions of the Oppressed; a Study of Modern Messianic Cults*. New York: Alfred A. Knopf.

Leenhardt, Maurice. 1979. *Do Kamo; Person and Myth in the Melanesian World*. Chicago: University of Chicago Press.

Lévi-Strauss, Claude. 1955. *Tristes Tropiques*. Paris: Plon.

　　1962a. *Le Totemisme Aujourd'hui*. Paris: Presses Universitaires de France.

　　1962b. *La Pensée Sauvage*. Paris: Plon.

　　1969. *The Raw and the Cooked; Introduction to a Science of Mythology*: I. tr. by John and Doreen Weightman. New York: Harper and Row.

Lévy-Bruhl, Lucien. 1951. *Les Fonctions Mentales dans les Sociétés Inférieures*. Paris: Presses Universitaires de France.

Macran, H. S. 1929. *Hegel's Logic of World and Idea*.

Mannheim, Karl. 1959. *Essays on the Sociology of Knowledge*. London: Routledge and Kegan Paul.

Mauss, Marcel. 1967. *The Gift; Forms and Functions of Exchange in Archaic Societies*. New York: W.W. Norton.

Mead, Margaret. 1930. *Growing up in New Guinea*. New York: Morrow.

　　1934. Kinship in the Admiralty Islands. *Anthropological Papers of the American Museum of Natural History*, 34, part 2, 183-358. New York.

1975. *New Lives for Old: Cultural Transformation—Manus, 1928—1953.* New York: Morrow. (First edition 1956).

1977. *Letters from the Field 1925-1975.* New York: Harper and Row.

Meier, Joseph P. 1907, 1908, 1909. Mythen und Sagen der Admiralitäts Insulaner. *Anthropos* 2, 3 and 4.

Merleau-Ponty, Maurice. 1967. *The Structure of Behavior.* Boston: Beacon Press.

Moss, Leonard W. and Stephen Cappannari. 1982. In Quest of the Black Virgin: She is Black because She is Black. In *Mother Worship: Theme and Variation.* James J. Preston, ed. Pp. 53-74. Chapel Hill: University of North Carolina Press, 53-74.

Murphy, John J. 1966. *The Book of Pidgin English.* London: W. R. Smith and Paterson Pty, Ltd. First Ed. 1943.

Neverman, Hans. 1934. Admiralitäts-Inseln. II. Ethnographie: A Melanesien. Ergebnisse der Südsee-Expedition, 1908-1910, G. Thilenius, Hamburg, Friederichsen, De Gruyter, vol. 3.

Parkinson, Richard. 1907. *Driessig Jahre in der Sudsee.* Stuttgart: Strecker and Schroeder.

Pike, Kenneth L. 1967. *Language in Relation to a Unified Theory of the Structure of Human Behavior.* The Hague: Mouton.

Pitt-Rivers, Julian. 1957. *People of the Sierra.* Chicago: University of Chicago Press.

Rabinow, Paul. 1977. *Reflections of Fieldwork in Morocco.* Berkeley: University of California Press.

Romanucci-Ross, Lola. 1963-67. Field notebooks of the Admiralty Islands-New Guinea Expedition (with translations, film and tape catalogues for Sori, Mokerang and Pere). (Library of Congress, with Margaret Mead collection).

1966. Conflits Fonciers à Mokerang, village Matankor des Iles de l'Amirauté. *L'Homme*, 6:2, 32-52.

1969. The Hierarchy of Resort in Curative Practices: The Admiralty Islands, Melanesia. *Journal of Health and Social Behavior*, 10:3, 201-210.

1973. *Conflict, Violence and Morality in a Mexican Village.* Palo Alto: Mayfield.

1978. Melanesian Medicine. *Culture and Curing.* Peter Morley and Roy Wallis, eds. London: Peter Owen.

1980a. Anthropological Field Research: Margaret Mead, Muse of the Clinical Experience. *American Anthropologist*, 82(2)

1980b. On the Researching of Lost Images. *Anthropology and Humanism Quarterly.* Vol 5, No. 1, 14-20.

1982. The Italian Identity and its Transformations. *Ethnic*

*Identity in Cultural Continuities and Change.* George De Vos and Lola Romanucci-Ross, eds. Chicago: University of Chicago Press. 198-227.

1983a.    Apollo   Alone   and   Adrift   in   Samoa;   Early   Mead Reconsidered. *Reviews in Anthropology.* Vol 10, No. 3, 85-92.

1983b.    The Impassioned Cogito; Shaman and Anthropologist as Healer of the Body and the Body Politic. Paper delivered at the International Congress of Anthropological and Ethnological Sciences, Phase II, Vancouver. August 18-25.

1983c.    Madness, Deviance and Culture. *The Anthropology of Medicine; from Culture to Method.* Lola Romanucci-Ross, Daniel E. Moerman and Lawrence R. Tancredi, eds. South Hadley, Mass: J. F. Bergin, and New York: Praeger Scientific, 267-284.

Salisbury, Richard F.   1958.   An 'Indigenous' New Guinea Cult. Kroeber Anthropological Society Papers.  18:67-68.

Schwartz, Theodore.  1962.  The Paliau Movement in the Admiralty Islands,   1946-54.   *Anthropological   Papers   of   the   American Museum of Natural History.* Part 2, 207-422. New York.

1963.   Systems   of   Areal   Integration;   Some   Considerations Based on the Admiralty Islands of Northern Melanesia. *Anthropological Forum* 1:1, 56-97.

1982.   Cultural Totemism. *Ethnic Identity: Cultural Continuities and Change.* George de Vos and Lola Romanucci-Ross, eds. Pp. 106-131. Chicago: University of Chicago Press, 106-131.

1983.   Anthropology, A Quaint Science. *American Anthropologist.* 85 (4), 919-929.

Spiegelberg, Herbert.  1960.  *The Phenomenological Movement* (2 vols). The Hague: Mouton.

Trumbull, Robert.   1977.   *Tin Roofs and Palm Trees.*  Seattle: University of Washington Press.

Wagner, Roy, 1981.  *The Invention of Culture.* Chicago: University of Chicago Press.

Wolfers, Edward P.   1975.   *Race Relations and Colonial Rule in Papua New Guinea.* Canberra: Australian National University.

Worsley, Peter.  1957.  *The Trumpet Shall Sound.* London: MacGibbon and Key.

Wylie, Lawrence.   1974.   *Village in the Vaucluse.* Cambridge, Mass.: Harvard University Press.

# Index

# RELATED BOOKS

**The Anthropology of Medicine**
*Lola Romanucci-Ross, Daniel Moerman,*
*Laurence R. Tancredi*

**In Her Prime**
A New View of Middle-Aged Women
*Judith Brown and Virginia Kerns*

**Transnationals and the Third World**
The Struggle for Culture
*Armand Mattelart*

**The Anthropology of Sport**
*Kendall Blanchard and Alyce Cheska*

**Development and Decline**
The Evolution of Sociopolitical
Organizations
*Henri J.M. Claessen, Pieter van de Velde and*
*M. Estellie Smith*

**Political Anthropology**
An Introduction
*Ted C. Lewellen*
Foreword by Victor Turner

**Women and Change in Latin America**
*June Nash and Helen Safa*

**Tribes on the Hill**
The United States Congress—Rituals &
Realities
*J. McIver Weatherford*

**Women's Work**
Development and the Division of Labor by
Sex
*Eleanor Leacock and Helen Safa*

**The Politics of Education**
Culture, Power, and Liberation
*Paulo Freire*